METHUEN'S MANUALS OF MOD
General Editor : Professor

★

PERSONALITY TESTS AND ASSESSMENTS

PERSONALITY TESTS
AND
ASSESSMENTS

BY

PHILIP E. VERNON

PROFESSOR OF EDUCATIONAL PSYCHOLOGY IN THE
INSTITUTE OF EDUCATION, UNIVERSITY OF LONDON

METHUEN & CO. LTD. LONDON
11 New Fetter Lane, E.C.4

First published in 1953
Reprinted 1957, 1962 and 1965

D 464 6·77

1·4

CATALOGUE NO. 02/5438/36

REPRINTED BY LITHOGRAPHY IN GREAT BRITAIN BY
JARROLD AND SONS LTD. NORWICH

TO
GORDON ALLPORT

FOREWORD

MOST of my own work in the field of personality assessment was done between 1928 and 1935, at which time such rapid developments were taking place that it seemed hardly possible to encompass them in a book. However, I attempted to provide a systematic survey of verbal tests, questionnaires and ratings in a monograph, which was published as a Report of the Industrial Health Research Board in 1938. This has long been out of print, and Chapters VII–IX of the present volume cover much the same ground. I am grateful to the Medical Research Council and to the Controller of Her Majesty's Stationery Office for permission to reproduce some of the material contained in that Report.

Since the 1930s, personality testing has become more stabilized. The exigencies of applied psychology in war-time showed that certain methods could be put to immediate use, under carefully controlled conditions, whereas many bright ideas were quite impracticable. It showed also that so-called ' clinical ' methods like the interview and projection techniques, in spite of their apparent advantages in yielding insight into the personality as an organized whole, are very subjective and untrustworthy tools for vocational purposes. Thus the time is now ripe for an overall appraisal of the various approaches to personality assessment, for noting the more solid achievements and the most promising lines for further development, and for dismissing the unsuccessful.

The 1940s have also seen some decline of interest in the assessment of individual personalities, and a greater emphasis on the psychology of people's behaviour in social groups. But however true it may be that the individual person behaves differently according to the structure of the group of which he is a member, the problem of assessment still remains. The results of most investigations in general and social psychology are still affected by personality differences among the people being studied, and these need to be measured. The employer or teacher, and the educational or vocational psychologist, still wish to find out the character, social and emotional qualities, the attitudes and interests, of prospective pupils, students, and employees. While this book tries to cover all such types of assessment, it does not deal specifically with the diagnosis of abnormal personalities, nor discuss clinical methods in detail. Some use is made of the evidence from tests of neurotic and psychotic patients, but chiefly in order to prove the worth of the tests among normal adults and children.

Though there are numerous and valuable reviews of *parts* of the field of personality assessment, and these are listed in the short bibliography at the end, no book dealing with the whole of it appears to have been published since Symonds's *Diagnosing Personality and Conduct* in 1931, and none at all by a British author. (Special mention should be made of R. B. Cattell's *Description and Measurement of Personality* and H. J. Eysenck's *Dimensions of Personality* ; but both of these are primarily outlines of the writers' own contributions.) I have tried to cover the majority of British publications, but the American literature is by now so vast that I have had to be highly selective. My judgments as to what to leave out are doubtless open to question, but I believe that sufficient references are supplied in the footnotes or the bibliography to enable the research worker to follow up any topic that I appear to have slighted. The book is written mainly for psychology students, but it avoids technicalities as far as possible and will, it is hoped, be useful to the intelligent layman who wishes to know what psychology can contribute to the important problem of personality assessment. Chapter I deals with fundamental theoretical and methodological matters ; it may,. if preferred, be read last rather than first. The final chapter sums up the practical implications of the survey.

My interest in personality psychology was first aroused by the writings of Gordon W. Allport, and I owe more than I can say to the stimulus of working with him during 1930–1931 and 1937. Thus I have ventured to dedicate this to him, although I have diverged from his views in many respects. I am particularly grateful also to Mark A. May and Henry A. Murray for their inspiration, and for the help that they gave with my studies while I was in America.

Acknowledgements are also due to the following for permission to quote illustrative items from published tests :—

Dr. E. A. Doll, The Training School, Vineland, New Jersey— *The Vineland Social Maturity Scale*. Dr. D. A. Laird, Colegate

University, Hamilton, N.Y.—*Personal Inventories B*2 *and C*3. Professor T. F. Lentz, Washington University, St. Louis, Mo.— *C-R Opinionaire.* Dr. E. J. Shoben and Genetic Psychology Monographs—*Scale of Parental Attitudes to Child Adjustment.* Dr. Lydia Jackson, London—*Test of Family Attitudes.* F. H. and G. W. Allport and Houghton Mifflin Co., Boston, Mass.— Allport's *A-S Reaction Study* and Allport-Vernon *Study of Values.* Stanford University Press—Strong's *Vocational Interest Blank,* Bernreuter's *Personality Inventory,* and Willoughby's *Emotional Maturity Scale.* Bureau of Publications, Teachers College, Columbia University, New York—G. B. Watson's *Test of Public Opinion* and Maller's *Character Sketches.* C. H. Stoelting Co., Chicago, Ill.—Woodworth's *Personal Data Sheet* and Pressey's *X-O Test.*

P.E.V.

CONTENTS

I

Introduction

IN bringing up children wisely, and guiding them into suitable educational careers and occupations, we have to take account of their personality qualities. The doctor will tell us their physical capacities and defects ; school examinations and psychological tests will give us at least an approximate indication of their educational abilities, intelligence and aptitudes along special lines. But many a child with high intellectual qualifications at 11 years does not fulfil his promise in a secondary grammar school through lack of perseverance, weak academic interests, or emotional instability. Other children who are dull according to tests, or in their school work, develop into worthy members of society owing to their sound personalities. In *Personnel Selection in the British Forces* [1] Dr. Parry and the writer have described the success of psychological methods of allocating recruits to jobs in the Services during the Second World War. But there were many individuals who did very much better, or less well, in some employment than had been predicted, largely because of the difficulties of making accurate personality assessments. For example, a little progress was made—but far too little—in diagnosing the men with poor morale or neurotic tendencies who were a liability to the army, or the potential leaders who would make good officers.

Cannot the psychologist, then, devise some tests of personality, analogous to tests of intelligence and other abilities, which could be applied by the teacher, the vocational or personnel officer, or others interested in the future of a pupil or employee ? Such tests would be of the utmost value too to Child Guidance Clinic workers, and to those concerned with abnormal personalities such as delinquents and criminals, neurotics or the insane. Much unhappiness and failure, not only in school or employment, but also in marriage, might be

---

[1] Cf. Bibliography. *N.B.*—Other references not listed in footnotes will be found in the Bibliography at the end of the book.

obviated by scientific personality testing. But though an enormous amount of research and experiment on tests has, in fact, been carried out by psychologists during the past thirty years or so, the answer to our question is indubitably negative. We shall see in this book that many personality qualities *can* be measured or diagnosed fairly effectively, but that the methods are far too elaborate and time-consuming, or far too dependent on the skill and experience of the psychologist, to be generally applicable for any practical purpose, or to be used by anyone not specially trained. True, it is possible to suggest some improvements on the unreliable methods that the average layman habitually employs. Moreover, the outlook is more hopeful in certain fields, such as the measurement of interests and attitudes. But in the writer's opinion it is safer to be pessimistic regarding the future of personality testing in general, and one of the objects of this chapter is to explain why.

DEFINITIONS OF PERSONALITY, CHARACTER AND TEMPERAMENT

Personality has been variously defined, and its nature and origins variously explained, as is shown by G. W. Allport in his *Personality—A Psychological Approach*. Here we mean by it, simply, what sort of a person is so-and-so, what is he like? Or as R. B. Cattell expresses it—personality is that which enables us to predict a person's behaviour in a given situation. While a man's intelligence, his bodily strength and skills are certainly part of his personality, yet the term refers chiefly to his emotional and social qualities, together with his drives, sentiments and interests. (Note, however, that this is much broader than the colloquial usage, whereby an individual is sometimes said to ' have personality ' if he is very domineering, impressive or attractive.)

Character is often used synonymously with personality, but is usually a more evaluative term. That is, it refers to certain traits of personality which are approved or disapproved, such as honesty, reliability, integrity, self-control and their opposites. The word ' temperament ' has also received diverse definitions, but is most usefully limited to the constitutional and inborn factors underlying personality—the instinctive drives, the effects of the endocrine glands or other physiological factors on a person's behaviour, and certain general tendencies which may be at least in part hereditarily determined, such as the strength or urgency of drives, excitability vs. placidity, and emotional instability. We cannot in fact ever observe temperament directly, since even in early infancy it is influenced and modified by the parents' or nurse's handling and other environmental factors. Nevertheless quite marked individual differences do occur in the personalities of young babies, also among brothers or sisters who have apparently been brought up alike. Hence the existence of innate temperamental factors seems a reasonable hypothesis.[1] (Like personality, temperament often has a narrower colloquial usage, namely, the unstable or hysterical traits commonly found among artists and actresses. But according to our view this is merely one kind of temperament. Indeed, very probably it is not innate at all, but is a kind of personality.)

THE STRUCTURE OF PERSONALITY

Personality develops, then, from the interaction of the living human organism with an environment that frustrates or encourages, and conditions its impulses. Psychoanalysts have shown how the manner of early handling, feeding, and weaning, the love and security that the parents may give or withhold, and the ' sanctions ' that society imposes, mould the growing child. Although their theories are largely unverified, con-troversial and unscientific (so that few, if any, definite associa-tions are established between particular methods of upbringing and later personality traits [2]), yet we may agree that an organized system or structure is built up which includes the conscious sentiments and interests, and the unconscious ' mechanisms ' or complexes, and which determines the child's or adult's behaviour in any situation. Much progress is indeed being made through the researches of medical and of ex-perimental depth psychologists towards formulating general

[1] Recently Eysenck and Prell have obtained strong evidence, from a study of twins, that emotional stability-instability is hereditarily deter-mined to at least the same extent as is general intelligence. Eysenck, H. J. and Prell, D. B., ' The Inheritance of Neuroticism : An Experimental Study '. *J. Ment. Sci.*, 1951, 97, 441–465.

[2] Cf. Orlansky, H., Bibliography.

principles of personality dynamics,[1] though this is not the place to describe such work. Special mention should be made, however, of Allport's principle of functional autonomy—the view that fresh mechanisms and interests continue to develop during a man's life-time and to become self-supporting. There is no justification for the implication that the motive forces of his behaviour invariably trace back to McDougallian instincts, or to Freudian complexes which are fixed during the pre-school years. The evidence presented in later chapters does not support the view that personality can only be understood if it is studied longitudinally or historically. Nevertheless this structure is fairly stable, and thus produces consistency of behaviour towards similar situations from time to time. (For example, Neilon [2] has compared personality sketches of 2-year-old children with independent sketches of the same individuals 15 years later, and found that judges could match or identify the one set with the other fairly successfully. In terms of the present writer's matching formula, the consistency of personality over this time is represented by a coefficient of 0·64.) It is the extreme complexity of the structure, and the fact that many of its links are repressed into the unconscious mind, which make it so difficult for us to understand a person's motives. Personal behaviour is always meaningful, and even at its most irrational (as in the neurotic or psychotic) it is logically determined by this structure. Yet it may appear to vary inexplicably. The same child may display very different characteristics at home, at play with his friends, in school classes under different teachers. And we interpret it so diversely that experimental investigations rarely yield correlations higher than 0·5 to 0·6 between assessments of a person's traits by different acquaintances or observers.

Research on leadership during and since the war has been particularly enlightening in showing that this quality of behaviour is not, as it were, a fixed ' property ' of the individual, but that it varies according to the kind of social group of which

[1] E.g. Sears, R. R., *Survey of Objective Studies of Psychoanalytic Concepts.* New York : Social Science Research Council, 1943. Cattell, R. B., *Personality.* New York : McGraw-Hill, 1950. Stagner, R., see Bibliography.

[2] Neilon, P., ' Shirley's Babies After Fifteen Years : A Personality Study '. *J. Genet. Psychol.*, 1948, 73, 175–186.

he is a member and the activities in which the group is engaged.[1] Other relevant studies, such as those of Hartshorne and May on honesty, will be cited in later chapters. But this does not mean, as some American writers have supposed, that personality consists of vast numbers of independent habits, specific to each situation. The consistency is there if we could but trace it. Nevertheless the traits or qualities of behaviour by which we describe people are, it must be admitted, very rough and over-simplified generalizations. We are far too apt to jump to conclusions, to ignore the complexities of structure, and to assume that people will always react in certain limited ways— that a boy who, say, is caught cheating in class is destined for a life of crime, whereas the cheating may have arisen from all sorts of motives. Hence experimental research reveals a tendency that Thorndike [2] called the ' halo effect '. If we rate or assess a number of people on several presumably distinctive traits (say good looks, intelligence, sociability, moral character), it is always found that the ratings overlap rather closely. Presumably we are influenced, unwittingly, by our general good or bad impressions of the people, and so attribute all the desirable traits to some, undesirable ones to others, almost regardless of their meaning.

PERSONALITY TRAITS

Since this book is mainly concerned with attempts to measure or judge personality traits, we must define the sense in which the term is used. Trait refers to any characteristic in which people differ or vary from one another. But such differences exist at many levels, as it were. There are physical character-istics, and objective features of behaviour such as speed of walking, amount of time spent at church or the cinema, etc. At the other end of the scale there are the psychoanalyst's mechanisms or complexes, which cannot be directly observed at all, but which are inferred as the underlying ' ganglia ' of personality structure. Personality traits lie between these extremes ; they are more general qualities of social and

---

[1] Cf. Carter, L., Haythorn, W., and Howell, M., ' A Further Investigation of the Criteria of Leadership '. *J. Abn. Soc. Psychol.*, 1950, 45, 350–358.
[2] Thorndike, E. L., ' A Constant Error in Psychological Ratings '. *J. Appl. Psychol.*, 1920, 4, 25–29.

emotional behaviour—the common features which we abstract from observing how people differ. And we would regard them (like Stagner) as descriptive rather than (like Allport) as explanatory. Cattell distinguishes between descriptive or ' surface ' traits, and underlying ' source ' traits. We would accept this, but doubt his claim to be able to determine source traits merely by factor analysis (cf. p. 12).

The scientific study and measurement of traits is exceedingly difficult, for several reasons. First, they are mostly very vague and ambiguous in meaning, and different people often include different modes of behaviour within any one trait. Such things as height and weight are objective ; any two observers would arrive at practically the same measurements. Mechanical ability, arithmetical attainment and the like, also comprise certain types of behaviour which can be fairly readily recognized and agreed upon by different observers (though even here the notorious unreliability of examinations shows that their objectivity is limited). Leadership, honesty, persistence, introversion, aggressiveness, timidity, etc., are still more complex. Behaviour which one person interprets as aggressive might be called adventurous by another, or limelight exhibitionism by another.

Our second difficulty is that they involve subjective interpretation. They are partly dependent on the observer. His own personality and viewpoint both influence what he notices in other people's behaviour, and his interpretations of the traits responsible for such behaviour.[1] For example, a Victorian parent sees naughty actions in a child, and attributes these to rebelliousness, where a progressive parent either notices nothing, or regards the actions as a sign of the child's initiative. We recognize this tendency in everyday life ; for example, we do not accept A's judgment of B at its face value if we regard A as a prejudiced person. And the more we penetrate behind the superficial behaviour characteristics to the underlying motives, the more subjective interpretation enters. The novelist, dramatist and biographer who excel in depicting personality do not merely give us a factual record of a man's actions over a period. They select the most significant incidents, and infer or intuit the man's feelings, desires, fears, ideas, and so integrate

[1] Cf. Vernon, P. E., ' The Biosocial Nature of the Personality Trait '. *Psychol. Rev.*, 1933, 40, 533–548.

the facts into a meaningful whole. Much the same is true of the psychoanalyst's or clinical psychologist's case study.

A third point, referred to above, is the artificiality of studying personality in isolation from society. This runs counter to one of the dominant trends in contemporary psychology. Nevertheless the applied psychologist or the layman continually makes judgments about individuals as though they possessed distinctive traits, attitudes, and interests in almost any social context. The extent to which success or failure in a job, or the development of neurotic or criminal tendencies, is determined by the qualities of the individual or of the group, is a matter for experiment rather than for theoretical argument.

Fourthly, we have seen that any particular piece of behaviour depends on such a multiplicity of factors in the personality structure and the environment, that no one reacts in accordance with a trait all the time. Nevertheless this does not mean that it is hopeless to try to measure personality traits or to assess people. For it is clear that some individuals behave more markedly and frequently than others do in a manner that most of us would call, say, timid, and that others are more bold or fearless. Of course we cannot measure timidity in absolute physical units as we can height, temperature, etc. But so long as we can arrange people in rank order for the trait, or agree that some are 'high', some 'low', the essential requirements of measurement are met.[1] The most fruitful approach (which originated in May and Hartshorne's investigations of character) has been described by the writer elsewhere as the trait-composite method.[2]

THE TRAIT-COMPOSITE APPROACH

Suppose we desire to obtain a measure of an individual's timidity-boldness : we first select a number of situations in everyday life to which people react either timidly or boldly, or devise special situations or tests which seem likely to bring out the trait (cf. Chaps. IV–VI). We must apply these to a large

[1] Cf. Banks, C., and Burt, C., 'Statistical Analysis in Educational Psychology '. *Current Trends in British Psychology* (edit. C. A. Mace and P. E. Vernon). London : Methuen, 1953.

[2] Vernon, P. E., 'Human Temperament '. *Eugen. Rev.*, 1932, 23, 325–331.

group of comparable people, not only to the one individual, and record their responses, since the only way of measuring the strength or weakness of his timidity in each situation is by seeing how he stands relative to the average and spread of scores in such a group, i.e. by reference to a statistical distribution. Here, then, we have a series of *samples* of the individuals' timid or bold behaviour. Next we present them with a questionnaire or ' paper-and-pencil test,' which contains, say, fifty questions about their past behaviour or their feelings under conditions which were likely to stimulate them to fear or bravery (cf. Chap. VIII). We get them to check the answer to each question which best describes themselves, and if they do this frankly one or more scores will be obtained which represent a sample of their own opinions about their timidity.

Thirdly, we ask other people who are well acquainted with the individuals to estimate timidity and other related traits on some form of rating scale (cf. Chap. VII). Here again we shall get better results if they base their assessments on actual behaviour that they have observed in the past, rather than on their personal subjective impressions. And we should try to get hold of acquaintances who will have diverse slants or viewpoints. The judgments of schoolfellows may afford one quite useful sample, but different samples should be collected from relatives, teachers or employers, or others who have observed them in various phases of their existence.

We now possess scores on, say, a dozen different samples of behaviour or opinion, and proceed to find by correlation methods the extent to which the samples ' hang together ' or are consistently associated. Thus if we take the schoolfellows' opinions and the questionnaire scores, we shall probably find some agreement, but perhaps no higher than a coefficient of 0·4. This indicates a slight tendency for those individuals who think that they behave timidly to be regarded as timid by their friends, although there are many exceptions. Different sets of ratings by associates may agree more highly, but this may be largely because they have similar biases. That is why it is important to get raters from various walks of life, even if the inter-correlations sink. The coefficients for the objective situations or tests are likely to be more irregular, yielding an average correlation with all the other samples of around 0·2 (in the writer's experience). But this should not surprise us in view of the previous discussion. Some samples may show virtually no agreement because they are so remote from the underlying personality structure (e.g. this might happen if we took softness of voice or weak handwriting pressure as tests of timidity). Other samples may have been affected by some unanticipated motive so that they are really reflecting quite different traits (e.g. dislike of the experimenter, or some unconscious compensatory mechanism, etc.).

The next step is now obvious, namely, to combine as many diverse, yet overlapping, samples as possible. This combination of scores is what we call a trait-composite, and this provides us with the best available measurement of the trait in which we are interested. Samples which fail to correlate positively with the rest are eliminated, leaving perhaps only half a dozen or so with a fairly high average inter-correlation. But one has to be very cautious at this stage, since omission of the more diverse samples necessarily narrows the scope of the composite and renders it less representative. Thus it would not do to use only ratings or opinions, although these would usually overlap quite highly. (This is a problem which statisticians have not yet solved even in the field of abilities ; and in the personality sphere, it looks as if the subjective judgment of psychologists and the practicability of the sample measures must largely determine the choice.) Provided, however, that we finish with half a dozen or more really varied samples, having an average inter-correlation of 0.30 or more, we can be satisfied that our composite scores have a ' theoretical validity ' of at least 0.85.

The notion of theoretical validity implies that the perfect criterion of our trait is a complete record of all the individual's behaviour of the timid-bold variety, together with his self-expressed ideas and wishes, and all the impressions that he makes on acquaintances, or interpretations that they offer (whether biased or not). Naturally we can never collect all this information, but if we have a representative set of overlapping samples, we can predict that other samples would overlap similarly, and that the correlation between our combined samples and the complete survey would amount to 0.85. Note that this approach forces us to realise that a test is not ' a miraculous instrument for revealing otherwise unsuspected qualities ' (cf. Vernon and Parry). It is either a good or a poor sample of the sort of behaviour, or opinion, which goes to constitute some trait. If this viewpoint were more generally adopted, less credence would be given to horoscopes, or physiognomical signs of personality, or to some of the very artificial tests of temperament and personality on which much time has been wasted in the past.

Though no really satisfactory external criterion of the validity of a personality test exists, the correlation between any sample and such a composite provides us with the best available evidence. In many experiments, tests have been validated by correlating with associates' ratings. But while this may be a useful first step, it really amounts to no more than comparing one imperfect sample of the trait with another biased sample. The same objection applies to comparisons with personality questionnaires.

Some psychologists would argue, with considerable justification, that this approach is still too vague and subjective to be of value, and that it would be better to do without the concept of traits. For example, Eysenck starts with the much more definite datum—the difference between neurotic patients and non-patients, or the difference between hysteric patients and dysthymic (anxiety and obsessional) patients, etc. He then proceeds to build up composites of tests which differentiate the groups as effectively as possible. Many other recognized ' syndromes ' or types of abnormal personality can be and have been used as criteria. Again, we can contrast delinquent with non-delinquent children, males with females, or children who succeed in grammar school with others (of the same intelligence and social background) who fail, and likewise develop batteries of predictive measures. This approach too, however, does not provide a sure and complete solution, for several reasons. First, it is doubtful how far the syndromes are distinctive ; many different, yet overlapping, classifications of mental patients are possible.[1] Neither schizophrenics, hysterics, nor juvenile delinquents constitute homogeneous or clear-cut groups.

[1] Several psychologists have applied factor analysis in an attempt to settle this problem. Unfortunately no two arrive at the same classification. Cf. Moore, T. V., ' The Essential Psychoses and their Fundamental Syndromes '. *Stud. Psychol. Psychiat. Cath. Univ. Amer.*, 1933, 3, 1–128. Burt, C. L., ' The Analysis of Temperament '. *Brit. J. Med. Psychol.*, 1938, 17, 158–188. Eysenck, H. J., see Bibliography. Wittenborn, J. R., ' Symptom Patterns in a Group of Mental Hospital Patients '. *J. Consult. Psychol.*, 1951, 15, 290–302.

Secondly, psychiatric diagnoses are subjective and unreliable, just like associates' ratings. Thirdly, there are numerous traits that we would like to measure which cannot be anchored to any syndrome. It is reasonable to regard mental patients as representing the extremes of certain normal personality tendencies. But where are we to find extreme cases of, say, tolerance vs. prejudice, impulsiveness-cautiousness, persistence, sense of humour, and so on ? Actually, both the trait-composite and the group-difference approaches are valuable, and should be regarded as complementary. A trait-composite for emotional stability might be based largely on measures which differentiate neurotics from normals and vice versa, one for persistence on tests which help to predict scholastic or job success.

FACTOR ANALYSIS IN THE FIELD OF PERSONALITY

The relations of these methods to factor analysis require some consideration. By statistical treatment of the correlations between personality tests or ratings it is possible to determine the common elements or factors, in the same way that g (general intellectual factor) is extracted from intelligence tests, v from verbal tests, k or S from spatial tests, and so on.[1] If we are studying two or more trait-composites or syndromes simultaneously, factorization will show whether they are independent, or whether they would be better combined or divided up differently. It helps, then, in mapping out the sphere of personality more parsimoniously, so that we do not waste our efforts in constructing composites for a lot of traits which come to much the same thing (e.g. boldness, aggressiveness, leadership, impulsiveness, initiative, self-confidence and sociability probably overlap considerably, and factorization might reduce them to a small number of more fundamental dimensions). Also factorization enables us to arrive at more accurate weighted trait-composite scores than the simple sum of results on a set of samples.

But statistically established factors may either be broad in content like our trait-composites, or they may be narrow. Thus

[1] Cf. Vernon, P. E., *The Structure of Human Abilities*. London : Methuen, 1950. For surveys of factor analysis in the field of personality, see Cattell, R. B., *Description and Measurement of Personality*. London : Harrap, 1946. Eysenck, H. J., *The Structure of Personality*. London : Methuen, 1953.

a combination of several tests of reaction time would give a clear factor, but this would be a very unimportant personality trait. Indeed the majority of factorial studies which have been made in the field of personality have been conducted with limited kinds of samples—associates' ratings, self-rating questionnaires, etc. Cattell has surveyed these studies very fully and has put forward a list of a dozen primary factors or ' source traits ' from his own analyses of ratings. But his attempts to equate others' results with his own involve considerable guesswork, and in later investigations where he did apply objective tests and questionnaires, these failed for the most part to group themselves convincingly under his primary factors.[1]

There is also the difficulty that an infinite number of solutions exist to any factorial problem. Cattell tries to decide the most appropriate set of rotations by Thurstone's criterion of Simple Structure, Eysenck by linking his factors to criterion groups (neurotics vs. normals, etc.). But it is still true to say that no two leading psychologists agree as to which are the best dimensions. Factors vary again in different groups. Most investigations have been done with male college students. But we could not expect, nor do we usually find, the same patterning among women, among unselected adults, among neurotic or other patients, or among children of different ages. Nevertheless it is possible to discover a modicum of agreement on two major dimensions, or at least a good deal of overlapping between different authors. Fig. 1 attempts to give a rough portrayal of such results. In accordance with factorial practice, traits shown at right angles are independent or uncorrelated, and those making small angles with each other are closely correlated. More than two dimensions are really needed, and dotted lines are intended to indicate spokes that project in various dimensions from the plane of the paper.

The most pervasive or far-reaching dimension might be termed *dependability*—a blend of persistence, purposiveness,

[1] Cattell, R. B., ' Primary Personality Factors in the Realm of Objective Tests '. *J. Person.*, 1948, 16, 459–487. Cattell, R. B., and Saunders, D. R., ' Inter-relation and Matching of Personality Factors from Behavior Ratings, Questionnaires, and Objective Test Data '. *J. Soc. Psychol.*, 1950, 31, 243–260.

stability and good character. As early as 1915 Webb[1] described such a factor—W or will-persistence, though this was based on ratings and was therefore certainly contaminated with halo or general good impression. Cattell's Factor C is similar; it combines such traits as emotionally stable, realistic and persevering. In another careful analysis of ratings, Reyburn and Raath[2] found separate Stable-Mature-Balanced and

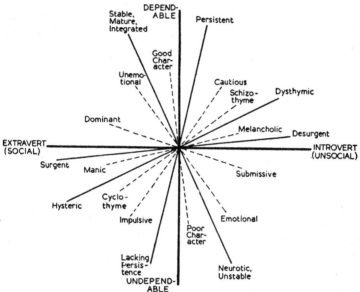

Fig. 1.—Diagram of Relations between Main Personality Dimensions.

Persistence factors, but these were quite closely correlated. Conscientious Effort was the most important of the syndromes arrived at in Sanford's elaborate research with children.[3] He attributed it to harmonious and integrated development of the Ego and Super-ego. More objective backing is forthcoming from

[1] Webb, E., ' Character and Intelligence '. *Brit. J. Psychol. Monogr. Suppl.*, 1915, No. 3.
[2] Reyburn, H. A., and Raath, M. J., ' Primary Factors of Personality '. *Brit. J. Psychol., Statist. Sec.*, 1950, 3, 150–158.
[3] Sanford, R. N., *et. al.*, ' Physique, Personality, and Scholarship '. *Monogr. Soc. Res. Child Devel.*, 1943, 8, No. 34.

Hartshorne and May's work. For though the correlations between their measures of honesty, persistence, self-control, co-operation, and consistency were low, yet there was a common element, which Maller [1] identified as ' readiness to forgo an immediate gain for the sake of a more remote but greater gain '. (Actually persistence showed least overlap with the other traits mentioned ; hence the ' good character ' aspect of dependability is shown by a dotted line on our diagram.) Brogden [2] factorized 29 character tests, and though he rotated them into half a dozen factors, it is clear that there must have been quite a strong common element or general factor. Several other researches have been done on persistence tests (cf. p. 83), and though here too some authors find very little overlapping, and others break down the trait into distinct group-factors or types of persistence, Ryans concludes that a general factor is justified. In a very thorough research on London secondary school boys, MacArthur [3] recently demonstrated a strong persistence factor in objective tests and ratings (together with subsidiary group-factors), and found that this, as well as intelligence, contributed to school achievement. Our notion of dependability corresponds, indeed, to Alexander's [4] X-factor of industriousness which, as shown elsewhere,[5] so largely determines educational and vocational success. It links too with Charlotte Bühler's conception of the ' work attitude ' among young children and with the ' sense of duty ' which, she considers, differentiates older and more mature from younger adults.[6] Finally our factor certainly overlaps with Eysenck's neuroticism factor, which was based on the contrast between normals and neurotic patients. For some of his best differentiating tests are usually accepted as tests of persistence.

[1] Maller, J. B., ' General and Specific Factors in Character '. *J. Soc. Psychol.*, 1934, 5, 97–102.

[2] Brogden, H. E., ' A Factor Analysis of Forty Character Tests '. *Psychol. Monogr.*, 1940, 52, No. 234, 39–55.

[3] MacArthur, R. S., *An Experimental Investigation of Persistence and its Measurement at the Secondary School Level*. Ph.D. Thesis, University of London, 1951.

[4] Alexander, W. P., ' Intelligence, Concrete and Abstract '. *Brit. J. Psychol. Monogr. Suppl.*, 1935, No. 19.

[5] Vernon, *op. cit.*, p. 11.

[6] Bühler, C., *From Birth to Maturity*. London : Kegan Paul, 1935. Frenkel, E., ' Studies in Biographical Psychology '. *Char. & Person.*, 1936, 5, 1–34.

Whether Burt's [1] factor of general emotionality—obtained from observations and ratings of children's emotional reactions—can also be identified with undependability is more doubtful ; it is therefore shown in Fig. 1 on a different plane. Note that our factor is not entirely independent of general intelligence (cf. p. 71), but we should need yet another plane to portray this.

The underlying core of the second main dimension, orthogonal to or independent from the first, is more controversial. For though it corresponds to the familiar extravert-introvert dichotomy, this conception has been variously interpreted. Jung's original notion of objective vs. subjective orientation is difficult to pin down, and we would suggest that the most clear-cut dimension is social-co-operative-liking people vs. unsociable. Factorial studies of personality questionnaires show that this type of introversion overlaps largely with neurotic tendencies. [2] Hence the angle on our Figure between Introversion and Instability is acute ; while Eysenck's own introvert dimension (derived from dysthymic vs. hysteric patients) is drawn at 90 degrees to neuroticism. Cattell's Factor F of Surgency (optimistic, sociable vs. melancholic, seclusive) is very close to our conception, as also are dichotomies based on manic vs. depressed patients, or on the Freudian oral-gratified and ungratified types. [3] Banks's [4] two major factors, obtained from ratings of women students, are emotional stability and 'euthymic-dysthymic'. Reyburn and Raath's [5] first factor was Spontaneity-Cheerful-Sociable, and Fiske [6] found a first factor

[1] Burt himself regards it as the innate temperamental element underlying (the inverse of) Webb's acquired character factor, W. It seems to be more akin to Cattell's Factor D–hypomanic vs. phlegmatic. Cf. Burt, C. L., ' The Factorial Analysis of Emotional Traits '. *Char. & Person.*, 1939, 7, 238–254, 285–299.

[2] Cf. Eysenck, Bibliography ; Vernon, P. E., ' The Assessment of Psychological Qualities by Verbal Methods '. *Industr. Hlth. Res. Board Rep.*, No. 83. London : H.M. Stat. Off., 1938.

[3] Goldman, F., ' Breast-feeding and Character Formation '. *J. Person.*, 1948, 17, 83–103.

[4] Banks, C., ' Primary Personality Factors in Women : A Re-analysis '. *Brit. J. Psychol., Statist. Sec.*, 1948, 1, 204–218.

[5] *Op cit.*

[6] Fiske, D. W., ' Consistency of the Factorial Structures of Personality Ratings from Different Sources '. *J. Abn. Soc. Psychol.*, 1949, 44, 329–344. In this investigation the most prominent second and third factors were named Emotional Maturity and Conformity. Our conception of Dependability partakes of both of these.

of Social Adaptability in ratings of clinical psychology students by staff, other students, and themselves. Burt,[1] however, distinguishes two bipolar emotional factors—sthenic vs. asthenic and pleasant vs. unpleasant. Kretschmer's [2] cyclothyme-schizothyme typology is even more difficult to place. It overlaps with Jung's description of extravert-introvert in many respects, but is quite different in others. Moreover it is not, as Kretschmer claimed, continuous with the distinction between manic-depressive insanity and schizophrenia (cf. p. 36). Cattell distinguishes it sharply from surgency, but as his cyclothyme Factor A is based on the traits Easygoing, Frank, Co-operative vs. Obstructive, Reserved, it seems impossible to disregard the overlapping. We have, therefore, shown it on our Figure by a dotted line.

Other traits which are certainly connected with, but should probably be considered as oblique to, extraversion-introversion are dominance-submissiveness (Cattell's Factor E), and impulsiveness-caution. There seems to be an obscure relation also with the masculine-feminine dichotomy, with the practical-verbal ($k:m$ vs. $v:ed$) factor in abilities, and with types of interests.[3] Obviously the situation is very confused. It might be cleared up by sub-dividing Dependability and Extraversion-Introversion into group factors, or by the addition of other independent dimensions. But there seems to be little prospect of different factorists agreeing. At least this brief survey has indicated that factor analysis is not yet in a position to supply a complete and acceptable map of personality. Though an invaluable tool, it cannot by itself answer the question—what trait composites should we try to measure ? Nevertheless it would be no mean achievement if these two factors alone could be firmly established and measured by practicable batteries of tests and ratings. Not only would it provide a foundation for more detailed personality studies, but also it would cover a great deal of what is needed in educational and vocational selection and guidance.

[1] *Op cit.*

[2] Kretschmer, E., *Physique and Character.* London : Kegan Paul, 1925.

[3] Cf. North, R. D., ' An Analysis of the Personality Dimensions of Introversion-Extroversion '. *J. Person.*, 1949, 17, 352–368.

PERSONALITY TYPES

Mention should also be made of the German typological approach. Representative doctrines are those of Jung with his sensation, thinking, feeling, and intuition as well as extravert-introvert, types; Kretschmer's cyclothyme-schizothyme; Jaensch's T and B, integrate and disintegrate, and the synthetic-analytic types of older writers; and Spranger's types of value (cf. p. 162). Such types are quite different from trait-composites or syndromes, that is, clusters of behaviour samples which are known to inter-correlate.[1] They are admitted to be idealizations or intuitive generalizations, whose value resides in their bringing together a whole set of phenomena and showing how they interact in the hypothetical typical person. They help in the understanding rather than in the exact description or measurement of people. For example, Kretschmer [2] interrelates physique, psychopathological syndromes, normal temperamental variations, certain characteristics of perception, imagery and movement, and styles of artistic and literary productions. But no one individual is supposed to show all these aspects, any more than we expect to meet pure and complete examples of such types as the aesthete, the Aberdonian or the absent-minded professor. The latter are referred to as 'stereotypes' by social psychologists; they are very similar to the German concept, though they possess even less logical or empirical backing. Kretschmer, Jaensch and their collaborators have carried out many experiments which claim to show differences between groups of people representing different types, though they seldom apply statistical tests of significance, or correlation techniques, for demonstrating just how closely the characteristics are linked. The present writer has surveyed some of the literature elsewhere, and shown how chaotic are

---

[1] They can, however, be expressed quantitatively by means of what Stephenson calls Q-technique. Stephenson shows also that there is no validity in the common objection that most of the traits or attributes of which a type is composed tend to be normally, not bimodally, distributed. Stephenson, W., 'Methodological Considerations of Jung's Typology'. *J. Ment. Sci.*, 1939, 85, 185–205. *Introduction to Q-Technique.* Univ. Chicago Psychol. Dept. (mimeographed), 1951.

[2] For a sympathetic appraisal of Kretschmerian typology, see Eysenck, H. J., 'Cyclothymia and Schizothymia as a Dimension of Personality. I. Historical Review.' *J. Person.*, 1950, 19, 123–152.

the results, due to the lack of exact specification of the persons and situations investigated, and of proper experimental con-trols.[1] Such work, together with the writings of Jung and Spranger, is full of interesting insights and hypotheses which would be worth following up by objective research. But it appears to contribute even less to the scientific assessment of personality than does the trait-composite, the syndrome or group-difference, or the factorial approaches.

This brings us to the extremely important and controversial question of how far personality can be measured. Is it not a Gestalt or totality, which is disrupted by our breaking it down into separate traits or factors ? ' The mere enumeration of a person's traits and habits does not give us the person himself, since it omits the essential aspect of organized structure. Each single characteristic has to be considered in relation to the whole.' [2] Allport has put the arguments very clearly for the idiographic, clinical, or intuitive approach to personality, as opposed to the nomothetic, analytic and psychometric approach; while Eysenck has forcefully supported the nomothetic position. Now we would agree that the clinical standpoint always operates in everyday life ; we see the individual as a unique and integrated whole, and we make our predictions about him, or advise him, in the light of our understanding of his past history and present structure. Every biographer or novelist, every vocational or medical psychologist who is concerned with personalities, does the same ; and they would regard a cross-section of a person's measurements on a series of separate traits as entirely inadequate. But unfortunately the factual evidence, some of which is surveyed in our next chapter, seems to show that every layman's or psychologist's insight into an individual's personality is different. The ' clinical ' approach is so subjective and unreliable that more accurate predictions can often be made by narrower, though more objective, methods. The present writer would not accept Eysenck's extreme position, since the objective methods themselves give very variable and far from certain results. But he would urge that clinical judgments would always be assisted, and often corrected, by making use of

[1] Vernon, P. E., ' The Rorschach Inkblot Test '. *Brit. J. Med. Psychol.*, 1933, 13, 179–200.

[2] Vernon, P. E., ' Can the " Total Personality " Be Studied Objectively? ' *Char. & Person.*, 1935, 4, 1–10.

such objective techniques and scientific tests as are available. Moreover, he would reject the view that these two approaches must necessarily be opposed. On the one hand, most of the hypotheses about personality to be investigated, and most of the ideas for possible tests, derive from the clinical (medical or vocational) psychologist, or from everyday-life observations. On the other hand, the psychometrist can devise appropriate objective techniques for validating or disproving these hypotheses.

For example, the lay or psychological interviewer can be given full freedom to use his ordinary methods of enquiry, and to apply his insight, and yet express his conclusions in terms of predictions, say, of success in some job, which can then be validated in the same way as a test. The matching method, described in Chap. IV, enables correlations to be calculated between two sets of ' wholistic ' data, such as impressions of the voice or of handwriting, and sketches of the personalities. Even the uniqueness of every personality could be covered, theoretically at least, by the standard psychometric approach ; for if sufficient traits were measured, each personality would show a different pattern or profile of scores. Cronbach [1] has suggested one technique for comparing patterns of scores, as distinct from isolated variables, and many other statisticians are interested in this problem.[2] Especially fruitful are the techniques based on ' correlations-between-persons ' or ' between-occasions ' (Q- and P-techniques) developed by Burt, Stephenson, and Cattell,[3] since these make possible the statistical treatment of structural properties of individual personalities. Not only cross-sectional but also genetic-dynamic patterns can be formulated quantitatively. With the influx, especially in America, of laboratory-trained psychologists into the fields of clinical and consulting psychology, we may hope for more rapid advances in bringing the two approaches together.

[1] Cronbach, L. J., ' " Pattern Tabulation " : A Statistical Method for Analysis of Limited Patterns of Scores, with Particular Reference to the Rorschach Test '. *Educ. Psychol. Measmt.*, 1949, 9, 149–171.

[2] Cf. Banks, C., and Burt, C., ' Statistical Analysis in Educational Psychology'. *Current Trends in British Psychology* (edit. C. A. Mace and P. E. Vernon). London : Methuen, 1953.

[3] Burt, C. L., and Watson, H., ' Factor Analysis of Assessments for a Single Person '. *Brit. J. Psychol., Statist. Sec.*, 1951, 4, 179–192. Cattell, R. B., *Personality*. New York : McGraw-Hill, 1950. Stephenson, W., *op. cit.*, p. 17.

II

The Interview : Its Reliability and Validity

THE interview is the method most frequently used for assessing personality either for educational or vocational purposes, and for the diagnosis of maladjusted children and mental patients. There may be a single formal session conducted by a headmaster, prospective employer, or a group of people, where a rough picture of the personality of the interviewee is obtained and recorded in the form of notes or a personality sketch, or used to guide the decision to accept or reject. Or there may be a series of interviews, interspersed with observations of behaviour in the school, factory, or clinic, leading to the completion of a school's or personnel manager's record card, or the writing of a full case-study. The more sophisticated vocational psychologist may sum up his impressions by rating a series of standard traits. The psychological processes involved in conducting interviews and making judgments of personality are well described by Oldfield [1] (cf. also Chap. VII), and several useful books have been published on the technique of interviewing. A general summary is given by Vernon and Parry.

The interview is also the most comprehensive of methods, since it makes more or less use of all the techniques which we shall discuss in subsequent chapters, though usually in a haphazard manner : observations of external appearance, of gestures, voice and other modes of expression, and of behaviour under the stress of the interview situation or in response to difficult questions ; evidence regarding behaviour and achievements in the past ; self-descriptive data regarding the interviewee's interests, social attitudes, etc. ; and reference is usually made to testimonials or assessments provided beforehand by associates. The psychiatric interview may in addition include some projection material, such as free association and analysis of dreams. It is this very multifariousness which makes its results so uncertain ; there is so much scope for the

[1] Oldfield, R. C., *The Psychology of the Interview*. London : Methuen, 1941.

interviewer to jump to false conclusions, and to be influenced by prejudices and unsound theories. A notorious instance of this was described by Rice.[1] Two interviewers tried to discover the reasons for the destitution of large numbers of persons applying for relief. One, a socialist, found that 39% of his cases were attributable to industrial conditions, 22% to drink. The other, an advocate of temperance, found 7% and 62% respectively under these headings.

The selection interview is obviously unsatisfactory, too, because it provides such an unrepresentative and limited sample of the interviewee's behaviour. He is keyed up to make a good impression, and subjected to a situation very different from that commonly occurring in his later school career or job. But in spite of all the adverse evidence the interview is likely to remain the major technique for the following reasons. First, it is almost universally accepted not only by employers and others who require assessments of personality, but also by people who are to be assessed. The former would resent being unable to exercise their own powers of ' summing up ', and the latter are suspicious of more impersonal (even if more efficient) techniques such as tests, examinations, or written information. Secondly, it is quicker and more economical than any method involving tests, and also more flexible or adaptable to new purposes or to special circumstances. The development and validation of a battery of tests involves protracted work by skilled psychologists, and if candidates of a different age or different educational or social background come forward, the whole process needs to be repeated. Tests and other methods more objective than the interview can certainly be of great use in research on personality, but it will rarely be possible to apply them for any practical purpose other than supplementing the interview.

RELIABILITY AND VALIDITY

Before proceeding, we should clarify the meaning of the terms ' reliability ' and ' validity '. When a layman states that a test or interview is reliable he usually means that its results are correct and useful. This, however, is what the psychologist calls

[1] Rice, S. A., ' Contagious Bias in the Interview '. *Amer. J. Sociol.*, 1929, 35, 420–423.

valid—the extent to which the method predicts, or correlates with, some external criterion. As shown in Chap. I, the validity of a test or interview can be investigated : (a) by its correlations with other samples of behaviour or opinion (e.g. ratings) which are presumed to cover the same trait or quality ; (b) by its correlation with a trait-composite or factor ; (c) by its capacity to discriminate between groups known on other grounds to differ in personality, such as different types of neurotic patients, or successes and failures in a job.

Reliability is used to indicate the trustworthiness or stability of the test itself, apart from its representativeness or capacity for predicting anything else. Different kinds of tests or judgments possess different kinds of reliability and unreliability, and it will be as well to list some of the main ones. In subsequent chapters the type that is mentioned should usually be clear from the context.

1. The agreement between two or more persons in their judgments of, or decisions about, the personalities or traits of a group of individuals or ‘ subjects ’. This applies to interview assessments, to diagnoses of mental patients by psychiatrists, to ratings, and to interpretations of personality based on projection tests, or expressive movements.

2. The agreement between two or more observers in recording specified types of behaviour ; also the agreement between two or more scorers in sorting the responses of subjects to projection tests into the same categories (apart from any interpretation of the behaviour or the responses).

3. The agreement between scores or ratings received by the same subjects when the test, interview, or other method is repeated. Any method can be investigated in this way, but it is seldom done, both because the subjects’ responses may differ when they meet a situation a second time, and because personality qualities themselves are admitted to be somewhat unstable or liable to fluctuation. This may be denoted as repeat reliability.

4. The agreement between scores derived from one half of the test and those from the other half (e.g. the corrected odd-even technique), or the consistency of responses to all the items (Kuder-Richardson technique). The comparison of scores on two alternate forms of a test given on different occasions is intermediate between Nos. 3 and 4. So is the method some-

times applied to ' time-sampling ' (p. 94), where records of behaviour on alternate days over a considerable period may be inter-correlated. This type of reliability—better termed consistency—chiefly applies to objective tests and question-naires, and to certain projection test scores (e.g. Rorschach). It can be studied too when a judge gives ratings on several items presumed to cover the same trait, as in third-person questionnaires (p. 109).

5. A number of tests such as the Haggerty-Olson-Wickman Behavior Schedules, Kent-Rosanoff word association, Strong Interest Blank, etc. are scored by the resemblance of the subject's responses to those of a given group (mental patients, people in different vocations, etc.). Such scores tend to be unstable unless the standardization group was very large. In this instance, reliability can best be established by what is called cross-validation. Two groups of, say, mental patients are used, and two scoring keys developed which differentiate them from normal persons. Group I is then scored on Group II's key, and vice versa. The reliability of the keys is shown by the extent to which each group is differentiated from normals by the other's key. It is generally recognized nowadays that the same kind of procedure should be applied in all validatory studies, particularly of batteries of tests. Validities established within a single group only are often very unreliable.

RELIABILITY OF THE INTERVIEW

Obviously no method of personality assessment can be valid unless it is first reasonably reliable in any or all of the above senses. No exact standards can be laid down, but lower coefficients of reliability are normally accepted in the field of personality than in that of abilities. Only Type 2 correlations are expected to approximate to 1·0. For the other types, ·70 upwards would be considered satisfactory, and ·50 to ·70 as low but passable. Coefficients of ·85 and over are suspiciously high, unless obtained from exceptionally thorough tests or from the combined judgments of several persons. They may indicate that the method is assessing some rather artificial or stereotyped quality which possesses poor validity.

Hollingworth carried out one of the first studies of the reliability (Type 1) of interviewing. Twelve sales managers interviewed 57 applicants independently and ranked them on : ' suitability for the position in question '. He states that every applicant received rankings most of the way from the top to the bottom of the list, though he does not quote any inter-correlations. Hartog and Rhodes's [1] study of interviewing of 16 candidates by two boards of experienced Civil Service examiners deserves particular notice, since it was typical of much employment or scholastic interviewing. Each board had the candidates' educational records, and questioned each candidate for quarter to half an hour. The four or five members recorded separate assessments of alertness, intelligence, and suitability of personality for the Civil Service, and after discussion reached a final percentage mark. Within each board there was fairly close agreement, but the two boards differed greatly, the correlation between their final marks being only $\cdot41\pm\cdot14$. The average discrepancy in marks was 12%, but it ranged from 1% to 31% for different candidates.

Other studies by Webb, Magson, Fearing, Cantril, Hill and Williams, and work carried out in the Services during the war, are summarized by Vernon and Parry. They mostly yield correlations between interviewers of around $\cdot5$ to $\cdot6$. It may be useful to illustrate this figure. If 2 schoolmasters independently interviewed 100 candidates for a grammar school, and each picked the 20 best in his opinion, they would agree on 9 of their choices only and disagree on 11. This reliability is low, but it is no lower than that usually found for ratings of personal qualities by acquaintances who have known the subjects for some time (cf. Chap. VII). In one investigation by Newman, Bobbitt, and Cameron,[2] much higher figures of over $\cdot8$ were obtained. Here the psychologist and psychiatrist interviewers of officer candidates had thoroughly analysed and specified beforehand just what qualities they were looking for. The reliability of psychiatric diagnoses (that is the assignation of patients to particular neurotic or psychotic categories) cannot readily be stated, since so much depends on the coarseness of the classification and on the heterogeneity of the patients.

[1] Hartog, P., and Rhodes, E. C., *An Examination of Examinations*. London : Macmillan, 1935.

[2] Newman, S. H., Bobbitt, J. M., and Cameron, D. C., ' The Reliability of the Interview Method in an Officer Candidate Evaluation Program '. *Amer. Psychologist*, 1946, 1, 103–109.

Quite commonly there is disagreement on 50% of cases.[1] Large variations are also found in the proportions of cases (from comparable populations) which different psychiatrists put into the various psychopathological groups.

VALIDITY OF THE INTERVIEW

The evidence regarding validity is still less favourable, though Vernon and Parry quote studies where particular psychologists or personnel selection officers (PSOs) were notably successful in picking recruits for Service employments or for officer training. Usually the PSO in the Army or Navy had a record of the candidate's success on a number of intelligence, educational, or aptitude tests, and his answers to a biographical questionnaire. After interviewing him for about quarter of an hour, he summarized his judgments of suitability in a final recommendation and, in some experiments, assessed his likelihood of success in that employment. The remarkable result of several such investigations was that the PSOs' predictions, although combining the indications from tests with judgments of experience, personality and interests, were on the average less valid than predictions based on the best tests alone. Since there were big individual differences in the selecting ability of different PSOs, it follows that several of them must have given much worse predictions than the tests. Stuit[2] quotes similar results from the U.S. Navy where interviewers did no better, or even worse, than ability tests. (No personality tests were used in these studies.)

Similarly McClelland[3] followed up pupils in Dundee secondary schools and showed that, if account had been taken of primary school teachers' judgments of industriousness or other personality qualities, the number of instances of bad selection would not have been reduced. No investigation seems to have been made of grammar school headmasters' interviews, but they would hardly be likely to do better than the teachers who had

[1] Cf. Ash, P., ' The Reliability of Psychiatric Diagnoses '. *J. Abn. Soc. Psychol.*, 1949, 44, 272–276.

[2] Stuit, D. B. (edit.), *Personnel Research and Test Development in the Bureau of Naval Personnel.* Princeton, N.J. : Princeton University Press, 1947.

[3] McClelland, W., *Selection for Secondary Education.* London : University of London Press, 1942.

known the pupils for some years. This does not mean that the teachers could not judge suitability for secondary schools at all, but that the valuable element in their judgments was already incorporated in the ordinary school marks. Himmel-weit's [1] research on the selection of students at the London School of Economics is even more devastating. Interview judgments by a board of university teachers showed zero validity when checked against degree marks 1 and 2 years later ; whereas a short entrance examination gave small positive predictions of success, and a battery of aptitude tests considerably better predictions.

Such experiments cannot always be accepted at their face value, for two technical reasons. First, the accepted candidates who are followed up may have been actually selected chiefly on the basis of the interview. In such a selected group the validity inevitably drops, whereas the validity of tests, etc., which were used only indirectly or not at all for selection, is less affected. Secondly, many writers compare the interview with the best of a number of tests, or with the best combination of a battery of tests. Such validity coefficients are by no means stable, especially if the group is small. Different tests might rise to the top on another occasion, and the same battery with the same weighting of its component parts would certainly give a much lower coefficient (a phenomenon known as shrinkage). These snags can be allowed for, but they are often forgotten by those who condemn the interview as worthless.

RESEARCHES INTO THE SELECTION OF CLINICAL PSYCHOLOGISTS AND OF CIVIL SERVANTS

The most comprehensive investigation of interviews, ability *and* personality tests yet made is that of Kelly and Fiske into the selection of candidates for training as clinical psychologists. Each candidate was studied for 7 days. So far results have been published for a group of 76 to 93 cases, who were carefully assessed after 2 years of their 4-year training, and again at the end of their training. Thus a somewhat different picture may emerge when larger numbers are available, or when success on the actual job can be determined. The coefficients quoted in

---

[1] Himmelweit, H. T., and Summerfield, A., ' Student Selection—An Experimental Investigation, II '. *Brit. J. Sociol.*, 1951, 2, 59–75.

Table I are averages of correlations with the 2-year and 4-year assessments. They are all very small and statistically unreliable, but this is to be expected in highly selected groups. The following conclusions are indicated :

TABLE I

AVERAGE VALIDITY COEFFICIENTS OF PROCEDURES USED
IN SELECTING CLINICAL PSYCHOLOGISTS

	Correlations	
	2 yr.	4 yr.
Paper qualifications only, judged by 2 psychologists . .	·17	·22
Paper qualifications + 1 hour's interview . . .	·15	·25
Judgments based on paper qualifications + a number of objective tests	·27	·28
Separate objective tests only : Miller Analogies . .	·17	·30
Certain scores on Guilford-Martin Personality Inventory	·22	·16
Strong Interest Blank, scored for psychologist . .	·25	·20
Strong Interest Blank, scored for clinical psychologist .	·32	·16
Judgments based on above data + a series of projection tests	·29	·26
Separate projection tests, each given by an independent tester		
Rorschach Inkblots	·12	·05
Thematic Apperception	·11	·12
Sentence Completion (group test) . . .	·19	·21
Ditto + a further intensive interview . . .	·27	·26
Judgments of a team based on all the above . .	·24	·30
Ditto after observing ' Situations ' tests (final prediction) .	·20	·33
Situations alone judged by 3 independent observers .	·27	·22

1. The addition of the first or second interview does not increase the validity of predictions. (Note that these judgments were not used for the actual selection of candidates.)

2. The study of paper qualifications and objective test scores gives almost as good predictions as any of the methods involving personal contact with the candidates. The collection of more data, or the bringing of additional judges into the decision, seldom improves, and may lower, the validity.

3. Certain objective tests are superior to any method involving ' clinical ' judgment, though we cannot say whether these would stand up as well on subsequent occasions. A battery of the best objective ability and personality tests might well achieve a validity of ·4. The Situations tests also give promising results (cf. group-observation methods, p. 96).

4. The projection tests are decidedly less valuable than the better objective ones, and the simplest group projection technique is better than the elaborate individual ones.

5. The degree of confidence felt by the judges in any method provided completely misleading indications of its true value.

Kelly and Fiske's explanation of these results is that the more data the judge of personality has to go on, the more he is likely to over-weight indicators that have poor significance, and to under-weight those with good validity. If their findings are confirmed, it would follow that diagnostic methods which claim to penetrate most deeply into the personality or to give the fullest insight, such as psychiatric interviews and batteries of projection tests, are of less value for practical predictive purposes than quite superficial but more objective methods. We are not, of course, denying the usefulness of psychiatric diagnoses of psychopathological conditions, nor the ability of psychiatrists to make moderately good predictions of the onset of neurotic breakdown. Hunt [1] shows that psychiatric screening of recruits in the American Services was of some value ; though in the absence of experimental evidence, we cannot state that other more objective methods might not have been more successful. Again, in Chap. X, we shall see that projection tests such as Rorschach and T.A.T. are of proved worth in differential diagnosis of mental patients. But all these methods which depend largely on subjective, intuitive assessment, appear to be of very dubious value for vocational predictions.

At the same time, Kelly and Fiske's work must be accepted with caution. The somewhat similar selection and follow-up of British candidates for the higher administrative Civil Service and Foreign Service, described by the writer elsewhere,[2] point to rather different conclusions. These candidates too underwent a cumulative procedure, though it was less elaborate (lasting only 2 to 3 days), and no objective personality tests were used. The criterion against which validity was measured consisted of assessments after they had spent 1½ to 2 years at the job. The specimen coefficients quoted in Table II

[1] Cf. Wittson, C. L., Hunt, W. A., and Stevenson, I., ' A Follow-up Study of Neuropsychiatric Screening '. *J. Abn. Soc. Psychol.*, 1946, 41, 79–82.

[2] Vernon, P. E., ' The Validation of Civil Service Selection Board Procedures '. *Occup. Psychol.*, 1950, 24, 75–95.

refer to 330 selected candidates. They are higher than Kelly and Fiske's, mainly because they have been corrected for selectivity. The following points emerge :

1. Objective tests and examinations have poor predictive value. Even the best combination of them would hardly give a coefficient greater than ·3. Personality tests might have helped. Thus the sociometric rating is promising.

TABLE II

VALIDITY COEFFICIENTS OF VARIOUS PARTS OF CIVIL SERVICE SELECTION PROCEDURE

Entrance examinations, or verbal intelligence tests (average coefficient)	·22
Observation of discussion among groups of candidates (average for 3 observers)	·32
Ditto + observation of committee and other exercises (2 observers)	·44
Consideration of all above evidence + individual interviews (2 interviewers) . . . . . . ,	·47
Sociometric ratings by candidates themselves . . .	·29
Final mark after discussion between 3 observer-interviewers . .	·50
Separate board considers all above evidence and re-interviews .	·58

2. With the accumulation of evidence from successive exercises (Situations), the validities rise.

3. The addition of interviews produces no appreciable improvement ; (but the judgments based on exercises may to some extent have been contaminated by interview data, as the interviews did not always come last).

4. A re-interview by an independent board (containing no psychologists) does improve the final predictions significantly.

Another relevant research into the assessment of children's personalities is briefly described by Burt. Using teachers' ratings as criteria, he found that objective tests and judgments based on projection material gave the poorest validities. Individual interviews combined with observation of behaviour were more successful, and observations in standard social situations (cf. p. 96) better still. But the combination of methods, after discussion among 3 or more observers and interviewers, gave the highest validity.

There is good evidence also for the value of one type of interviewing in the follow-up studies of cases given vocational guidance by the National Institute of Industrial Psychology (cf. Vernon and Parry). A few tests of abilities are employed, but the recommendations are based mainly on the psychologist's synthesis of information from the school and the parents, and from an interview with the candidate. Over 90% of those who follow the recommendation are found to be satisfied and satisfactory in their jobs some years later, as compared with some 50% of those who go against the recommendation. It is possible that fuller tests of ability together with some personality tests would do better than this, but it is difficult to see how these could be chosen and applied when an unlimited range of occupations is under consideration. Here (as also in Civil Service selection and in Burt's investigation), the interviewer follows a systematic procedure designed to bring out the most relevant traits and interests, but makes little use of psycho-analytic interpretations or of projective testing. This may have something to do with the, apparently, more valid results.

CONCLUSIONS

We may conclude that many interviews given by untrained, and also some by very highly trained, persons are of little or no value for the practical assessment of personality. Nevertheless the method does give useful results in some circumstances. Unfortunately we know little about choosing good interviewers and training them. Clearly it is desirable to develop more objective methods, despite the difficulties pointed out in the previous chapter, and despite the fact that they do not seem to help much in increasing one's insight into or understanding of people. In guidance, counselling or therapeutic situations they cannot be expected to replace the overall picture of the develop-ment and structure of personality provided by the systematic interview and case-study ; yet they should often help to correct biased judgments or undue confidence on the part of the interviewer. In selection situations where large numbers of candidates are involved, and where scientific follow-up is possible, they might well improve on current interview procedures. It would be better indeed if the interview was confined to assessing certain traits which cannot readily be covered by other methods, that is—treated as one test whose results are combined with those of other tests. This approach is used, for example, in the selection of officers for the American Army, sometimes also in the British Civil Service and in secondary school selection. Jenkins describes the American officer boards, where the interviewers do not explore experience or background but look for and assess only those aspects of manner and speech, and social traits which are readily brought out in an interview situation. It is worth remembering that the object of selection is usually to pick people who will impress employers, colleagues, and subordinates favourably—not merely individuals who will do the job well. Often, therefore, the interview may constitute a useful analogous exercise (cf. p. 99).

We can now turn to a discussion of the more objective methods, or at least a selection of them. There has been so much ingenuity in the construction of tests, and so much experimentation often leading to variable or contradictory results, that we shall consider only those whose value, or lack of value, appears to be best authenticated. Elsewhere the writer has pointed out that psychological tests derive initially from the methods we normally employ in judging people in everyday life, or in interviewing them, though they are refined in a number of ways. ' A psychological test, by presenting a standardized task or situation, elicits a sample of the testee's behaviour which can be objectively scored and compared with norms of performance, and which has been proved to be predictive of future occupational or other behaviour.' In the field of personality this is an ideal rather than an actuality. Few tests have reached a stage where application and scoring are as standardized as in testing, say, intelligence ; and few have trustworthy norms, except for specialized groups such as American university students. Reliabilities are low, as already pointed out, and validities very difficult to establish. It is best, perhaps, to ask not what tests are available, but what methods show most and least promise in the scientific study of personality.

III

Physical Signs of Personality

PHYSIOGNOMY

HOW far are outer physical characteristics indicative of personality traits? Height and weight, body build, dimensions of the head and bumps on the skull, shape of profile, height of forehead, size of jaw, colour of hair and eyes, shape of the fingers, lines on the palm—all these at various times have been regarded as significant, and still play a part in popular lore. Red hair is sometimes said to show irritability, blue eyes—innocence; the jaw reveals determination or weakness, the forehead intellect, and so on. The ancient Greeks attributed to people the characteristics of animals which they resembled. For example, people with aquiline features were noble, but grasping, like eagles. Lavater and the physiognomists made careful studies of the features of outstanding people—artists, philosophers, soldiers, criminals—on the assumption that others who resembled them physically would be similar psychologically. The phrenologists analysed personality into a series of propensities and faculties, the strength of each of which was represented by the protuberance of a certain section of the skull. We should also mention, in passing, the astrologers' claim that personality is influenced by the stars under which one is born, since a remarkable number of people, particularly women, appear to find this credible. Many of our epithets for personality—martial, saturnine, lunatic, etc., derive from such superstitions.

When these alleged correlations are put to experimental test, scarcely a single one shows the slightest value. D. G. Paterson's *Physique and Intellect* gives a useful summary of the evidence. In general there is no agreement between measurements of any physical characteristic and judgments of personality given by acquaintances. For example, Paterson and Ludgate [1] asked

[1] Paterson, D. G., and Ludgate, K. E., ' Blonde and Brunette Traits : A Quantitative Study '. *J. Personnel Res.*, 1922, 1, 122–128.

94 students to assess people well known to them on 26 traits, and, on dividing these people into blondes and brunettes, found no appreciable difference in any trait. There was no support for the common belief that blondes are more domineering, dynamic, or impatient. The claims of German racial theorists regarding the superiority of Nordic physical types to Mediterraneans are equally baseless. These so-called races are distinguished not only by colouring of hair and eyes, but also by shape of skull ; Nordics being dolichocephalic or long-headed, Mediterraneans brachycephalic or broad-headed. But experiment has shown no relation between length or breadth of skull and either intelligence or other psychological qualities.

Another influential physiognomical theory was that of Lombroso, the Italian criminologist, who claimed that criminals belong to a degenerate physical type, which can be recognized by characteristic features or stigmata. But he omitted to enquire how often these same stigmata occur in non-criminals. Later research certainly shows poor physique and physical defects to be somewhat more common among criminals and delinquents, but there is no distinct criminal type.

Palmistry and Chirognomy. Psychologists often classify these along with astrology, phrenology and physiognomy as mere charlatanry. Recently, however, C. Wolff[1] has provided plausible reasons why certain dimensions of the hand and fingers, and lines on the palm, might be affected by endocrinological and neurological conditions, and thus indirectly reflect health, temperament, and intelligence. She describes a well-controlled experiment in reading from the hands alone ; her judgments of the personality traits of 24 students agreed with their self-judgments (an obviously unsatisfactory criterion) to a small but statistically significant extent. So far her methods have not been confirmed by others, and it is doubtful whether most professional palmists work on equally sound principles.

Readers may object that they themselves or their acquaintances have had remarkably accurate character-readings from palmists, phrenologists, and the like. Quite apart from fraud, there are good reasons why this is possible. First, there are a number of vague characteristics which anyone will accept as applying to themselves, e.g. ' strong sense of humour, abilities

[1] Wolff, C., ' Character and Mentality as Related to Hand-Markings '. *Brit. J. Med. Psychol.*, 1941, 18, 364–382.

not fully appreciated by others', etc. Morgenthaler[1] gave copies of a single phrenological diagnosis to 10 women, independently; on the average each of them considered that 70% of its statements accurately described herself. Secondly, the character reader seldom bases his judgments solely on specific features of the hand or head. There are numerous other clues—conversation, manner, dress, etc., and these contribute to a total impression which, as we shall see in the next chapter, may be much more revealing. Thirdly, we are apt to remember a few striking coincidences much more clearly than a large number of inaccurate statements.

Nevertheless there are some positive findings to be mentioned. First, there are gross pathological conditions such as cretinism and acromegaly, where disorders of the endocrine glands result both in physical and psychological abnormalities. The cretin (who has not received thyroxin treatment) is both mentally defective and sluggish in temperament. Again, men with very feminine, or women with very masculine, physique do tend to show some of the emotional qualities and interests of the opposite sex, according to Terman and Miles ;[2] though there are far too many exceptions for this to be a safe generalization in judging people. Secondly, there are slight positive correlations between height or weight, also size of head, and intelligence or academic ability on the one hand, and leadership or aggressive traits on the other. Galton and Pearson found that Honours students at Cambridge had heads some 2% larger in volume than ordinary or Pass Degree students. Industrial executives, political and religious leaders have been shown to be significantly taller and heavier than others less successful in their careers. The highly intelligent children studied by Terman[3] were generally superior in physique and health to average children of the same age, not—as is sometimes supposed—puny prodigies. The most thorough experiment was that of Murdock and Sullivan,[4]

[1] Morgenthaler, W., ' Ueber populäre Charackterdiagnostik '. *Schweiz. med. Wochenschrift*, 1930, 60, 351–360.

[2] Terman, L. M., and Miles, C. C., *Sex and Personality*. New York : McGraw-Hill, 1936. W. H. Sheldon (cf. p. 37) has also described a feminine physical type in men and its personality correlates.

[3] Terman, L. M., *et. al.*, *Genetic Studies of Genius*, Vol. I. Stanford, California : Stanford University Press, 1925.

[4] Murdock, K., and Sullivan, L. R., ' A Contribution to the Study of Mental and Physical Measurements in Normal Children '. *Amer. Phys. Educ. Rev.*, 1923, 28.

who found correlations of $+\cdot14$ to $\cdot16$ between the heights and weights of 600 children and their intelligence test scores.

But it should not be concluded that physical size means a large brain and that a large brain indicates intelligence. It is at least as likely that the more intelligent and successful individuals have usually been brought up in more favourable circumstances, and so tend to be superior in health and physique. Although in the evolution of animal species, increase in size of forebrain or cerebrum goes with increase in intelligence, and although the white human race has larger brains than certain primitive peoples such as Australian aboriginals, there is no proven correlation among whites. It has been suggested that complexity of convolutions or other features of the brain, rather than mere size, underlie intelligence. But in fact physiologists cannot, at present, tell us anything about the intellectual or other personality characteristics of an individual from examining his brain, except in cases of disease or gross abnormality. We need hardly add that there is no justification for any of the claims of the phrenologists. Not only is it untrue that mental capacities and personality traits depend on particular sections of the cerebrum, but also the strength of a faculty would not affect the size of that section, nor produce any swelling visible on the skull surface.

TYPES OF BODY BUILD

A third and more important correlation is that between body build and certain traits which may be roughly labelled introversion-extraversion. The notion of physical and temperamental types has a lengthy history, well described by Roback [1] in his *Psychology of Character*. Shakespeare summed it up :

> Let me have men about me that are fat ;
> Sleek-headed men and such as sleep o' nights :
> Yond Cassius has a lean and hungry look ;
> He thinks too much : such men are dangerous.

The best-known modern formulation is that of Kretschmer,[2] who found that a majority of schizophrenic patients were of

[1] Roback, A. A., *The Psychology of Character*. New York, Harcourt, Brace, 1927.
[2] Kretschmer, E., *Physique and Character*. London : Kegan Paul, 1925.

asthenic or leptosome (tall-thin-pale) and athletic (intermediate) build, whereas a majority of cycloid or manic-depressive patients were of pyknic (rotund-florid) physique. He extended this generalization to normal persons, claiming that asthenics tend to be schizothyme or quiet, sensitive, reserved in temperament, whereas pyknics are cyclothyme or emotionally labile, genial, and sociable. He also classified historical figures by body build, stating that they show distinctive philosophies or interests. For example, realists, humorists, and materialistic scientists tend to be pyknic, while romantics, idealist philosophers and metaphysicians tend to be asthenics.

Now we cannot accept Kretschmer's theories without qualifications. Later surveys, even of psychotic patients, do not always confirm his findings, particularly when age is controlled. (For manic-depressive insanity tends to occur later in life than schizophrenia, when more people are fat.) So far as geniuses are concerned, it is easy to pick out cases that fit ; no check was made on those that didn't. It is questionable, again, whether deductions based on psychotics apply to normals. Indeed by an ingenious adaptation of factor analysis (termed criterion analysis), Eysenck [1] has shown that schizophrenia and cycloid insanity cannot be regarded as extreme forms of a normal schizothyme-cyclothyme dimension. He did find, however, that the neurotic conditions of hysteria and dysthymia (anxiety+obsessional) are continuous with the normal, and that patients belonging to these extreme groups are to some extent differentiated by bodily build. Perhaps the most striking results among normals are those of Burt,[2] who prefers Viola's classification of build into macrosplanchnic (predominance of trunk over limbs) and microsplanchnic (predominance of vertical over horizontal dimensions), to Kretschmer's. He quotes correlations of ·32 in adults and ·26 in children with his sthenic-asthenic or extravert-introvert emotional factor.

Another controversial point is just what index of physical type to use. Kretschmer himself has a complicated series of criteria for classification, whose application appears somewhat

[1] Eysenck, H. J., *The Scientific Study of Personality*. London : Routledge, 1952. A better name would be ' rotation to a criterion ', since it does not, in fact, involve any analysis of the criterion.

[2] Burt, C. L., ' The Analysis of Temperament '. *Brit. J. Med. Psychol.*, 1938, 17, 158–188.

subjective. Moreover, his theory implies that every individual falls definitely into one of four distinct types, rather than that build is a matter of degree ; (the fourth type is the dysplastic or irregular). Other writers have suggested various more objective and quantitative morphological indices. Eysenck compared a large number of bodily measurements by factor analysis, and found the following simple index to be representative :

$$\frac{Height \times 100}{6 \times Chest\ Diameter}.$$ The average male adult obtains an index of 100, while asthenics range up to about 130, pyknics down to about 70.

In recent years an ingenious threefold classification of build and temperament has been put forward by Sheldon.[1] It is based on the relative development of three bodily components : endomorphy (roundness, softness), mesomorphy (hardness, muscularity) and ectomorphy (delicate, ' linear ' physique with weak development of both visceral and somatic structures). An individual is photographed from standard positions. From measurements of the pictures he is assigned a threefold rating on a 1 to 7 scale, indicating his standing on each component. For example a definite pyknic, on Kretschmer's system, might be 7 1 1, and a moderate asthenic 2 4 6. Sheldon's temperamental classification, which is claimed to correspond closely to the physical, is based on thorough clinical interviewing and observation. By means of ratings on 60 traits the relative prominence of viscerotonia (sociable, affectionate, love of comfort), somatotonia (vigorous, assertive, love of muscular activity), and cerebrotonia (reserved, love of privacy and mental activity), is determined. Sheldon's original correlations are obviously spurious, and later work suggests that the connection between his physical types and personality traits amounts to the usual figure of around ·2 to ·3.[2] Investigations have been made

---

[1] Sheldon, W. H., and Stevens, S. S., *The Varieties of Temperament.* New York : Harper, 1942. See also, Hunt, J. McV., Bibliography.

[2] Cf. Child, I. L., and Sheldon, W. H., ' The Correlation Between Components of Physique and Scores on Certain Psychological Tests '. *Char. & Person.*, 1941, 10, 23–34. Fiske, D. W., ' A Study of Relationships to Somatotype '. *J. Appl. Psychol.*, 1944, 28, 504–519. Smith, H. C., ' Psychometric Checks on Hypotheses Derived from Sheldon's Work on Physique and Temperament '. *J. Person.*, 1949, 17, 310–320. Child, I. L., ' The Relation of Somatotype to Self-ratings on Sheldon's Temperamental Traits '. *J. Person.*, 1950, 18, 440–453.

into the somatotypes of officer candidates and air-force pilots, but there seems to be no evidence that they are of any value in selecting men of suitable temperament. Like Kretschmer's types, somatotypes probably depend considerably on age.

PSYCHOSOMATIC AND ENDOCRINOLOGICAL RELATIONSHIPS

Although these small positive correlations are almost the only examples of direct relations between physique and personality, we should not forget the complex network of interactions between the physical and the emotional known as psychosomatics.[1] Adler pointed out that many persons suffering from an organic defect of speech, or the senses, or from a deformity, strive to compensate for this inferiority, and even develop special talent in the very field of their weakness. Demosthenes's impediment of speech and Beethoven's deafness are stock examples. People of very small stature not infrequently display excessive assertiveness or talkativeness. But there is, of course, no straightforward correlation here between some physical condition and a psychological quality. Rather it is a dynamic situation which differs widely in different individuals and which, while it may be traced out clinically, can hardly be expressed statistically. Demosthenes's impediment may have been one factor in making him a great orator ; in someone with a different personality it might just as well lead to shyness and taciturnity. Nevertheless one interesting research by Faterson [2] did yield a correlation of ·23 between the scores of students on an inferiority self-rating questionnaire (cf. p. 127) and the numbers of bodily defects or symptoms of disease elicited in medical examinations of these students. Another physical fact to which Adler attached much importance was order of birth. Being the oldest or youngest child in a family may affect personality development in various ways, but as Jones's [3] survey of the literature shows, no safe generalizations are possible. There does,

[1] Cf. Dunbar, H. F., *Emotions and Bodily Changes*. New York: Columbia University Press, 1938.

[2] Faterson, H. F., ' Organic Inferiority and the Inferiority Attitude '. *J. Soc. Psychol.*, 1931, 2, 87–101.

[3] Jones, H. E., ' Order of Birth in Relation to the Development of the Child '. *A Handbook of Child Psychology* (edit. C. Murchison). Worcester, Mass. : Clark University Press, 1931.

however, seem to be a slight tendency for only children to be more susceptible to maladjustment and delinquency than others.

There is some connection, again, between lefthandedness (and possibly left-eyedness) and personality. Certainly an undue proportion of delinquent and of educationally backward children are left-handed. But we cannot say whether left-handedness is a symptom of nervous and temperamental instability, or whether some young children with maladjusted personalities tend unconsciously to express their revolt against society by contrariness over handedness. Burt[1] gives an excellent discussion of the complex nature and origins of handedness. Certain sensory deficiencies are often the product of neurotic, rather than of purely physiological, conditions. Thus Eysenck finds defective dark adaptation or night vision useful as a measure of neuroticism. Similarly Slater[2] obtained poor visual acuity more frequently among neurotic patients than among normals.

Peptic ulcer is the most notorious example of a psychosomatic disorder. A large proportion of ulcer patients (though by no means all) tend to show a characteristically drawn and anxious facial expression, and to be asthenic in physique. They are often highly vigorous and ambitious people who drive themselves to the detriment of their health and digestion ; and the development of the ulcer often follows some serious disappointment or frustration in their lives[3] But it is hardly possible to say how far physical factors underlie the psychological, or vice versa. Certain forms of asthma and many other diseases have similarly been shown to be associated with, or to be unconscious expressions of, psychological mechanisms. Yet there is no one-to-one connection which would justify the diagnosis of people who are liable to particular illnesses as always belonging to particular personality types.

The notion that bodily chemistry underlies temperament goes back to the Greeks and Romans, to Hippocrates and Galen.[4] The four classical types of temperament—sanguine, choleric,

---

[1] Burt, C. L., *The Backward Child.* London : University of London Press, 1937.

[2] Slater, E., and Slater, P., ' A Heuristic Theory of Neurosis '. *J. Neurol. Neurosurg. & Psychiat.*, 1944, 7, 49–55.

[3] Cf. Davies, D. T., and Wilson, A. T. M., ' Observations on the Life-History of Chronic Peptic Ulcer '. *Lancet*, 1937, 1353–1360.

[4] Cf. Smith, M., ' The Nervous Temperament '. *Brit. J. Med. Psychol.*, 1930, 10, 99–174.

melancholic, and phlegmatic—were attributed to the relative prominence of four bodily fluids or humours—blood, yellow bile, black bile, and phlegm. The modern version of this doctrine is based on the discovery of the vital effects of the endocrine glands and their secretions on growth, health, and the emotions. Berman,[1] for example, not only describes a pituitary, a thyroid, and other types of personality in whom these glands are said to be dominant, but also claims to diagnose the types to which historical personalities belonged. And he attributes criminality and insanity largely to glandular disorders. Now it is certainly false to regard each hormone as responsible for some particular set of traits, although it may well be true that disturbances in the normal equilibrium of bodily chemistry do influence the emotions and behaviour. (Equally, personality maladjustment may in some cases bring about endocrine malfunction.) It is far too simple, for example, to regard the sex glands as determining masculine and feminine temperamental characteristics, or their efflorescence during puberty as producing the well-known instability of adolescence. For psychologists recognize that these sex differences and adolescent traits vary widely in different societies and are largely culturally determined. In other words, they are matters of personality, not only of temperament. It is, therefore, much too optimistic to expect a system of blood tests, or X-rays of the glands, to provide us with anything more than very rough indications of personality trends. Almost the only well-substantiated result is that disorders of the endocrine system, particularly of the pituitary, are found in a considerable proportion, perhaps 20%, of children showing serious delinquency or maladjustment.[2] But it is not clear whether such disorders can be diagnosed easily and objectively, nor how frequently they occur in psychologically normal children. Some investigators claim a correlation between alkalinity of body fluids and emotional stability, but this is denied by others.[3]

[1] Berman, L., *The Glands Regulating Personality*. New York : Macmillan, 1928.

[2] Cf. Healy, W., and Bronner, A. F., *New Light on Delinquency and its Treatment*. New Haven, Conn. : Yale University Press, 1936. Lurie, L. A., ' Endocrinology and Behavior Disorders of Children '. *Amer. J. Orthopsychiat.*, 1935, 5, 141–153.

[3] Cf. Gilchrist, J. C., and Furchtgott, E., ' Salivary pH as a Psychophysiological Variable '. *Psychol. Bull.*, 1951, 48, 193–210.

One would expect that persons with high basal metabolism would in general be more active and energetic than those who live at a lower rate. An investigation by Dispensa was unpromising, but both Sanford and Herrington provide confirmatory evidence.[1]

Another plausible theory which may help to link biochemical factors with bodily build and temperament is that some people are dominated by the sympathetic nervous system, others by the parasympathetic. ' Sympathicotonics ' are supposed to be more dominating, impulsive, active, while ' vagotonics ' are more anxious, depressed, and cautious. A large amount of work has been done with such indices of autonomic activity as basal metabolism, pulse, respiration, blood pressure, salivation, tendency to flushing, and sweating, etc. Unfortunately these variables fluctuate widely from day to day, and are mostly very specific, thus it is difficult to get reliable diagnostic measures on reasonable numbers of cases. And though factor analysis has been applied, there is no agreement as to what are the main physiological ' dimensions '.[2] Nevertheless the evidence suggests a general physiological activity factor, and an autonomic imbalance or sympathetic vs. parasympathetic factor. Sanford finds that parasympathetic response does link with asthenic build and (negatively) with social, outgoing, lively personality traits. Similarly Eysenck, using Wenger's best index—the salivation rate—found it to be higher among hysteric than dysthymic patients. He admits that this might be due to greater anxiety at being tested among dysthymics, which would inhibit salivation. Darling [3] considers that measures of psychogalvanic response (cf. below) and of blood pressure in children (which tend to be inversely related) correspond to parasympathetic and sympathetic activity. The

[1] Dispensa, J., ' Relationship of the Thyroid with Intelligence and Personality '. *J. Psychol.*, 1938, 6, 181–186. Sanford, R. N., *et. al.*, ' Physique, Personality and Scholarship '. *Monogr. Soc. Res. Child Devel.*, 1943, 8, No. 34. Herrington, L. P., ' The Relation of Physiological and Social Indices of Activity Level '. *Studies in Personality* (edit. Q. McNemar and M. A. Merrill). New York : McGraw-Hill, 1942.

[2] Cf. Darling, R. P., ' Autonomic Action in Relation to Personality Traits of Children '. *J. Abn. Soc. Psychol.*, 1940, 35, 246–260. Wenger, M. A., ' Studies of Autonomic Balance in Army Air Forces Personnel '. *Compar. Psychol. Monogr.*, 1948, 19, No. 4. Cattell, R. B., *Personality*. New York : McGraw-Hill, 1950. Sanford, R. N., *op. cit.* Herrington, L. P., *op. cit.*

[3] *Op cit.*

difference between them correlated to about ·3 with ratings on Activity, Alertness, Co-operativeness, and Attention.

Two other theories should be mentioned. McDougall [1] considered that introversion arises from inhibition of the lower by the higher nervous centres, and that this is released to some extent by chemical influences ; in other words, the extravert is normally in a state akin to mild intoxication. This has not led to any useful tests (cf. p. 79). Finally, there are Jaensch's T (tetanoid) and B (Basedowoid) types, which are believed to depend on the parathyroid and thyroid glands, and on calcium metabolism.[2] Originally derived from differences in eidetic imagery, the types are claimed to show not only distinct sensory and perceptual characteristics, but also different bodily physique and structure of the capillaries. (As pointed out in Chap. I, few of these correlations were based on any convincing evidence). Jaensch later expanded his theories into an elaborate system of integrate and disintegrate types ; the former were synthetic, intuitive people, the latter more analytic and inflexible. During the Nazi régime his typology became entangled with so-called racial psychology, and hardly merits further consideration.

THE PSYCHOGALVANIC REFLEX AND ELECTROENCEPHALOGRAPHY

At one time it was hoped that the psychogalvanic reflex would provide a significant clue to emotional traits (cf. Fig. 2). The electrical resistance of some part of the body, usually the hand, is measured continuously by a Wheatstone Bridge apparatus, and it shows marked fluctuations (which are outwith conscious control) when the person is stimulated, say, by an electric shock, or by the threat of a shock, or by emotionally toned words in a free association experiment (cf. p. 172). Like the pulse, blood pressure and respiration, or muscular tonus (cf. p. 53), it is affected by psychological tensions. Thus it is often included in so-called Lie Detection instruments. Unfortunately, however, there is no simple association between the reflex and any

---

[1] McDougall, W., ' The Chemical Theory of Temperament Applied to Introversion and Extroversion '. *J. Abn. Soc. Psychol.*, 1930, 24, 293–309.

[2] Jaensch, E. R., *Eidetic Imagery and Typological Methods of Investigation*. London : Kegan Paul, 1930.

particular mental state. The PGR is the end result of a variety of factors—circulatory, postural, sweat secretion and temperature, not to speak of the thickness of the cuticle, the position of the electrodes, and other vagaries of the apparatus ; and it is elicited to varying extents in different people by a great variety of stimuli. Thus, although twenty or more experiments on the psychological correlates have been published, their

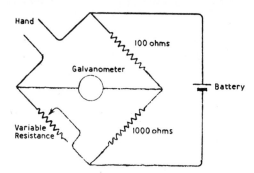

Fig. 2.—Psychogalvanic Reflex. Electrodes are attached to the back and palm of the subject's hand, or to two fingers, and are connected to a battery by a Wheatstone Bridge circuit. The variable resistance is then adjusted until no deflection appears in the galvanometer ; the subject's resistance (multiplied by 10) can be read off. When a stimulus is applied the resistance tends to drop, and the galvanometer needle moves.

results are largely contradictory. Perhaps the most thorough work is that of Darrow and Heath.[1] Neither initial, nor average resistance, nor total drop in resistance during the application of a series of standard stimuli, show any clear relation to other tests or ratings of emotional traits, though rapid recovery rate from stimulation appears more promising. Since there is a definite tendency for more emotional word associations to evoke bigger responses than less emotional,[2]

[1] Darrow, C. W., and Heath, L. L., ' Reaction Tendencies Relating to Personality '. *Studies in the Dynamics of Behavior* (edit. K. S. Lashley). Chicago, Ill. : Chicago University Press, 1932.

[2] Cf. Smith, W. W., *The Measurement of Emotion*. London : Kegan Paul, 1922.

the average or percentage response per stimulus is often considered to give a measure of ' emotionality '. Some studies bear this out, but others, including those of Darrow and of the writer, fail to do so and suggest more connection with social, extraverted, traits. We would conclude that the PGR may be of value in clinical studies of the associations or other stimuli which arouse most tension in an individual, but that it can hardly be employed as a generalized test of any identifiable personality trait.

The electroencephalograph, which records the overall electrical activity of the brain in the living subject, has also been less fruitful as an objective indicator of mental phenomena than was anticipated. The main rhythm—the alpha waves— does develop with age during early childhood, but is apparently unrelated to intelligence. Walter [1] claimed to be able to distinguish visual thinkers from verbalizers among adults by means of their EEG records, though this has not been confirmed. One very useful finding is the appearance of certain abnormal wave forms in almost all epileptics ; and the EEG is now regularly employed in diagnosing this condition. Similar abnormalities occur in some 60% of psychopaths, and in considerable proportions of delinquents and criminals, but only in 5–10% of normal stable adults.[2] But it turned out to be quite useless in the selection of air-crew. Although then we have here a reliable test of some condition of the brain which underlies certain mental abnormalities, its significance for personality is still obscure.

In conclusion : although this chapter is so largely negative, it would be as incorrect to say that physical characteristics are unrelated to personality as it would be to claim that a large jaw always means strength of will, or that slender fingers always indicate an artistic nature. What we have shown is that, with rare exceptions, no isolated physical or chemical symptom has any invariable significance. Hence any system of personality diagnosis based on such signs is certain to be false. None the less, many anatomical or biochemical factors may exert an important influence in the development of the individual

[1] Walter, W. G., ' Electro-Encephalography '. *Recent Advances in Psychiatry*. London : Churchill, 1944.

[2] Cf. Hill, D., and Watterson, D., ' Electro-Encephalographic Studies of Psychopathic Personalities '. *J. Neurol. & Psychiat.*, 1942, 5, 47–65.

personality. Some of these—such as body build, and certain chemical, psychogalvanic and EEG measures—might occasionally be included in appropriate trait composites, although they do not constitute samples of behaviour in the sense described in Chap. I. We shall see, also, in the next chapter that the features, hands and body may, when subjectively interpreted, be expressive of personality.

IV

Expressive Movements

IN judging personality from external appearance we normally rely more on an unanalysed impression of the general balance of facial and bodily proportions than on specific signs, also on the movements or play of the features and limbs during conversation, walking, or other behaviour. Consider first, however, what can be deduced from the total static appearance as given in photographs of individuals otherwise unknown to us. In numerous experiments observers have been asked to rank sets of ' photographees ' for intelligence or other traits, or to identify such characteristics as vocations, or to decide which of a number of emotions the photographee is expressing. The last of these is fairly easy. Adults and older children are usually quite successful in naming the more primitive emotions—anger, fear, laughter, disgust, etc., rather less so in judging the more subtle expressions such as disillusionment (though much depends on the aptness of the particular photograph). However, this is an artificial type of experiment. Landis [1] has shown that actors (who usually supply the photographs) can readily portray a number of stereotyped and conventional expressions, but that unsophisticated persons subjected to highly emotional situations do not necessarily assume any such consistent or recognizable expressions. In fact we depend as much on the context or total situation in judging facial expressions of emotions as on the features themselves : witness the difficulty of telling what the people on a cinema screen are expressing if one enters in the middle of a film, until one has had time to pick up the thread of the plot. Even if, as Charles Darwin suggested, there were consistent and universal muscular adjustments for each main emotion, it would not necessarily follow that more permanent traits would be revealed by similar contractions. The highly

[1] Landis, C., ' The Interpretation of Facial Expression in Emotion '. *J. Gen. Psychol.*, 1929, 2, 59–72.

irritable or the good-humoured individual might or might not habitually show the expressions typical of anger or happiness, respectively.

The ranking of photographs for intelligence gives very low average correlations of $+\cdot10$ or less with intelligence test scores, though some raters achieve fairly high correlations and others negative coefficients. There is no tendency for psychologists, teachers, or doctors to do any better at this than other judges, and women are no more successful than men. It is found, however, that most judges agree more closely with one another than with the true order; in other words, that there is a fairly widespread convention as to what the intelligent or dull person looks like—a convention which is largely fallacious. Pintner [1] questioned his judges and found that they relied on a diversity of signs such as bright eyes, wearing spectacles, also on resemblances to acquaintances. Judgments of personality traits such as sociability, efficiency, energy, humour, etc., may be slightly more successful, though it is, of course, more difficult to get an objective criterion of accuracy, and most investigators have employed ratings by associates. Burt [2] obtained coefficients ranging up to $+\cdot37$ for certain traits, though the average was only $+\cdot18$; and the present writer obtained an average of only $\cdot01$ when rankings of 10 students' photographs on 4 traits were compared with composite measures of these traits. It was noticeable that the judgments of the different traits—intelligence, artistic interests, sociability and efficiency—overlapped considerably; and that the 5 students who received the highest average judgments on all traits were all smiling when photographed, whereas the 5 with low judgments all happened to be caught frowning or with solemn or disagreeable expressions. Uhrbrock has published similar results, and Thornton shows that wearers of spectacles tend to be rated especially high in intelligence, industriousness, and honesty. [3]

[1] Pintner, R., ' Intelligence as Estimated from Photographs '. *Psychol. Rev.*, 1918, 25, 286–296.

[2] Burt, C. L., ' Facial Expression as an Index of Mentality in Children '. *Child Study*, 1919, 12, 1–10.

[3] Uhrbrock, R. S., ' Estimating Intelligence from Photographs '. *Proc. IX Intern. Cong. Psychol.* Princeton, N.J. : Psychol. Rev. Co., 1930, 451–452. Thornton, G. R., ' The Effect of Wearing Glasses upon Judgments of Personality Traits of Persons Seen Briefly '. *J. Appl. Psychol.*, 1944, 28, 203–207.

Landis [1] and several other investigators have obtained virtually no agreement between judgments of vocational success from photographs and actual success.

This shows the worthlessness of asking for photographs with applications for jobs, except perhaps in choosing a private secretary or a mannequin. If the applicant puts on a pleasant smile when being photographed he is likely to be credited with all the desirable traits of intellect and character, whereas a less fortunate pose will damn him with most employers. Although it is true that some judges are more accurate than others, this ability to judge is highly variable and uncertain. Success at one set of photographs, or at one trait, is very little indication of success at other sets, or other kinds of judgments (cf. p. 118).

At the same time, this method of correlating rankings with external criteria of the photographees' traits is open to serious criticism. It is likely that most individuals do reveal some aspects of their personalities in static photographs, though they do not all provide any reliable evidence of the same aspects. In another experiment the writer listed 30 traits in random order, 6 of which were known from a previous investigation to be particularly applicable to each of 5 photographees. Judges managed to match 33% of these traits with the appropriate photograph, and this represents a moderate agreement, equivalent to a correlation of ·32.[2]

A famous study of stereotypes was made by Rice.[3] Nine photographs, including a French premier, a senator, a bootlegger, and a Russian Bolshevik were given to several groups of judges to fit or match with their titles. Many of the matches revealed the existence of biased or stereotyped opinions as to what such people should look like. Thus one of the photographees had a beard, and the majority called him the Bolshevik; but the Russian himself presented a distinguished foreign

[1] Landis, C., and Phelps, L. W., ' The Prediction from Photographs of Success and of Vocational Aptitude '. *J. Exper. Psychol.*, 1928, 11, 313–324.

[2] This and other matching coefficients quoted below are contingency coefficients. Burt's matching formula : $\sqrt{\dfrac{c-1}{t-1}}$ (where c=correct choices, t=number of choices) yields higher correlations, for example ·41 in this experiment ; (cf. Vernon and Burt, Bibliography).

[3] Rice, S. A., ' " Stereotypes " : A Source of Error in Judging Human Character '. *J. Personnel Res.*, 1926, 5, 267–276.

appearance, and the majority identified him as the French premier. Nevertheless one quarter of all the judgments were correct, where one ninth would be expected by pure chance, suggesting therefore that people do to some extent conform to our stereotypes, or that our judgments do have some slight validity. Arnheim, Gahagan, and the present writer [1] carried out numerous experiments where small sets of photos of unknown writers, politicians, or other persons had to be matched with excerpts from their writings, with their professions, with short case-studies, specimens of handwriting, records of their voices and so forth, and in almost all of these a considerable superiority to chance success was found, corresponding to coefficients of around ·4. Yet another technique which works well is to get the judges to write free characterizations of the photographees in their own words. Most of the sketches appear to contain a good deal of accurate material, and this can be proved objectively by asking other judges who know the original photographees to guess which sketch refers to which person.

In this field of expression the matching method [2] is an advance on methods which deal with one trait at a time. But it has various weaknesses. Although numerous judges can be used, they cannot deal with more than about half a dozen personalities at once. Hence their success is very variable, depending largely on the heterogeneity of the particular personalities. It is better for each judge to match several sets of material, chosen at random. When matching, say, photographs with character sketches or case-studies, it often happens that some single phrase in a sketch happens to give the clue. A remark about health or stature, neatness, maturity, etc., may allow an identification, without any real consideration of the personality as a whole or the appearance as a whole. Other photographs in the set which do not happen to fit in with the judges' stereotypes may never be matched correctly except by a process of elimination.

[1] Arnheim, R., ' Experimentell-psychologische Untersuchungen zum Ausdrucksproblem '. *Psychol. Forsch.*, 1928, 11, 1–132. Gahagan, L., ' Judgments of Occupations from Printed Photographs '. *J. Soc. Psychol.*, 1933, 4, 128–134. Vernon, P. E., ' Can the " Total Personality " be Studied Objectively ? ' *Char. & Person.*, 1935, 4, 1–10.
[2] Cf. Vernon, Bibliography.

EXPRESSIVE MOVEMENTS

One would expect to get better judgments from observations of living, moving people, or from motion pictures, than from static photographs. It is useful to distinguish here between expressive and adaptive behaviour. The latter implies reactions to particular situations, where we are interested in *what* an individual does and *why*, i.e. in his aims and achievements. While the former connotes *how* he acts, regardless of the ' content ' of his behaviour. It includes facial expressions, gestures, postures, poses ; also voice and style of speech, hand-writing and literary or artistic style (though not the content of what is said or written). Dress and furnishings of a room are among the other characteristics which to some extent reflect the personality of the owner. Naturally the two types of behaviour overlap, and we commonly rely on both content and style in judging a person ; but it is not difficult to separate them for research purposes.

In an attractive book, *A Mirror of Personality*, J. G. Vance [1] writes : ' Almost everything we do gives some clue to the hidden self, and particularly everything which just happens without premeditation.' Part of Freud's *Psychopathology of Everyday Life* is devoted to showing that apparently aimless movements are no more determined by chance than are slips of the tongue or lapses of memory, and that they unwittingly reveal inner traits and wishes. A full discussion and classification is given by Allport and Vernon in *Studies in Expressive Movements*.

To a larger extent than is commonly recognized, these modes of expression depend on the conventions and customs in which the individual has been reared. Thus the clergyman's voice, the army officer's gait and straight back, the Bohemian artist's clothes, the stenographer's painted finger-nails, the Frenchman's free—and the Englishman's restricted—use of his hands in conversation, have little significance for personality. They are useful, of course, in enabling one to identify the social groups to which an individual belongs. But one needs to be familiar with national, occupational, or social class differences before one can observe genuine individual differences. Similarly, the graphologist must know the script which a writer was originally

[1] London : Williams and Norgate, 1927.

taught, and base his interpretations on deviations from this model. Movements are much affected also by health or fatigue, and by environmental restrictions such as the pressure of clothes or furniture on the body or, in the case of writing, the kind of pen-nib and paper.

This does not mean, however, that our non-adaptive movements are merely specific learned habits. Thus every adult's writing differs from what he or she was originally taught in a manner peculiar to himself. Moreover, this individual style does not depend only on the finger and wrist muscles and nerves, for it reappears if one writes on the blackboard, or with the left hand, or with the toe on a smooth sand surface. Handwriting is a particularly useful mode of expressive movement to study because it leaves a permanent trace ; it is a crystallized gesture. But the same conclusions hold good for any other mode. How they arise, and how far they reflect either conscious traits or unconscious tendencies, is too complex a psychological problem to be considered here. Only in rare instances, such as obsessional hand-washing, can the clinical psychologist trace fairly clearly the origin of any particular movement.[1] And this means that the interpretation of any expression is highly subjective and uncertain. The obvious deductions—that a loud voice shows domineeringness, a flabby handshake weakness, an illegible handwriting disorderliness, are probably as often as not untrue. Many expressions are compensatory. Sometimes different parts of the body are contradictory, as when a shy and nervous person controls his face and voice but gives himself away with his hands or feet. And intentional distortion of manner, or playing a part, is not difficult ; many people, such as salesman, largely live by it.

Probably our judgments of temporary emotions or moods are reasonably successful, in that they enable us to get on with one another in daily life, without too many misunderstandings. But, as in the case of the features, it does not follow that more permanent traits can be inferred or intuited. One thing we do know from experiment is that there is a strong trend towards reliability and consistency. Allport and Vernon measured the speed, extension, and pressure of a large number of simple

[1] Cf. Krout, M. H., ' A Preliminary Note on Some Obscure Symbolic Muscular Responses of Diagnostic Value in the Study of Normal Subjects '. *Amer. J. Psychiat.*, 1931, 11, 29–71.

movements, in walking, writing, drawing, etc., and found quite high correlations between different occasions and different muscle groups. Moreover, the man who was expansive in having large handwriting tended to draw large figures on the blackboard or with his foot in sand, to take big strides in walking, and to overestimate angles when his lower arm was rotated. In addition to this ' areal ' or expansive quality of movement, it was possible to establish a quality of ' centrifugality ' or ' outward-tendency ', and a factor of force or emphasis. Similarly, a series of experiments by Wolff [1] showed that independent judges could match different modes of expression with some success—motion pictures of bodily actions, records of the voice, profiles, handwritings, and styles of retelling a story.

Investigations which try to correlate judgments or measurements of expressive movements with ratings by associates, test scores or other criteria of personality, generally give positive but not very good results. Cleeton and Knight [2] had a number of people sitting silent on a platform. Judgments by observers on several traits gave an average correlation of only +·23 with friends' ratings, but this was noticeably better than the average validity of ·00 for several measurements of physiognomical features which were studied in the same experiment. Eysenck, Himmelweit, and Petrie [3] find no good differentiation on a number of simple expressive movement tests between neurotic and normal adults or children, but claim more promising results with psychotic patients. Estes [4] took motion pictures of several pairs of subjects engaged in such actions as removing coat and shirt, holding a lighted match, and wrestling with each other. These subjects had been very comprehensively studied and assessed previously in Murray's [5] research, thus it was possible to show that judgments

[1] Wolff, W., *Expression of Personality*. New York : Harper, 1943.

[2] Cleeton, G. U., and Knight, F. B., ' Validity of Character Judgments Based on External Criteria '. *J. Appl. Psychol.*, 1924, 8, 215–231.

[3] Eysenck, H. J., *The Scientific Study of Personality*. London : Routledge, 1952. Himmelweit, H. T., and Petrie, A., ' The Measurement of Personality in Children '. *Brit. J. Educ. Psychol.*, 1951, 21, 9–29.

[4] Estes, S. G., ' Judging Personality from Expressive Behavior '. *J. Abn. Soc. Psychol.*, 1938, 33, 217–236.

[5] Murray, H. A., *et. al.*, *Explorations in Personality*. New York : Oxford University Press, 1938.

based on the films alone agreed significantly with independent evidence about their personalities. One of the most interesting points was that university teachers and professional psychologists were rather poor judges of the films, artistic and literary people better than average. In Wolff's study, free characterizations of the subjects were written by judges who observed their modes of expression, and these were identified by acquaintances of the subjects—with varying success. Wolff found that subjects themselves often failed to identify their own modes of expression (e.g. their voices), but nevertheless showed strongly emotional reactions to them. For example, they wrote longer and more favourable or unfavourable characterizations of them than they did of other people's. This suggested that some modes reflect, not the conscious personality structure, but deeper tendencies which the subject is unwilling to accept. However, Huntley,[1] who confirmed most of the experimental results, points out that they could be more simply explained by ' ego-involvement '. A subliminal or partial recognition of one's own voice might be sufficient to evoke the same halo effect that occurs in ordinary self-ratings.

Another approach is that of Enke,[2] who claims characteristic differences between the expressive movements of pyknics and asthenics, which are therefore presumably related to temperament. Pyknics tend to be more unrestrained, smooth, flexible, and varied both in gestures and postures, play of the features, voice, and handwriting. For example, in carrying a full glass of water across a room, asthenics are said to move cautiously with ' anguished ' expressions, pyknics to be more slap-dash.

Numerous techniques of recording the tension of various muscle groups, and its variations, have been devised,[3] and there is much evidence pointing to a connection between such tension and emotional tension. Jacobsen,[4] for example, bases his

[1] Huntley, C. W., ' Judgments of Self Based upon Records of Expressive Behavior '. *J. Abn. Soc. Psychol.*, 1940, 35, 398–427.

[2] Enke, W., ' Die Psychomotorik der Konstitutionstypcn '. *Zsch. f. ang. Psychol.*, 1930, 36, 237–287.

[3] Cf. Davis, R. C., ' Methods of Measuring Muscular Tension '. *Psychol. Bull.*, 1942, 39, 329–346.

[4] Jacobson, E., *Progressive Relaxation*. Chicago : University of Chicago Press, 1929. ' The Neurovoltmeter '. *Amer. J. Psychol.*, 1939, 52, 620–624.

treatment of neurotic and unstable patients largely on the practice of progressive muscular relaxation. He describes an instrument—the neurovoltmeter—for summating action potentials, and thus measuring the total contraction tendencies of, say, the relaxed arm. As yet, however, there is no direct

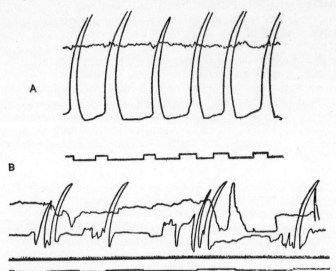

Fig. 3.—Motor Reactions on a Luria Apparatus of: (A) a stable, and (B) an unstable subject, during a free association test. In each record the upper line represents the pressure of the left hand resting passively; the next line shows the compression by the right hand of a rubber bulb as the subject responds to each stimulus; the bottom line indicates the time between the stimulus word and the response.

(Reproduced from *The Nature of Human Conflicts*, by A. R. Luria. By permission of Liveright Publishers. Copyright 1932.)

demonstration that individual differences correlate with recognizable differences in personality. The Russian psychologist, Luria,[1] reports very striking results from free word association tests in which the subject presses a bulb with his right hand as he gives each response, and also rests his left hand on a surface which records involuntary tremors or pressure

[1] Luria, A. R., *The Nature of Human Conflicts*. New York: Liveright, 1932.

variations. This continuous record from both hands shows irregularities when highly emotional verbal stimuli are given (in this respect it is quite similar to the psychogalvanic reflex), or when the subject is under strain, and even more marked disorganization occurs among neurotics (cf. Fig. 3). These effects are widely confirmed in the literature, though it can scarcely be said that they have yet led to a simple and straightforward test. Clarke, and Albino [1] report correlations between neuroticism and right-hand, and left-hand disturbances, respectively, during word association tests. Several studies of muscular tension in young children have been carried out by Duffy,[2] where the pressure of the hand on a rubber bulb was recorded during reaction time and other tests. She claims correlations of around ·5 with assessments of the children's excitability and emotionality.

VOICE SPEECH, AND HANDWRITING

The voice is an interesting form of gesture which happens to be made by the throat muscles, and to be audible instead of visible. Intonation and dynamics ; speed, rhythm, and continuity ; pronunciation ; vocabulary and choice of words, and style all provide important clues in our reactions to one another's personalities.[3] Pear [4] has pointed out the rôle of the voice in judgments of social class and, in an experiment over the radio, found that occupation and age can be guessed fairly accurately. Dusenbury and Knower [5] showed that emotions can be expressed by, and recognized from, tone of voice as accurately as from facial expressions. Asthenic or pyknic

[1] Clarke, A. D. B., *The Measurement of Emotional Instability by Means of Objective Tests*. Ph.D. Thesis, University of London, 1950. Albino, R. C., ' The Stable and Labile Personality Types of Luria in Clinically Normal Individuals '. *Brit. J. Psychol.*, 1948, 39, 54–60.

[2] Duffy, E., ' The Measurement of Muscular Tension as a Technique for the Study of Emotional Tendencies '. *Amer. J. Psychol.*, 1932, 44, 146–162.

[3] Cf. the analyses by Newman, S., and Mather, V. G., ' Analysis of Spoken Language of Patients with Affective Disorders '. *Amer. J. Psychiat.*, 1938, 94, 913–942 ; and Moses, P. J., ' The Study of Personality from Records of the Voice '. *J. Consult. Psychol.*, 1942, 6, 257–261.

[4] Pear, T. H., *Voice and Personality*. London : Chapman and Hall, 1931.

[5] Dusenbury, D., and Knower, F. H., ' Experimental Studies of the Symbolism of Action and Voice, II '. *Quart. J. Speech*, 1939, 25, 67–75.

physique can be identified with moderate success,[1] and different types of psychotics show many characteristic differences in voice and speech.[2] The most extensive study was that of Allport and Cantril,[3] where sets of three speakers read identical passages to large audiences, either from behind a curtain, or through microphone and loudspeaker. Various characteristics of the speakers were known, and the listeners tried to match these with the voices. Occupations, political affiliations, specimens of handwriting, and photographs were identified only slightly better than chance would allow (coefficients of around ·2). But high or low scores on tests of ascendance-submission and extraversion-introversion were correctly matched 47% of times (vs. 33% by chance), and short descriptions of the total personalities of the speakers were even better recognized, the correlations being ·29 and ·41 respectively. As in experiments with photographs, judges tend to have common stereotypes about voices, whether or not these are correct.

In the field of speech, much work has been done on the development of vocabulary, grammatical forms and length of sentences, with age. More relevant to personality are Piaget's observations on the egocentricity and dogmatism of the language of young children, and their inability to conceive impersonal causation. As Sanford [4] suggests, there may well be significant differences among adults in these same qualities, which might be measured from their conversation. We commonly regard rate of speaking as indicative of impulsiveness-deliberation, and fluency or facility as characteristic of extraversion, and there is some slight supporting evidence. Rogers (cf. p. 70) found that oral fluency did not overlap at all with fluency in written tests, when general verbal ability was held constant ; the former, but not the latter, correlated around ·3 with ratings on such traits as cheerfulness. Johnson [5] discusses

---

[1] Cf. Fay, P. J., and Middleton, W. C., ' Judgment of Kretschmerian Body Types from the Voice as Transmitted over a Public Address System '. *J. Soc. Psychol.*, 1940, 12, 151–162 ; Moses, *op. cit.*

[2] Cf. Newman and Mather, *op. cit.*

[3] Allport, G. W., and Cantril, H., ' Judging Personality from Voice '. *J. Soc. Psychol.*, 1934, 5, 37–55.

[4] Sanford, see Bibliography. Cf. also Henle, M., and Hubbell, M. B., ' "Egocentricity" in Adult Conversation'. *J. Soc. Psychol.*, 1938, 9, 227–234.

[5] Johnson, W. B., ' Studies in Language Behavior, I. A Program of Research '. *Psychol. Monogr.*, 1944, 56, No. 2, 1–15.

a number of quantitative measures of language, such as the Type/Token ratio—the number of different words over total words. One of the most promising is the Verb/Adjective ratio, which has been shown by Busemann [1] to correlate positively with ratings of emotional stability. Again Balken and Masserman [2] find the highest proportion of verbs in the speech of anxiety neurotics, the lowest among hysteric patients. Much investigation needs to be done into the consistency of speech measures; it is only too likely that a person's style varies greatly in different contexts and different social situations.

In the ordinary interview, the interviewer not only has the full range of modes of expression to judge from, but can also take account of the content of what the interviewee says. The fact that interview judgments are often so inconsistent and inaccurate, even with this additional data, indicates that expressive movements and voice alone are too readily misinterpreted to yield any easy test of personality which would possess high validity.

For this reason one would not expect the analysis of handwriting to be as useful as graphologists claim, though it has the advantages not only of permanence but also of being more spontaneous and less liable to intentional distortion or disguise than any other mode of expression. It has the disadvantage that only about a quarter of the population are sufficiently fluent writers to have developed a mature, individual, style. Graphologists admit that children's and poorly educated adults' scripts are much less revealing, though H. J. Jacoby believes that even the scribblings of pre-school children are to some extent diagnostic. (His book, *Analysis of Handwriting*,[3] may be recommended for a general review. Allport and Vernon, and Bell, survey the psychological literature.)

We must distinguish clearly between the older graphological systems which attributed significance to specific signs or details (such as length of t-bars, height of upper and lower ' projections ', etc.) and more modern methods based on the work of

[1] Busemann, A., *Die Sprache der Jugend als Ausdruck der Entwicklungsrhythmik.* Jena : Fischer, 1925.

[2] Balken, E. R., and Masserman, J. H., ' The Language of Phantasy '. *J. Psychol.*, 1940, 10, 75–86.

[3] London : Allen and Unwin, 1939.

Klages and Saudek, which emphasize the dynamic pattern of the script as a whole, its flow and rhythm, its control and drive. Objective investigations in which measurements of details are correlated with ratings of the writers give results as negative as do studies of physiognomical signs.[1] Nevertheless there seem to be a few significant relations, e.g. backhanded slope, relatively small capital letters, and insufficient space between lines, tend to go with certain traits of emotionality or introversion.[2] Many psychologists concluded from the early investigations that the whole of graphology was mere quackery. Some of their other studies have shown a complete lack of understanding of the graphologist's aims and methods (e.g. several which prove that untrained judges can guess the sex of the writer in about 66% of cases, where 50% could be got by chance). On their side, graphologists have been somewhat unwilling to submit to the requirements of scientific experimentation, and are apt to use an esoteric jargon for describing personality which renders validation very difficult. They claim that the usefulness of graphology is proved if the writers themselves, or their acquaintances, accept their personality sketches as accurate. This is quite unconvincing to the psychologist.

The possibilities of a more Gestalt-like approach are shown by Wolff's and Arnheim's work, already mentioned, and by Bobertag's[3] study. Here several graphologists analysed handwriting specimens and wrote case-studies describing the personalities of the writers. Friends of the writers then matched or identified these with an average success of 80%, where only 20% would be expected by chance. In a similar experiment Theiss[4] had untrained judges match scripts with thumbnail personality sketches. His enquiries showed that half the judges relied on the general pattern of the writing, while a third

[1] Cf. Hull, C. L., and Montgomery, R. B., ' An Experimental Investigation of Certain Alleged Relations between Character and Handwriting '. *Psychol. Rev.*, 1919, 26, 63–74.

[2] Cf. Land, A. H., ' Graphology, a Psychological Analysis '. *Univ. of Buffalo Stud.*, 1924, 3, 81–114. Harvey, O. L., ' The Measurement of Handwriting Considered as a Form of Expressive Movement '. *Char. & Person.*, 1934, 2, 310–321.

[3] Bobertag, O., *Ist die Graphologie zuverlässig?* Heidelberg, Kampmann, 1929.

[4] Theiss, H., ' Experimentelle Untersuchungen über die Erfassung des handschriftlichen Ausdrucks durch Laien '. *Psychol. Forsch.*, 1931, 15, 276–358.

employed more specific signs. Powers,[1] also Cantril and Rand [2] in other matching experiments got moderately good results from professional graphologists, and poorer ones from non-graphologists. Stein Lewinson [3] was able to predict failures in college work and personality maladjustment with considerable success from her analyses of the handwritings of women students. Eysenck [4] found that a graphologist could to some extent predict the answers of neurotic patients to a personality questionnaire, and could match her analyses with personality diagnoses written by psychiatrists. Some of the patients appeared to express themselves in their writing much more completely than others, and some questions were much better guessed than others. In a later research,[5] another graphologist (considered to be professionally skilled) entirely failed to differentiate the handwritings of a group of neurotics from those of normals. There is plenty of evidence, however, that certain types of psychotics show strongly differentiated handwriting characteristics. This is summarized by Bell.

In conclusion it should be pointed out that modern graphology is a highly skilled art and science. The amateur who attempts to apply it after reading one or two books is unlikely to give diagnoses of any value at all. Many so-called professionals are also inept, and there is no ready means of distinguishing the bad from the good. The best undoubtedly are able to produce very penetrating diagnoses of some (though not all) mature writers. But even they are limited in what they can cover. For example, handwriting gives little scope for the recognition of special talents, or social attitudes. It may chiefly be expected to throw light on the emotional structure, conscious and unconscious, of the personality, on character integration and neurotic mechanisms. How completely these are expressed in graphic movements we do not yet know.

---

[1] Powers, E., cf. Allport and Vernon, Bibliography.

[2] Cantril, H., and Rand, H. A., ' An Additional Study of the Determination of Personal Interests by Psychological and Graphological Methods '. *Char. & Person.*, 1934, 3, 72–78.

[3] Cf. Munroe, R., Stein Lewinson, T., and Waehner, T. S., ' A Comparison of Three Projective Methods '. *Char. & Person.*, 1944, 13, 1–21.

[4] Eysenck, H. J., ' Graphological Analysis and Psychiatry : An Experimental Study '. *Brit. J. Psychol.*, 1945, 35, 70–81.

[5] Eysenck, H. J., ' " Neuroticism " and Handwriting '. *J. Abn. Soc. Psychol.*, 1948, 43, 94–96.

Handwriting pressure and its variations constitute an important element in graphological analysis. Usually they are

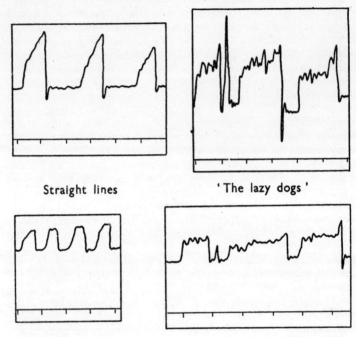

Straight lines   'The lazy dogs'

Fig. 4.—Handwriting Pressure Variations as Expressive of Personality. Two students — one an immature, self-assertive, extravagant and unstable individual, the other a colourless, quiet, agreeable and dependable person — drew some short straight lines and then wrote a sentence containing the words 'the lazy dogs'. These records show remarkable differences between the writers in the application of pressure to the point of the pencil while carrying out the same simple tasks, differences which appear to be characteristic of their personalities.

(Reproduced from *Studies in Expressive Movement*, 1932, by G. W. Allport and P. E. Vernon, by permission of The Macmillan Company.)

judged by the thickness of the trace made by the nib, or the depth of indentation of the paper. Numerous instruments have been devised for giving more accurate records both of point-pressure (on the paper) and grip-pressure (of the hand on the pen) ; though almost all of these have the disadvantage of interfering to some extent with normal writing movements. Such records show marked individual differences both of average pressure and of pattern, which appear to reflect the personalities of the writers (cf. Fig. 4), and which are characteristically distorted in some organic and functional disorders. Both Allport and Vernon, and Pascal,[1] quote correlations of ·5 to ·6 between point-pressure and such traits as Energy and Expressiveness. More systematic exploration of the possibilities of such apparatus is badly needed.

Two other methods developed out of graphic movements by clinical psychologists deserve mention. Mira's [2] myokinetic diagnosis (P.M.K.) requires the patient to draw with each hand in turn series of straight, zigzag and circular lines of standard form, in various spatial directions. Half-way through each task his vision is blocked, and the subsequent kinaesthetically-guided movements naturally tend to diverge from the original form. The type of drift is claimed to throw light on inner emotional and aggressive trends. Bender's [3] Visual-Motor Gestalt test gives scope for distorted perception as well as inaccurate motor reproduction of shapes. It is based, like the Binet Memory for Designs, on observation and drawing of a number of simple figures. Characteristic disturbances occur in cases of nervous and mental disorder. Similarly Bühler [4] has described abnormal features in responses to the Stanford-Binet Ball and Field test among neurotic children. There is little evidence as to the diagnostic possibilities of such tests in more normal personalities.

Artistic productions and literary style might logically be considered here, but are more conveniently postponed to the chapter on projective techniques (pp. 180, 192).

[1] Pascal, G. R., ' Handwriting Pressure : Its Measurement and Significance '. *Char. & Person.*, 1943, 11, 235–254.

[2] Mira, E., ' Myokinetic Psychodiagnosis '. *Proc. Royal Soc. Med.*, 1940, 33, 173–194.

[3] Bender, L., ' A Visual Motor Gestalt Test and its Clinical Use '. *Res. Monogr. Amer. Orthopsychiat. Ass.*, 1938, No. 3. See also Pascal, G. R., and Suttell, B. J., *The Bender-Gestalt Test.* New York : Grune and Stratton, 1951.

[4] Bühler, C., ' The Ball and Field Test as a Help in the Diagnosis of Emotional Difficulty '. *Char. & Person.*, 1938, 6, 257–273.

BEHAVIOUR DURING PERFORMANCE TESTS

One of the chief difficulties in direct, objective, testing of personality is that subjects so readily guess the object of the test, correctly or incorrectly, and tend to modify their normal behaviour in order to make a favourable impression. There is much to be said, therefore, for more indirect tests where subjects think that their abilities are being tested, and do not realize that at the same time their expressive movements and manner of performance are being observed. Discussing the methods of personality assessment available in the 1920s, Burt [1] wrote : ' The most helpful suggestions are to be gained, not from any formal or quantitative work, but rather from an alert attention to his method of attack . . . his confidence, heedlessness, his readiness to co-operate, his attitude when faced by difficulty or doubt ; the sidelights so secured are often far more illuminating and far more correct than any single score on a scale.'

Most psychologists who have written about individual Binet, Merrill-Palmer, or performance tests, have stressed the value of observing the child's reactions to difficulties and his social behaviour in the testing situation. And many test record sheets contain rating scales for the personality traits which commonly emerge. Goodenough [2] found that negativism, shyness, and distractibility in young children, as rated by different testers at successive tests, are fairly reliable, at least over short periods. Most children do not behave entirely differently on different occasions or with different testers. On the next page is reproduced a fairly comprehensive rating sheet which the writer uses in any suitable test or interview situation with adults. It follows the principle of Freyd's graphic rating scales (cf. p. 107). A cross or tick is made on each of the vertical lines in order to express rapidly the approximate standing of the subject on each quality. Additional items may be added for particular tests, e.g. the Porteus Mazes. It should be completed directly after the testing session and supplemented by descriptive notes.

[1] Burt, C. L., *The Young Delinquent*. London : University of London Press, 1925.
[2] Goodenough, F. L., ' The Emotional Behavior of Young Children during Mental Tests '. *J. Juven. Res.*, 1929, 13, 204–219.

Although the tester can base his judgments on the full range of expressive movements, including conversation, the method has serious limitations. The subject is in an unusual situation, and there is no guarantee that he will react to the problems set before him in the same manner as he habitually reacts in daily life. Particularly in testing adults, it is difficult to produce a natural, spontaneous, atmosphere. It is only too easy, also, to jump to conclusions from slight evidence, to misinterpret facial, vocal, or other expressions, or to be biased by chance resemblances to acquaintances, by general like or dislike of the testee, or by hasty first impressions, etc. On the other hand the psychologist usually has the advantage of coming fresh to each testee, uninfluenced by previous knowledge of him. Clearly everything depends on his impartiality, experience, and intuitive skill.

In one experiment by the writer,[1] 25 students were observed by 3 testers (2 of them quite inexperienced) in three different performance test sessions. The average agreement between their impressions, determined by the matching of personality sketches, was represented by a correlation of ·72. They also rated the subjects on Practical Intelligence, Quickness, and Impulsiveness, Extraversion-Introversion, and Emotional Stability. The average inter-correlation of ·56 shows a considerable amount of variation either in the subjects' behaviour or in the testers' interpretations. Nevertheless the correlations of the summed judgments with composite measures of the same traits averaged ·50 (·43 to ·61), showing a very promising validity.

The method can be made still more useful by including a wide variety of tests which will stimulate the subjects to display more significant behaviour. Ordinary individual intelligence, educational and performance tests are hardly provocative enough. It can also be developed in such a way as to yield quantitative indices at least of certain traits, and thus reduce the amount of subjective judgment. A good example of this is the Q or Quality score in the Porteus Mazes,[2] based on the number of times the subject crosses or touches the printed lines, cuts corners, starts to go up wrong turnings, lifts his pencil, etc. Porteus states

[1] Vernon, *op. cit.*, p. 49.
[2] Porteus, S. D., *Qualitative Performance in the Maze Test.* Vineland, N.J. : Smith Printing House, 1942.

GENERAL RATING SCALE FOR QUALITATIVE OBSERVATIONS DURING TESTING AND INTERVIEWING

Name.. Date................... Examiner ....

ACTIVITY

Excited, restless, unable to keep still	Impulsive
Quick and vivacious	
	Stable
Calm and deliberate	Cautious
Inert and listless	Inhibited

Poses, motor attitudes..

Tics .... Nail-biting .... Twitchings ....

Fiddling with material............... Clothes............... Hands............... Feet.............

Peculiar expressions..................................Excessive wrinklings...................................

MOVEMENT

Fluent and graceful	
Accurate and well-controlled	Quick stride and movements
Angular and awkward	Slow stride and movements
Clumsy	

PHYSIQUE AND BEARING

Impressive in bearing	Healthy looking, well developed and nourished
Satisfactory impression	
Unimpressive	Unhealthy, feeble physique

Forceful, efficient, energetic, upright posture and gait
Slouching gait
Weak, inefficient movements and bearing

Plump (pyknic)proportions	Florid
Well and symmetrically proportioned	
Thin (asthenic)	Pale

PERSONAL APPEARANCE AND EXPRESSION

Attractive and good-looking (positive reaction)

Pleasant	Sensual ....
Uninteresting, indifferent attractiveness	
Ugly and repulsive (negative reaction)	Effeminate ....

| Strong expressiveness of face and gestures | Frank |
| Expressionless | Secretive |

Quick and strong sense of humour	Cheerful, optimistic
Slow but sure	Depressed, melancholy
Unable to see humour	

Mature, serious, philosophical	Excitable, irritable
	Even-tempered
Immature, childish	Calm, phlegmatic

PERSONAL CARE

Fastidious in dress, over-manicured
Good taste, neat and clean
Passable and inconspicuous
Careless in dress and cleanliness
Slovenly and unkempt

SPEECH

Voice resonant, pleasing, well-modulated	Clear, fluent, distinct
Hard, harsh, pinched	Stutters, stammers

Expresses meaning directly, grammatically, with facility
Unable to express himself, ungrammatical

Accent...

Garrulous, over-talkative	
Rather voluble	Brilliant in talking, wide vocabulary
Seldom speaks of own accord	Dull and stolid, narrow vocabulary
Reticent, taciturn	

SELF-ASSERTION

Pompous and overbearing	
Complacent	Decisive
Self-confident and possessed	
	Wavering
Self-critical and deprecatory	
Embarrassed, bashful, self-conscious	Contrasuggestible
Anxious, apprehensive	
Submissive, retiring	Suggestible

CO-OPERATIVENESS

Willing to co-operate in every respect ; enters into spirit

Reserved and formal
Constrained and suspicious, outside the situation
Surly and hostile

Scrupulous, punctual and regular in attendance and application
Industrious

Easy-going, indifferent
Lazy and irregular

ALERTNESS AND CONCENTRATION

Intelligently attentive, wide-awake
Concentrated

Absent-minded
Easily distracted, inattentive

TEST REACTIONS : PLANNING

Analytical	
Serious but unsystematic	Profits by past experience
Trial and error	
Haphazard	Repeats same mistakes

EMOTION

Wild and unrestrained emotional behaviour and remarks
Wilful and childish reactions, capricious
Some loss of self-control and overt emotion
Humorous and unconcerned
Serious, philosophical
Repressed and inhibited

SPECIAL CHARACTERISTICS..

....

....

65

that delinquents and adult criminals make an average of two to three times as many such errors as normal controls, but this has not yet been independently confirmed. Foulds,[1] for example, finds few differences between neurotic and normal adults, though different types of neurotics show some characteristic differences, particularly in speed of maze performance.

A series of measurements indicative of emotional reactions to psychomotor and performance tests, together with rating scales, were devised by Biesheuvel [2] and his associates in selecting South African Air Force pilots during the last war. It is claimed that these helped in choosing men with suitable personalities as well as aptitudes. However, the evidence is equivocal, for similar methods tried out in the USAAF gave very meagre correlations of ·1 to ·2 with the criterion of passing vs. failing pilot training. In fact they were scarcely superior to judgments based on appearance alone.[3] Similarly M. D. Vernon [4] attempted to develop methods of gauging liability to breakdown under stress. Subjects worked at a dotting machine (cf. p. 85) at high speed for several minutes, and at other tests likely to induce strain, and records were made of their performance in successive half-minutes. From the upward or downward, or irregular trend, and from qualitative observations, a somewhat subjective rating of stability was reached. But no good evidence of the predictive value of these ' trend tests ' is available. Other more objective techniques are described in Chap. VI.

Even in group paper-and-pencil tests of abilities there is some scope for individual differences in manner of performance, which may express the testees' personalities without their being aware of it. Some people check multiple-choice answers only when they are certain, others guess more wildly. Guilford and Lacey [5] have shown that a consistent error-score factor (distinct from ability at the tests as such) may be extracted,

---

[1] Foulds, G. A., ' Temperamental Differences in Maze Performance. Part I. Characteristic Differences Among Psychoneurotics '. *Brit. J. Psychol.*, 1951, 42, 209–217.

[2] Biesheuvel, S., ' An Observational Technique of Temperament and Personality Assessment '. *Nat. Inst. Personnel Res. Bull.*, 1949, 1, No. 4.

[3] Guilford, J. P., and Lacey, J. I., *Printed Classification Tests*. Army Air Forces Aviat. Psychol. Prog. Res. Rep. No. 5. Washington, D.C. : U.S. Government Printing Office, 1947.

[4] Cf. Vernon and Parry.

[5] *Op cit.*

which they term ' carefulness '. In her research on student selection, Himmelweit [1] found such an error score to add appreciably to the prediction of subsequent degree results. Conceivably this might be useful too in selecting grammar school pupils by objective group tests, but it has not yet been tried. (The pupils and their teachers would, of course, have to be kept in ignorance, otherwise the very careless might be trained to modify their test behaviour.)

In conclusion it would seem that the evidence for objective indices is somewhat less favourable than that for subjective judgments of manner of performance by experienced testers. But much more research is needed.

[1] Himmelweit, H. T., and Summerfield, A., ' Student Selection—An Experimental Investigation, II '. *Brit. J. Sociol.*, 1951, 2, 59–75. Cf. also Brown, W. M., ' A Study of the " Caution " Factor and its Importance in Intelligence Test Performances '. *Amer. J. Psychol.*, 1924, 35, 368–886. Manson, G. E., ' Personality Differences in Intelligence Test Performance '. *J. Appl. Psychol.*, 1925, 9, 230–255. Fruchter, B., ' Error Scores as a Measure of Carefulness '. *J. Educ. Psychol.*, 1950, 41, 279–291.

V

Simple-Behaviour and Cognitive Tests

THERE is no hard and fast distinction between the indirect tests of the previous chapter and many of the tests described below such as oscillation, will-temperament, dotting machine, and the group observation methods. However, most of the tests in this and the subsequent chapter were devised to measure directly, or to sample, particular traits or types of behaviour. It will be apparent that early workers in the field of objective tests (probably influenced by the highly analytical trend of German experimental psychology) resorted chiefly to very simple sensory, motor, or ideational tests. Particularly in Britain, the development of mental testing was dominated by C. E. Spearman, and most of the work on personality, apart from that of Burt, was restricted by his narrow views of temperament. He laid it down that there were three main factors or dimensions [1] :

> p—perseveration, the tendency to inertia, or hang-over effect, in mental processes, as contrasted with the ability to switch quickly from one process to another ;
> f—fluency or quickness and richness of mental associations ;
> o—oscillation or variability in the performance of any task.

The very elementary tests of these factors, together with the analogous temperament tests constructed by Downey in America, were generally unreliable and highly specific. They showed little overlap with one another, and they had scarcely any bearing on the personality qualities of everyday life. Thus the majority of more recent tests, as shown in Chap. VI, have approximated more closely to natural samples of behaviour.

---

[1] There was also, of course, Webb's W or will-character factor, but this was based on ratings, not tests. A useful summary of the work of the Spearman school is given by Wynn Jones, L., *An Introduction to Theory and Practice of Psychology*. London : Macmillan, 1934.

SPEED AND FLUENCY

The first question to ask is whether some people are consistently quick or slow in all their actions and thoughts. In other words, is there a factor of personal tempo, possibly related to extravert-introvert temperament, which could be measured by reaction time, tapping or other dexterity tests, or speed of walking, or quickness at intelligence or other tests ? The writer has discussed the evidence elsewhere,[1] and has shown that considerable consistency does exist, both among manual and cognitive tests, but that to a greater extent speed is specific to particular kinds of activities. For example, different measures of reaction time correlate very closely, also different tapping tests ; but reaction times give much lower correlations with tapping. The same is true when records are made of normal speed of movement, in walking, speaking, writing, etc., as distinct from maximum speed. Thus Rimaldi [2] repeated and extended Allport and Vernon's investigation by giving 59 tests of normal speed to a group of students. He analysed his results into a series of multiple factors representing different types of speed. But in fact almost all his inter-correlations were positive, so that it would be justifiable to recognize a small general factor, together with group factors for quickness at special types of activity.

Schwegler, Notcutt,[3] and the present writer have obtained small correlations between various speed or fluency tests and extraversion among children and adults ; and Kretschmer's claim for quicker movements and reaction times in pyknics than in asthenics has had some confirmation. Himmelweit [4] points out that most dexterity tests can be scored for speed *or* accuracy, and that these two measures are largely independent, or even negatively related. When a choice is given, hysteric

[1] Vernon, P. E., *The Structure of Human Abilities*. London: Methuen, 1950. Cf. also Allport and Vernon, Bibliography.

[2] Rimaldi, H. J. A., ' Personal Tempo '. *J. Abn. Soc. Psychol.*, 1951, **46**, 283–303.

[3] Schwegler, R. A., 'A Study of Introvert-Extrovert Responses to Certain Test Situations '. *Teach. Coll. Contr. Educ.*, 1929, No. 361. Notcutt, B., ' Perseveration and Fluency '. *Brit. J. Psychol.*, 1943, **33**, 200–208.

[4] Himmelweit, H. T., ' Speed and Accuracy of Work as Related to Temperament '. *Brit. J. Psychol.*, 1946, **36**, 132–144.

patients tend to do better on tests scored for speed, dysthymics on tests scored for accuracy.

In the intellectual, as distinct from the motor, field it is quite difficult to separate speed from ' power ', i.e. from general intelligence. However, such tests as those mentioned below usually yield a factor for fluency of mental associations (Spearman's f), over and above g and v factors, which may have some significance for personality. Here also some investigators sub-divide it into more specialized types.[1] Examples of fluency tests used by Cattell, Stephenson and Studman, Thurstone, Eysenck, Rogers, and others [2] include :

> Writing as many words as possible in a minute beginning with the letter S ; or words ending with ' tion ' ;
> Writing as many names of animals, birds, plants, as possible, in a minute each ;
> Writing adjectives to describe a house ; listing names of round objects ;
> Giving associations to inkblots ;
> Speed of free word association, or numbers of words in continuous association ;
> Suggesting objects which could be inserted at a certain spot in a picture.

Normal speed of reading, and productivity in writing compositions, or in building words from a given set of letters, have also been used ; and several of the above tests have been applied orally. It has been shown that manic patients score higher in f than melancholics, and Cattell [3] claims that his battery of written tests scores as highly as ·6 with assessments of ' surgency ' among normal subjects. Probably this is largely attributable to halo (cf. p. 5), for no one else has approached this figure. Petrie [4] found that f tests do not differentiate between hysterics and dysthymics, and an extensive and thorough research by Rogers [5] gave negative results. He

---

[1] Cf. Vernon, *op. cit.*

[2] Cattell, R. B., *A Guide to Mental Testing*. London : University of London Press, 1936. Stephenson, W., Studman, G. L., *et. al.*, ' Spearman Factors and Psychiatry '. *Brit. J. Med. Psychol.*, 1934, 14, 101–135. Thurstone, L. L., ' Primary Mental Abilities '. *Psychometr. Monogr.*, 1938, 1. Rogers, C. A., *A Factorial Study of Verbal Fluency and Related Dimensions of Personality*. Ph.D. Thesis, University of London, 1952.

[3] *Op cit.*   [4] See Eysenck, Bibliography.   [5] *Op cit.*

applied a large variety of fluency tests and personality ratings to a representative group of 14-year-olds. His oral fluency tests did show some relation to ' surgent ' traits, but his written ones none at all. It has been shown by Bousfield and Sedgwick [1] that the production of responses in a typical fluency test tends to follow an exponential curve, and the constants for such a curve might be identified with the total reservoir of the subject's responses and with their rate of exhaustion. Rogers found no evidence that these more analytic fluency measures gave any better correlations with personality traits.

INTELLIGENCE AND PERSONALITY

As mentioned in Chap. I, general intelligence itself overlaps to some extent with the emotional and moral sides of personality. For example, in Terman's *Genetic Studies of Genius*,[2] the gifted children tended to have a wider range and better quality of interests than average, to be superior on character tests and ratings, and in emotional adjustment (though those with the highest I.Q.s of all were somewhat more liable than the rest to show difficulties of adjustment). Conversely, mental defectives are certified on grounds of social inadequacy and emotional instability as well as of low intelligence, and these qualities are to some extent associated.[3] Among adults, again, intelligence is quite clearly connected with cultural interests, and small positive correlations have been found with such attitudes as internationalism, tolerance, liberal, or progressive opinions, etc.[4]

An extremely tangled situation exists in the field of psychopathology, and we can review it only rather superficially, since its bearing on the assessment of normal personalities is

[1] Bousfield, W. A., and Sedgwick, C. H. W., ' An Analysis of Sequences of Restricted Associative Responses '. *J. Gen. Psychol.*, 1944, 30, 149–165. This equation was first put forward by Thomson, G. H., and Thompson, J. R., ' Outlines of a Method for the Quantitative Analysis of Writing Vocabularies '. *Brit. J. Psychol.*, 1915, 8, 52–69.

[2] Stanford, Calif. : Stanford University Press, 1925.

[3] Cf. Doll, E. A., ' Preliminary Standardization of the Vineland Social Maturity Scale '. *Amer. J. Orthopsychiat.*, 1936, 6, 283–293. O'Connor, N., and Tizard, J., ' Predicting the Occupational Adequacy of Certified Mental Defectives '. *Occup. Psychol.*, 1951, 25, 205–211.

[4] Cf. Allport, G. W. ' The Composition of Political Attitudes '. *Amer. J. Sociol.*, 1929, 35, 220–238.

limited.[1] On most intelligence tests the scores of neurotics differ
little if at all from those of normals; but psychotics, especially
those of the organic type, are distinctly poorer. Performance
declines also in aphasic conditions, or with brain injury, and
to some extent with age; (indeed much of the deficit among
psychotics may be an age effect). But this deterioration is
certainly more marked on some kinds of tests than others, and
is usually least on tests of what Cattell [2] calls 'crystallized'
intelligence, such as Vocabulary, whose level represents, as it
were, what intelligence has achieved in the past. Tests of
'fluid' intelligence, which are most affected, include speeded
tests, tests involving complex abstraction or conceptualization,
spatial judgment and orientation, memory (e.g. of digit series),
etc. Several deterioration indices have been devised which
contrast scores on tests that 'hold' and 'don't hold', for
example, the Babcock-Levy, the Shipley-Hartford, and the
Wechsler-Bellevue.[3] Unfortunately such indices are not very
reliable, and although they show considerable group differences,
they give very low correlations with one another in individual
diagnosis. (It is seldom realized that difference scores are
always much less reliable statistically than are the separate
scores from which they are derived; also, that two such scores
obtained from two imperfectly correlated sets of tests may
scarcely correlate at all with one another.) [4] Naturally the

[1] Useful reviews are given by Hunt, J. McV., Bibliography, and Brody,
M. B., 'A Survey of the Results of Intelligence Tests in Psychosis'. *Brit.
J. Med. Psychol.*, 1942, 19, 215–261.

[2] Cattell, R. B., 'The Measurement of Adult Intelligence'. *Psychol.
Bull.*, 1943, 40, 153–193.

[3] Babcock, H., and Levy, L., *Revision of the Babcock Examination for
Measuring Efficiency of Mental Functioning*. Chicago, Ill.: Stoelting,
1940. Shipley, W. C., 'A Self-administering Scale for Measuring Intel-
lectual Impairment and Deterioration'. *J. Psychol.*, 1940, 9, 371–377.
Wechsler, D., *The Measurement of Adult Intelligence*. Baltimore, Md.:
Williams and Wilkins, 3rd edit., 1944.

[4] Discrepancies between school achievement and intelligence level are
often regarded as giving an index of some personality factor such as
industriousness. These too are apt to be very unreliable when measured
by single attainment and intelligence tests. The Achievement Quotient
is particularly unsatisfactory; educational attainment should be compared,
not with M.A. or I.Q., but with predicted attainment based on the regres-
sion of attainment on intelligence. Cf. Chapman, J. C., 'The Unreliability
of the Difference between Intelligence and Educational Ratings'. *J. Educ.
Psychol.*, 1923, 14, 103–108.

type of deterioration differs in different psychopathological conditions, and elaborate systems of diagnosis have been based on discrepancies between the various Wechsler-Bellevue sub-tests, concept-formation tests, particular Stanford-Binet items, and so forth.[1] Rabin and Guertin [2] have surveyed the Wechsler literature, and concluded that there is little or no prospect for the success of any mechanical system of differential diagnosis based on profiles of performances on cognitive tests. Yet at the same time it may well be true that an experienced clinical psychologist can, from studying a patient's pattern of responses to diverse tests, obtain useful insights into his mental condition, and thus assist in making the psychiatric diagnosis. In spite of the enormous amount of material available in clinics and mental hospitals, and the hundreds of investigations that have been published, we still seem to have no thoroughly established quantitative indices. The contradictory and confusing results arise, no doubt, partly because patients in any one psychiatric group are never homogeneous and entirely distinct from other groups, partly because of the influence on test performances of poor co-operation during mental illness, and partly because of the difficulties of making allowance for age and previous education.

The same conclusion holds for variability or range of scores on different tests. Many psychologists working in Child Guidance Clinics believe that a wide scatter of passes and fails on the Stanford-Binet or Terman-Merrill scales is indicative of maladjustment ; and numerous measures of variability for this or for the Wechsler scale have been proposed. Jastak [3] has discussed the evidence, and concluded that Binet scatter is not diagnostic, although certain items such as Digits Backward and Memory for Designs tend to offer special difficulties to abnormal children. Unevenness in the performance of recruits at various intelligence, mechanical and educational tests was studied during the war, and could not be found to have any significance for personality. In his Progressive Matrices test

[1] Cf. Rapaport, Gill, and Schafer, Bibliography.

[2] Rabin, A. I., and Guertin, W. H., ' Research with the Wechsler-Bellevue Test : 1945–1950 '. *Psychol. Bull.*, 1951, 48, 211–248.

[3] Jastak, J., *Variability of Psychometric Performances in Mental Diagnosis.* New York : J. Jastak, 1934. ' Problems of Psychometric Scatter Analysis '. *Psychol. Bull.*, 1949, 46, 177–197.

(1938), Raven [1] provides an index of unreliability or irregularity of score pattern ; this too appeared to bear no relation to neuroticism. Other kinds of variability will be considered later when we come to Spearman's oscillation factor.

Is the difference between Vocabulary or *v*-tests, and more abstract intelligence or spatial (*g* and *k*) tests of any value in personality assessment ? Several studies suggest that scores on Kohs Blocks, Porteus Mazes, Picture Completion, also Progressive Matrices, are relatively high among delinquents, but lowered among neurotics. For example, Earl [2] claims that the profile of scores on Binet Vocabulary, a verbal absurdities test, Kohs Blocks and Dearborn No. 3 Formboard, is particularly useful (with the assistance of qualitative observations) in diagnosing instability and social inadequacy among morons. Himmelweit,[3] however, finds the ratio of Vocabulary to Matrices scores to relate to introversion, dysthymics obtaining larger ratios than hysterics.

Another possible lead is provided by the concept-formation or sorting tests of Goldstein and Scheerer, Weigl, Vigotsky, Berg, and others.[4] Brain-injured and schizophrenic patients, it is claimed, can cope with these at the concrete or perceptual level but cannot realize or formulate abstract principles of classification. Actually no one has proved that these are anything more than rather unreliable tests of *g*, though it would be worth investigating whether the perceptual vs. the conceptual approach is a consistent personality variable.[5] In the typical sorting test the subject is presented with a series of objects which can be classified in various ways (for example, wooden blocks of different shapes, sizes, and colours), and he is told to sort them or to pick out those which are similar to certain standard objects. If he has mastered one principle of

[1] Raven, J. C., *Progressive Matrices*. London : Lewis, 1938.

[2] Earl, C. J. C., ' A Psychograph for Morons '. *J. Abn. Soc. Psychol.*, 1940, 35, 428–448.

[3] Himmelweit, H. T., ' The Intelligence-Vocabulary Ratio as a Measure of Temperament '. *Char. & Person.*, 1945, 14, 93–105.

[4] Goldstein, K., and Scheerer, M., *Tests of Abstract and Concrete Thinking*. New York : Psychological Corporation, 1945. Hanfmann, E., ' A Study of Personal Patterns in an Intellectual Performance '. *Char. & Person.*, 1941, 9, 315–325. Berg, E. A., ' A Simple Objective Technique for Measuring Flexibility in Thinking '. *J. Gen. Psychol.*, 1948, 39, 15–22.

[5] Cf. Hanfmann, *op. cit.*

classification, e.g. by colour, he is given a new and more complex problem, and the process is repeated. Such tests are thus considered to involve not only the capacity for abstracting and generalising, but also flexibility in shifting to fresh principles. Whether or not this is true, flexibility and its converse—rigidity or inertia of mental processes—have played an important part in the development of temperament tests.

PERSEVERATION AND RIGIDITY

Some of the earliest tests were based on sensory functions, for example, slowness of dark adaptation, or low speed of fusion of colours on a colour wheel. It was claimed that melancholic patients showed greater perseveration at such tests than manics, but this was not borne out by later research. (Nor, incidentally, has any connection been found between any perseveration tests and the perseverative tendencies that occur in certain types of psychosis.) More popular were motor perseveration tests, where the subject writes certain letters or figures at maximum speed, and then reverses the letters or writes them in some unusual way. The decrease in speed of performance is taken as a measure of the perseverative effect of the normal performance. Examples include :

> Copying prose with and without dotting the i's and crossing the t's ;
> Doing simple 4-rule sums, but substituting $+$ for $-$ and $\times$ for $\div$ signs, and vice-versa ;
> Writing SS. . for half-minute, 88. : for half-minute, then S8S8. . for 1 minute ;
> Writing ee. . . forwards, and ee . . starting at the ' wrong ' end, then alternating.

Mirror drawing, which involves the breaking down of established eye-hand co-ordinations, is also sometimes regarded as a p test. There has been much dispute as to the best measure of decrement or hang-over ; all the scores tend to be affected by initial speed of writing or copying, unless appropriate correction is made.[1] After correction, the correlations between different

[1] Cf. Walker, K. F., Staines, R. G., and Kenna, J. C., ' The Influence of Scoring Methods Upon Score in Motor Perseveration Tests '. *Brit. J. Psychol.*, 1945, 35, 51–60.

tests seldom reach statistical significance (unless the tests are very similar), and they vary so widely in different researches using the same tests that it is extremely dubious whether any genuine factor of perseveration can be said to exist.[1] Lankes and Bernstein [2] obtained correlations as high as ·5 between pooled test scores and self-ratings or assessments of perseverative behaviour in daily life, but correlations with measures of introversion or of depressive tendency (with which perseveration has been identified) have generally been negligible. An entirely different claim was put forward by Pinard,[3] namely, that both very high and very low perseverators are more difficult, unreliable, and lacking in self-control and perseverance than subjects obtaining moderate scores. In other words, perseveration itself is not a significant trait, but abnormal reactions to *p* tests correlate to some extent with personality abnormality. Both Cattell [4] and Eysenck provide some independent confirmation of this.

More recently both Walker, Staines, and Kenna and Cattell [5] have stated that the alternation type of test and the miscellaneous sensory tests are useless, but that 'creative effort' tests, where the subject has to break down some well-established habit (such as i : t and $+ -$) are more consistent, and that they measure a quality of 'disposition rigidity'. Cattell obtained negative correlations around ·4 between a battery of such tests and ratings of Dominance and Character Integration, implying that the person with strong Ego development is more flexible and capable of modifying his habits. He argues, too, that there are important racial temperamental differences between Nordics and Mediterraneans in this trait. So far no other evidence of the validity of disposition-rigidity tests seems to have been published.

[1] Cf. Jasper, H. H., ' Is Perserveration a Functional Unit Participating in All Behavior Processes '. *J. Soc. Psychol.*, 1931, 2, 28–51. Notcutt, B., *op. cit.*, p. 69.

[2] Lankes, W., ' Perseveration '. *Brit. J. Psychol.*, 1915, 7, 387–419. Bernstein, E., ' Quickness and Intelligence '. *Brit. J. Psychol. Monogr. Suppl.*, 1924, No. 7.

[3] Pinard, J. W., ' Tests of Perseveration '. *Brit. J. Psychol.*, 1932, 23, 5–19, 114–126.

[4] Cattell, R. B., ' The Riddle of Perseveration '. *J. Person.*, 1946, 14, 229–267.

[5] Walker, K. F., Staines, R. G., and Kenna, J. C., ' P-tests and the Concept of Mental Inertia '. *Char. & Person.*, 1943, 12, 32–45. Cattell, *op. cit.*

Yet another conception of rigidity is put forward by Lewin and Kounin,[1] who regard it as the main characteristic differentiating the personalities of feeble-minded from normal children. When given a choice of drawing tasks they tend to persist longer at a single task, where normal children prefer a change. Perseveration was also demonstrated at card-sorting tests, and lack of flexibility on a concept-formation test, especially among defective adults. But how far such tests represent a consistent trait of personality, or how far they merely reflect lack of intelligence, has not been investigated.

Luchins [2] suggests that inefficient methods of education may produce rigid rather than flexible minds, and he has devised a number of paper-and-pencil concept-formation tests. Subjects are given a series of problems and find that these can be solved by the application of one principle. Half-way through the principle alters, but the original ' set ' may delay, or entirely prevent, them from realizing this. Note that the interfering set in such tests is established temporarily during the course of the test, whereas in perseveration tests it consists of a fully automatized habit. An investigation by Oliver and Ferguson [3] suggests that the former largely depend upon *g*, whereas the latter do involve a separate factor. Frenkel-Brunswick argues that highly prejudiced or ethnocentric persons tend to be rigid or intolerant of ambiguities in the perceptual sphere, and experiments by Rokeach with a problem similar to Luchins's provide some rather slight support for this.[4]

Luchins's tests also bear a considerable resemblance to some of the tests, described later, which have been proposed as measures of suggestibility. The notion of interference enters into a great variety of psychological phenomena, for example in retroactive inhibition, in positive and negative transfer, in

[1] Lewin, K., *A Dynamic Theory of Personality*. New York : McGraw-Hill, 1935. Kounin, J. S., ' Experimental Studies of Rigidity '. *Char. & Person.*, 1941, 9, 251–282. Their topological theory of personality rigidity is strongly criticised by Werner, H., ' The Concept of Rigidity : A Critical Evaluation '. *Psychol. Rev.*, 1946, 53, 43–52.

[2] Luchins, A. S., ' Proposed Methods of Studying Degrees of Rigidity '. *J. Person.*, 1947, 15, 242–246.

[3] Oliver, J. A., and Ferguson, G. A., ' A Factorial Study of Tests of Rigidity '. *Canad. J. Psychol.*, 1951, 5, 49–59.

[4] Adorno, T. W., Frenkel-Brunswick, E., *et. al.*, *The Authoritarian Personality*. New York : Harper, 1950.

memory for incompleted tasks,[1] in conditioning, and in the sets observed in psychophysical experiments. In all of these there are, no doubt, individual differences in flexibility, but it seems extremely unlikely that they all depend on one and the same trait.[2] Nor is there any good evidence that any of the tests we have mentioned reflect any socially important trait. Even the traditional *p* tests are so boring to the subjects, so troublesome to give and score, and of such dubious validity, that no psychologist seems to make any practical use of them.

OSCILLATION AND VARIABILITY

Fluctuations of performance have been measured in a large number of tests such as reaction time, simple addition sums, cancellation, muscle tone, handwriting, tapping and other motor tasks, usually with disappointing results. The Mean Variation or Standard Deviation of a long series of reaction times is said to be much higher in unstable mental patients than among normals, since they find it difficult to maintain the necessary concentration. But it is not clear how far this difference arises merely from their lack of experience in doing reaction times. To measure oscillation in addition and other similar tasks, the subject works continuously, but makes a tick, say every 15 seconds, to show the amount done. Considerable practice, or fatigue, effects may occur, but fluctuations can be measured from a moving average. Day-to-day variations can also be obtained, though naturally a large number of records is needed if the oscillation scores are to achieve reasonable reliability. There is some doubt as to whether absolute

[1] In a factorial study of tests of persistence, Rethlingshafer included tests of memory for incompleted tasks and some of Cattell's alternating type of *p* tests. Both of these showed appreciable loadings (·35 to ·45) on her ' willingness to continue ' factor. Other motor and sensory perseveration tests and a perseveration questionnaire yielded a distinct factor, or else were wholly specific. It is a pity that this interesting research with 29 tests was carried out on only 38 students. Rethlingshafer, D., ' Relationship of Tests of Persistence to Other Measures of Continuance of Activities '. *J. Abn. Soc. Psychol.*, 1942, 37, 71–82.

[2] Further useful discussions of rigidity, particularly in the abnormal field, are given by Werner, *op. cit.*, and Fisher, S., ' An Overview of Trends in Research Dealing with Personality Rigidity '. *J. Person.*, 1949, 17, 342–351.

or relative variability should be measured, but whatever the method, correlations between variability at different (simple) tasks are generally so low as to cast doubt on the existence of any consistent trait.[1] Nor is there any good evidence that such tests are diagnostic of emotional instability in general. One of the best results is that of Walton,[2] who found a correlation of — ·28 between oscillation among schoolchildren on 4 tests, and teachers' ratings of steadiness of character. In another research with several types of variability, Connor[3] found some differentiation between maladjusted and normal children, but no correlation with tests or ratings of instability among normals. More promising results obtained with more complex and realistic tests are described in the next chapter.

Another type of fluctuation is the reversals that occur when looking at ambiguous perspective figures like the Necker cube, the staircase, or shadow-windmill. McDougall[4] suggested that extraverts have a slower rate of reversal than introverts, and that this rate is decreased by an extraverting drug such as alcohol. While there is some evidence of these tests differentiating manic from schizophrenic patients, they fail to distinguish hysteric and dysthymic neurotics; and several experiments show no correlations with self-rating tests of extraversion-introversion among normals.[5]

Some exceptions to our general condemnation of sensory and motor tests are provided by the work of Eysenck and his collaborators. They have shown that certain tests of muscular co-ordination give quite promising correlations with normality vs. neuroticism. Presumably, good muscular control tends to be associated with emotional stability. Thus neurotics often perform badly on the Track Tracer and the O'Connor Tweezer

[1] Cf. Cockett, R., *Variability in Human Task Efficiency.* Ph.D. Thesis, University of London, 1950.

[2] Walton, R. D., ' Individual Differences in Amplitudes of Oscillation and Their Connection with Steadiness of Character '. *Brit. J. Psychol.*, 1939, 30, 36–46.

[3] Connor, D. V., *The Effect of Temperamental Traits upon Intelligence Test Performance.* Ph.D. Thesis, University of London, 1952.

[4] McDougall, W., and Smith, M., ' The Effects of Alcohol and Some Other Drugs during Normal and Fatigued Conditions '. *Med. Res. Counc. Spec. Rep.*, No. 56. London : H.M. Stat. Office, 1920.

[5] Guilford, J. P., and Hunt, J. M., ' Some Further Experimental Tests of McDougall's Theory of Introversion-Extroversion '. *J. Abn. Soc. Psychol.*, 1932, 26, 324–332.

Dexterity tests. Again, N. O'Connor and Tizard [1] found that the Heath rail-walking test gave the best indication of ' employability ' or ' work success ' in a large battery of tests applied to feeble-minded youths. This test [2] measures the distance a subject can walk along 4-, 2-, and 1-inch rails without falling off. Most striking is the body-sway test [3] of static ataxia and suggestibility. The subject stands with his eyes closed, and a thread is attached to his back which connects with a pointer and records on a smoked drum. The amount of sway is considerably higher in the average neurotic patient than in normals. But the effect is enhanced when a gramophone record is played reiterating the suggestion : ' You are falling, falling forwards . . .' Correlations as high as ·6 with Eysenck's neuroticism factor have been obtained among adults, and the test has some diagnostic value among maladjusted children.

PERCEPTUAL TESTS

Brief mention should be made of the numerous tests which have been claimed, by Continental typologists, to differentiate between pyknics and asthenics, or integrates and disintegrates, and so forth. Form vs. colour dominance is usually measured by exposing sets of coloured shapes for a fraction of a second with a tachistoscope, and seeing whether subjects more readily perceive and recall the colours or the forms. Tachistoscopic perception of complex visual material has also been used to classify people into synthetic (vague perception of the whole) or analytic (precise perception of details). Other tests aim to show the capacity for spreading the attention, as contrasted with concentrating on a single task. The Gottschaldt figures, in which the subject has to pick a given shape out of a complex Gestalt, is presumed to involve flexibility in manipulating configurations. None of the work done in this field gives satisfactory evidence that such perceptual types or tendencies are consistent, or that they bear any close relation to personality. The most thorough study of a large number of perceptual tests

[1] *Op cit.* p. 71.

[2] Heath, S. R., ' Clinical Significance of Motor Defect, with Military Implications '. *Amer. J. Psychol.*, 1944, 57, 482–499.

[3] Hull, C. L., *Hypnosis and Suggestibility*. New York : Appleton Century, 1933.

was that of Thurstone,[1] in which several factors were isolated, including : Perceptual Closure, Flexibility with Configurations, Susceptibility to Visual Illusions, Oscillation of Reversible Perspective Figures, etc. But there is no confirmation for his suggestion that some of these factors might differentiate successful leaders or administrators, or good and bad readers.

JUNE DOWNEY'S WILL-TEMPERAMENT TESTS

This series of tests [2] had a considerable vogue in the 1920s, but the results were as unsatisfactory as those of p and o tests, and they are now regarded as little more than a psychological curiosity. A dozen traits were supposed to be measured by elementary tests based on handwriting, which were given in group form or, better, individually. For example :

Speed of Movement.—Tested by normal speed of hand-writing.

Flexibility.—By ability to disguise writing, and to copy a model rapidly.

Care and Accuracy in Detail.—By time spent spontaneously on disguises and accuracy of copying.

Impulsiveness.—By tendency to write larger and faster under distraction, e.g. with eyes closed.

The tests were in fact based on a careful study of graphological systems, and Downey herself found that the pattern or profile of scores on the various tests provided an illuminating picture of her subjects' personalities. However, in numerous researches the separate scores were shown to have low reliability coefficients of around ·5, and little or no agreement was obtained between these scores and ratings by acquaintances on the relevant traits.

Possibly our criticism of the tests described in this chapter may seem unduly harsh, because their authors did not usually expect them to be diagnostic of everyday life personality qualities. Rather they were concerned with fundamental temperamental tendencies. We would say, however, that the attempt to measure inborn factors was a misguided one. Most

[1] Thurstone, L. L., *A Factorial Study of Perception.* Chicago, Ill. : Chicago University Press, 1944.
[2] Downey, J. E., *The Will-Temperament and its Testing.* Yonkers, N.Y. : World Book Co., 1924.

psychologists nowadays admit that intelligence can be tested only as a product of heredity and environment. Similarly, in the field of personality we can never really separate what is innate from what is acquired, and even if we could test the former it would scarcely help us in any of the practical problems of predicting people's behaviour.

VI

Miniature and Real Life Situation Tests

IN order to obtain more realistic samples of behaviour, which will yield quantitative scores, the psychologist is usually forced to simplify and restrict the testing situation. This may lead to considerable artificiality ; hence subjects may in fact react to ' miniature ' situations very differently from the way they would react in more natural circumstances. Thus it very commonly occurs that the validity of an objective personality test varies widely in different researches, depending on slight variations in the manner of application or in the attitudes of the subjects to being tested. And although quite promising results have been achieved with many of the tests described in the first half of this chapter, few if any of them can be trusted to work in the same straightforward manner as tests of intelligence and special abilities. The observational methods mentioned later in the chapter are less restricted, but are consequently more open to the vagaries of human judgment. And they, too, constitute only limited samples of the general behaviour tendencies or traits which we are trying to measure. Thus, as pointed out in Chap. I, numerous, varied samples are desirable ; and as each of these may require elaborate arrangements and materials, successful objective personality testing is chiefly confined to experimental researches.

PERSISTENCE TESTS

One of the first attempts was Fernald's [1] test of endurance, which consisted simply in recording the length of time a subject would stand with his heels raised off the ground. The median time for normal students was 36 minutes, whereas among a group of prisoners the median was only 15 minutes. Other versions of this test depend on the subject's holding his breath as long as possible, or sitting with one leg outstretched and the

[1] Fernald, G. G., ' An Achievement Capacity Test '. *J. Educ. Psychol.*, 1912, 3, 331–336.

foot raised an inch above another chair, or maintaining a grip on a hand dynamometer equivalent to two-thirds of his own maximum grip. Several of these have worked well in Eysenck's researches, and have correlated quite highly with his stability-neuroticism factor. Dysthymics also show somewhat greater persistence than hysterics. Howells [1] similarly applied a battery of tests of resistance to bodily pain and fatigue, which showed some value in the prediction of academic grades. Obviously such tests have to be ' put across ' in such a way as to stimulate the subjects' efforts, and their results might be seriously affected if, for instance, the subjects thought they were being applied for selection purposes.

Several other tests have been developed in which subjects are given some difficult manipulative puzzle or intellectual problem, and the time they are willing to spend on it is recorded. [2] Wordbuilding or hard intelligence test items have been used, and a promising Number Series test for adults, where the subjects are told that some of the problems are insoluble, is described by French. [3] Here, too, the motivation of the subjects is vital. MacArthur [4] showed that results differ somewhat when the tasks are given individually, or in group situations where a subject can compare himself with his fellows. He found it best to avoid suggesting that persistent trying was desirable, and instead to supply some similar alternative employment for his subjects to go on to when they had spontaneously spent as long as they wished on the original task.

A useful variant, which must be given individually, is Morgan and Hull's [5] Maze test. This consists of grooves cut in a board, and covered by a movable piece of card with a small hole in it so that the subject can see only half an inch of the board around his stylus. By inserting or removing blocks, the experimenter can set four problems of increasing difficulty,

---

[1] Howells, T. H., " An Experimental Study of Persistence," *J. Abn. Soc. Psychol.*, 1933, 28, 14–29.

[2] Cf. Hartshorne and May, and Ryans, Bibliography.

[3] French, J. W., ' The Validity of a Persistence Test '. *Psychometr.*, 1948, 13, 271–277.

[4] MacArthur, R. S., *An Experimental Investigation of Persistence and its Measurement at the Secondary School Level*. Ph.D. Thesis, University of London, 1951.

[5] Morgan, J. J. B., and Hull, H. L., ' The Measurement of Persistence '. *J. Appl. Psychol.*, 1926, 10, 180–187.

the last being insoluble. Instead of scoring objectively by time, the tester applies a 9-point rating scale which describes various degrees of persistence and hard work or of fiddling and wanting to quit. The writer obtained good validity for this test among students, but substituted a very difficult fourth problem for the insoluble one in order to avoid tricking them.

Thornton [1] considers that the correlations between such tests are too low to justify the conception of a common factor of persistence, and claims that withstanding-discomfort tests and keeping-on-at-a-task tests, etc., yield separate factors. But investigations such as those of Ryans, MacArthur [2] and others do support a general factor in all types of persistence tests, together with small group factors in particular types (cf. p. 14). Moreover, a battery of persistence tests correlates not only with teachers' or acquaintances' ratings (at least among children), but also with scholastic success (over and above any effects of intelligence), and—inversely—with emotional instability or neuroticism.

EMOTIONAL STABILITY

Several tests have been devised to elicit instability or variations of performance in more ' provoking ' situations than those characteristic of *o* (oscillation) tests. The McDougall-Schuster dotting machine exposes to the subject a sequence of small circles, irregularly spaced, in each of which he puts a dot with a pencil or stylus. The circles move faster and faster, and sooner or later the subject breaks down. But he may continue systematically dotting every second or third circle, or he may lose his head and make feeble jabs, or give up. Smith, Culpin, and Farmer [3] gave the test to telegraphists, and scored it by the total dots up to the point where five consecutive circles were missed. These scores correlated from ·33 to ·46 with assessments of neuroticism based on clinical interviews. Neurotics with obsessional tendencies, however, tended to score

---

[1] Thornton, G. R., ' A Factor Analysis of Tests Designed to Measure Persistence '. *Psychol. Monogr.*, 1939, 51, No. 229.

[2] *Op cit.*

[3] Smith, M., Culpin, M., and Farmer, E., ' A Study of Telegraphists' Cramp '. *Industr. Fat. Res. Board Rep.*, No. 43. London : H.M. Stat. Office, 1927.

highly. The validity of this particular score requires confirmation ; it may be that, as in Morgan and Hull's Maze test, observations of manner of reacting to difficulties would be more useful. The fact that such motor co-ordination tests as rail-walking and manual dexterity are done badly by neurotics (cf. p. 79) gives some support.

Cattell's [1] C.M.S. (Cursive Miniature Situation) test is a much more elaborate version of dotting, in which the subject crosses out or encircles various kinds of lines and patterns which pass before him at a rapid rate. If he keeps his head and chooses the most profitable sets of lines, he can raise his score considerably. Possibly the task is a bit too sophisticated except for intelligent and/or experienced subjects. But Cattell claims remarkably good differentiation between psychotic, delinquent, and normal adults. Unfortunately the scoring is so tedious that no one else has tried to confirm the value of the test. Probably there is scope for a test intermediate in complexity between the McDougall and the Cattell, which could be scored by electric counters. Kehr in Germany, and Freeman [2] in America, have described discriminatory reaction tests which likewise put the subject in ' stress ' situations, and which appear to have given good results. Freeman compares the performances under difficult, with those under easy conditions, and measures the time taken to recover efficiency after the stress period.

Instability of performance at learning tests is also promising. Thus Ball [3] finds that the learning curves of unstable or neurotic boys at a high-relief finger maze are much more irregular than those of normals. Rey [4] describes similar results with a learning problem based on a kind of formboard which can be solved only by trial and error. Neither test as yet gives a quantitative

[1] Cattell, R. B., ' An Objective Test of Character-Temperament '. *J. Gen. Psychol.*, 1941, 25, 59–73.

[2] Kehr, T., ' Versuchsanordnung zur experimentellen Untersuchung einer kontinuierlichen Aufmerksamkeitsleistung '. *Zsch. f. ang. Psychol.*, 1916, 11, 465–479. Freeman, G. L., ' Suggestions for a Standardized " Stress " Test '. *J. Gen. Psychol.*, 1945, 32, 3–11.

[3] Ball, R. J., ' An Objective Measure of Emotional Instability '. *J. Appl. Psychol.*, 1929, 13, 226–256.

[4] Rey, A., ' D'un procédé pour évaluer l'éducabilité '. *Arch. de Psychol.*, 1934, 24, 297–337. Cf. also Zangwill, O. L., ' Some Clinical Applications of the Rey-Davis Performance Test '. *J. Ment. Sci.*, 1946, 92, 19–34.

scc.e for instability, and inspection of the curves needs to be supplemented by qualitative observations of the children's reactions to difficulties. But a more practicable and more objective test might be developed along these lines. Thiesen and Meister [1] report an experiment on maze learning under frustrating conditions—namely, no solution possible and criticisms by the tester. Alterations in blood pressure and psychogalvanic response during stress appeared to relate to inability to tolerate frustration, and to school adjustment in general ; but only 10 children were tested. Mirror drawing is another learning task which has, at various times, been alleged to show freedom from perseveration, or emotional control, or adventurousness vs. timidity, or yet other traits. Actually it correlates moderately with intelligence ; and in a research by the writer a score based on the number of errors during the first four trials correlated better with a trait-composite of ' impulsiveness ' than with one of ' emotionality '.

SUGGESTIBILITY

As early as 1916 Brown [2] showed that the correlations between a number of tests supposed to involve suggestibility were very low and irregular, and subsequent research has confirmed the lack of generality of this trait. Eysenck considers that it includes at least three distinct traits which he calls primary, secondary, and prestige suggestibility. Primary suggestibility is best measured by the body-sway test, described on p. 80. The Chevreuil pendulum test of ability to hold a bob steadily at the end of a string, despite suggestions, is similar ; also possibly the autokinetic phenomenon. These and other tests correlate with susceptibility to hypnosis and, as already mentioned, with neuroticism. (Note that all neurotics tend to be more suggestible, in this sense, than normals, not only hysterics. Contrary to common psychiatric opinion, dysthymics obtain higher average scores.)

Secondary suggestibility includes the numerous visual,

---

[1] Thiesen, J. W., and Meister, R. K., ' A Laboratory Investigation of Measures of Frustration Tolerance of Pre-Adolescent Children '. *J. Genet. Psychol.*, 1949, 75, 277–291.

[2] Brown, W., ' Individual and Sex Differences in Suggestibility '. *Univ. Calif. Publ. ·Psychol.*, 1916, 2, No. 6.

cutaneous, olfactory, and other tests, such as Binet's progressive lines and weights, where the subject is led to anticipate a series of increasing stimuli ; his suggestibility is measured by the number of stimuli that he judges larger after the actual increase has stopped. Acceptance of suggestions in recalling a picture (' Aussage ' test), or suggestions that certain objects can be seen in inkblots, also fall under this heading, though the amount of positive correlation among such varied tests is low. Secondary suggestibility appears to have no correlation with emotional traits or syndromes, but (at least among children) it correlates negatively with intelligence to a marked degree.

' Prestige ' suggestibility has been measured by giving an attitude or opinion questionnaire, then repeating it while informing the subjects that most people, or certain important people, answer each question in such a way. It is scored by noting how often the subject changes his previous response in the direction suggested. Ferguson [1] has found that scores obtained from several such tests are moderately consistent. But there is no evidence to show that suggestibility to prestige in everyday life (e.g. to political speakers, to doctors or ministers, to newspapers, advertisements, or fashions) can be predicted by tests of this, or of any other type.

LEVEL OF ASPIRATION

This is an important concept in modern personality theory, which refers to the goals or standards at which a person aims.[2] Some people are highly ambitious, optimistic, or confident, while others, whose actual capacity may be no less, are more realistic and cautious, or else unduly pessimistic and afraid of failure. It has been studied by setting some task which provides considerable scope for improvement, and in which the subject can readily gauge how well or badly he is doing ; for example, simple addition sheets, substitution tests, or such manual tests as the pursuitmeter. This task is done for, say, ten 1-minute

[1] Ferguson, L. W., ' An Analysis of the Generality of Suggestibility to Group Opinion '. *Char. & Person.*, 1944, 12, 237–243.

[2] Cf. Hunt, Frank, Bibliography. The procedure here described is that used by Himmelweit, H. T., ' A Comparative Study of the Level of Aspiration of Normal and of Neurotic Persons '. *Brit. J. Psychol.*, 1947, 37, 41–59.

periods. After each period the subject guesses his own score (A) ; he is told his actual score (B), and guesses what his score will be in the next period (C). The differences between A and B yield a measure of what is called Judgment Discrepancy, and differences between C and the previous achievement B yield a Goal Discrepancy score. Other measures such as Responsiveness and Rigidity are derived from the number of times the estimates (C) go up or down in accordance with achievement, or remain unaltered.

Unfortunately the results from different tests are rather unreliable and inconsistent, though Lewin [1] claims that this can be overcome by standardizing the technique and scoring, and the motivation of the subjects. There is some evidence of lowered aspiration or discrepancy scores among cripples and physically handicapped children, among pupils or students who are failing in their work, and students affected by poor economic circumstances.[2] Males usually score higher than females. Himmelweit [3] found that Goal Discrepancy tends to be higher and Judgment Discrepancy lower in dysthymics than in hysterics, but the results of aspiration tests have been less favourable in subsequent researches by this author and Eysenck. In any case the discovery of plausible and interesting group differences does not necessarily show that the method is of any real value for individual diagnosis ; and Gardner [4] obtained very small (though meaningful) correlations between individual scores and ratings on a number of relevant traits. Thus it seems to the writer that aspiration tests are based on oversimplified and trivial situations ; that reactions to them are extremely chancy and have little bearing on the manner in which a person's self-esteem operates in his real-life behaviour.

The same criticism applies to the early attempts of Moore and Gilliland [5] to test ' aggressiveness '. One of their tests was based on the subject's ability to carry out oral addition sums while

[1] Cf. Hunt, Bibliography.

[2] Cf. Rotter, J. B., ' Level of Aspiration as a Method of Studying Personality, III. Group Validity Studies.' *Char. & Person.*, 1943, 11, 255–274.

[3] *Op cit.*

[4] Gardner, J. W., ' The Relation of Certain Personality Variables to Level of Aspiration '. *J. Psychol.*, 1940, 9, 191–206.

[5] Gilliland, A. R., ' A Revision and Some Results with the Moore-Gilliland Aggressiveness Test '. *J. Appl. Psychol.*, 1926, 10, 143–150.

looking the tester straight in the eye ; another on the speed and the aggressive or neutral content of free associations to such words as ' enterprise, success, danger ...' The correlations between the various sub-tests were low and sometimes negative, in a research by the writer with college students. Although small positive validity coefficients were obtained with a trait-composite for Dominance or Leadership, the tests were clearly too artificial, and too greatly affected by the personal relations between tester and subject, to be worth following up.

OBJECTIVE TESTS OF INTERESTS

Interests are generally assessed by some form of questionnaire (cf. Chap. IX), but Fryer's book on interests describes a number of attempts to test them through objective measures of behaviour. Other possible approaches are listed by Cattell and Heist [1] ; for example :

> Fraction of income and/or leisure time spent on each of a number of types of interest ;
>
> Free association tests with words representing various types, scored by speed of response and/or psychogalvanic reflex ;
>
> A large sheet of miscellaneous pictures and photographs is presented ; the subject studies these and is scored by the number he recalls belonging to different types ;
>
> Reading a passage concerned with an interest which contains nonsense words ; scored by failure to notice and cross out such words ;
>
> Subject studies pages containing statements relevant to types of interests, and irrelevant words ; strength of interest expected to be shown by failure to recall irrelevant material, but the reverse was found.

Cattell and his colleagues applied a dozen such tests in an attempt to measure twelve types of interests and attitudes among small groups of students. The inter-correlations were so low that, though it might be feasible to build up a battery of the best objective tests for giving a composite measure of some

---

[1] Cattell, R. B., *et. al.*, ' The Objective Measurement of Attitudes '. *Brit. J. Psychol.*, 1949, 40, 81–90. ' The Objective Measurement of Dynamic Traits '. *Educ. Psychol. Measmt.*, 1950, 10, 224–248.

single type of interest, it would obviously be impracticable to use such batteries in assessing numerous different types, e.g. for vocational purposes.

One kind of objective test, however, which does offer considerable promise is the test of information or knowledge about a given field. No doubt such tests depend on aptitude and training as well as interest, but they do tend to correlate with other interest measures, and they do help in the prediction of vocational or educational success. Fryer describes a number of early tests, particularly of mechanical information, which were employed in the American Army in 1918. Cattell [1] provides a set of fifteen short information tests dealing with the following fields : Travel, Sport, Commercial, Mechanical, Scientific, Things of the Mind, Rural-Naturalistic, Religious, Literary, Artistic, Decorative, Sensual, Sex, Social, and Home. These are not sufficiently thorough, nor well enough standardized, to be recommended for immediate use, but they provide a useful starting point. Tests of general information about everyday mechanical and electrical matters were of considerable value in allocating British recruits during the war,[2] and are being adapted by educational psychologists in some areas for selecting boys for technical education. The American Air Force psychologists also designed information tests covering technical and other types of interests. Items which best differentiated successful from unsuccessful pilots and navigators were picked out, and used in a revised test, which made a valuable contribution to aircrew selection.[3]

Peel and Lambert [4] have published an ingenious combination of information and ' miniature situation ' test for measuring academic vs. technical interests, to be used in selecting for different types of secondary education. Several blocks of questions are given, in each of which the pupil is told to answer half only. Thus he may choose to answer mostly technical, or mostly literary questions, and his score is based

[1] Cattell, R. B., *A Guide to Mental Testing.* London : University of London Press, 1936.

[2] Cf. Vernon and Parry.

[3] Cf. Guilford, J. P., and Lacey, J. I., *Printed Classification Tests.* Army Air Forces Aviat. Psychol. Prog. Res. Rep. No. 5. Washington, D.C. : U.S. Government Printing Office, 1947.

[4] Peel, E. A., ' Assessment of Interest in Practical Topics '. *Brit. J. Educ. Psychol.*, 1948, 18, 41–47.

on the proportion of choices as well as on their correctness.
For example :

> Write the meaning, and if necessary make a rough drawing,
> of *three* of the following words : monastery, brake,
> actor, clawhammer, optician, hacksaw.

Another cognitive test of relevance to personality is the
George Washington Test of Social Intelligence.[1] This group test
was devised by Moss, Hunt, and Omwake to measure the
ability to understand and get along with people; it can be used
with high school or college students. The five sub-tests involve :

> Selecting the best responses in various social problem
>   situations ;
> Recognizing the emotions underlying verbal statements ;
> True-False statements about human behaviour ;
> Memorizing and recalling names and photographs of people ;
> Choosing the best completion to humorous stories.

Primarily the battery measures the same general intelligence as
ordinary verbal tests, but it has also given useful correlations of
around ·4 with assessments or other tests of social extraversion.

MORAL KNOWLEDGE OR JUDGMENT, AND CHARACTER, TESTS

Large numbers of paper-and-pencil tests have been published
in America,[2] including vocabulary tests based on ethical, or
conversely on criminal or slang terms ; tests of biblical and
religious knowledge ; ranking offences in order of seriousness ;
and comprehension tests (presented either verbally or pictori-
ally), where children are asked the proper thing to do in various
moral situations. E.g. :

> If someone steals your lunch you should :
>   Steal another lunch to even it up ;
>   Report it to the teacher ;
>   Cry about it ;
>   Say nothing about it.

[1] Moss, F. A., *et. al.*, *George Washington Social Intelligence Test.* Washington, D.C. : George Washington University, Center for Psychological
Service, 1930.

[2] Symonds (cf. Bibliography) provides an excellent description.

Such tests attain good reliabilities and inter-correlations, but the fact that they are heavily weighted with intelligence indicates that they are unlikely to be highly predictive of ' good character '. Burt and others have pointed out that delinquents often know as well as non-delinquents what society regards as right or wrong. Nevertheless in Hartshorne and May's investigation, described below, a battery of tests, which correlated ·70 with intelligence, did correlate ·35 with a battery of objective tests of honesty. In other words, the information and judgment tests were rather more valid than teachers' ratings of the same children's honesty.

As described by Symonds, several miniature situation tests of honesty and cheating were developed by Voelker, Cady, Raubenheimer, and others in the 1920s. For example, children (or college students) may be given a straightforward attainment test ; unknown to them a copy of their answers is taken, and this is used to check the marks when they score their own papers. Alternatively the self-marked scores are compared with the scores on an exactly parallel test marked by the tester. Peeping tests set the children to trace mazes or carry out other tasks with the eyes closed. As these tasks are impossible without vision, successful performance gives a measure of cheating. In the Overstatement test, children are given a list of book titles, several of which are plausible but fictitious. The number they claim to have read is again supposed to show dishonesty.

Such tests may strike the reader as thoroughly obnoxious ; but one research in the field of character, using these and many other extremely ingenious tests, was of outstanding importance, namely, Hartshorne and May's Character Education Inquiry. This included not only rather artificial classroom situations, but also a variety of real-life situations, which were so arranged as to yield quantitative scores for character. For example, games were arranged at parties which gave scope for cheating. Children were sent on standard errands and given excess change, so that the amount they appropriated could be measured. Opportunities were provided for doing work for, and giving away things to, other children, or for being selfish. Several of the persistence tests described above, together with ethical judgment tests, and ratings of children by one another (cf. p. 113) or by teachers, were also employed.

When the results of different honesty measures, or persistence or altruism tests, were inter-correlated, the agreement was often so low that the authors concluded that there is no such thing as good character in general, rather that children should acquire specific good habits in specific situations. Yet most of the correlations were in fact positive, so that it is equally legitimate to think of honesty, persistence, etc., as general underlying factors, which can be measured by combining the results of a number of different tests, that is by trait-composites. Moreover, there was positive overlapping between several different composites constructed for measuring honesty, persistence, service and self-control, and consistency of behaviour. Thus a kind of super-composite representing character in general would be justifiable (cf. p. 14), although this manifests itself so differently in different situations that no single test could be taken as a valid index.

OBSERVATIONAL AND TIME-SAMPLING TECHNIQUES

Olson, Goodenough, Thomas,[1] and others in America have shown that it is possible to measure personality traits even more directly, and in less ' miniature ' types of situations, than did Hartshorne and May. An observer can record every instance of some specified form of behaviour, say aggressiveness, among children in a nursery school group. But it is usually more convenient to do this at regular time intervals. Olson and Cunningham define time-sampling as : ' systematic recording of a definitely delimited unit of behavior described in terms of action over a stated time interval, yielding quantitative individual scores by means of repeated time units '. And they describe applications of this technique to some forty types of behaviour. For example, Parten [2] studied social participation among 34 nursery school children. She first drew up a list of categories of participant behaviour including solitary play, onlooker behaviour, organized group play, etc. She

[1] Olson, W. C., and Cunningham, E. M., ' Time-Sampling Techniques '. *Child Devel.*, 1934, 5, 41–58. Thomas, D. S., *Some New Techniques for Studying Social Behavior*. New York : Teachers College, Columbia, Bur. Publ., 1929. Cf. also Arrington, Bibliography.

[2] Parten, M., ' An Analysis of Social Participation, Leadership, and Other Factors in Pre-school Play Groups '. *Instit. Child Welfare Monogr. Ser.* Minneapolis : University of Minnesota Press, 1931.

then observed each child for 1 minute a day for 60 days (distributing each child's minutes throughout an hour's school period), and ticked off the category of behaviour into which he fell during that minute. A score for social participation was thus derived from the numbers of minutes in which he had been engaged in each category. It was found in this and other such studies that time-sample scores possess good reliability ; for example, participation scores on odd-numbered days correlated highly with scores on even-numbered. Moreover, they predict future behaviour of the same type, or else other types which one would naturally expect to be related (e.g. leadership, talkativeness, laughter, and physical activity) in a consistent fashion. Time-sampling is reliable or consistent too, in the sense that two observers making records of the behaviour of the same children agree very closely provided that they are thoroughly trained, and that the behaviour is defined sufficiently unequivocally. Thomas shows that such consistency is higher when highly specific and objective activities are recorded (e.g. total physical contacts with other children) rather than activities which involve some interpretation (e.g. number of social contacts). But the latter are certainly more meaningful and useful for personality study.

The technique is mainly applicable among very young children, both because their behaviour is less complex than that of older children or adults, and easier to classify consistently, and because they can readily be observed without becoming self-conscious ; (if a one-way observation screen is available, they need not know that they are being watched at all). It has been extended to older children in a research by Olson,[1] who recorded the nervous habits, nail-biting, nose-picking, head-scratching, tics, etc., of children in class, unknown to them. Though it was difficult to get high observer-consistency, a reliable total score was built up, which bore some relation to teachers' ratings of behaviour difficulty. Newcomb [2] applied a similar technique to a study of extraverted and introverted

---

[1] Olson, W. C., ' The Measurement of Nervous Habits in Normal Children '. *Instit. Child Welfare Monogr.* No. 3. Minneapolis : University of Minnesota Press, 1929.

[2] Newcomb, T. M., ' The Consistency of Certain Extrovert-Introvert Behavior Patterns in 51 Problem Boys '. *Teachers College Columbia Contr. Educ.*, No. 382, 1929.

behaviour at a boys' summer camp. It might well be used with adults in a factory situation or committee ; indeed it overlaps with time and motion and accident studies, with Mass Observation, and with recent work on social dynamics of groups, though these are not, of course, concerned with personality differences. Such research is much more troublesome than would appear at first sight because of the difficulties of defining significant behaviour sufficiently rigidly, of securing impartial and consistent observers, and ensuring that their presence does not affect the behaviour of the individuals they are observing. Nevertheless it has yielded results of the greatest value in, for example, Murphy's study of sympathy and aggressiveness among young children, D. E. M. Gardner's comparison of the personalities of 5- to 10-year-old children taught in progressive and orthodox schools, and Lewin's investigations of the effects of frustration and of authoritarian, *laissez faire* and democratic club leadership on boys' social behaviour.[1]

GROUP OBSERVATION TECHNIQUES

Burt describes a research carried out during the First World War, where 53 12- to 14-year-old children were assessed on a number of traits (Emotional Stability, Extraversion, Leadership, Delinquent Tendencies, etc.) by several independent observers employing different techniques. These judgments were validated against exceptionally thorough teachers' ratings. The average coefficient for judgments based on interviews was ·44, and for those based on projection, questionnaire, and other tests was only ·27. Considerably more successful—the coefficients averaging ·54—were observations of children in specially arranged, but natural, situations such as a tea-party and a visit to the Zoo. ' On these occasions a number of stock little crises were stage-managed, so that each child's reactions to typical everyday emergencies could be observed.' No further details are given, but similar observational methods were applied in

---

[1] Murphy, L. B., *Social Behavior and Child Personality*. New York : Columbia University Press, 1937. Gardner, D. E. M., *Testing Results in the Infant School*. London : Methuen, 1942. *Long Term Results of Infant School Methods*. London : Methuen, 1950. Lewin, K., Lippitt, R., and White, R. K., ' Patterns of Aggressive Behavior in Experimentally Created " Social Climates " '. *J. Soc. Psychol.*, 1939, 10, 271–299.

assessing students engaged on biological field-work.[1] Clearly these investigations were forerunners of important later developments.

In the 1930s, German military psychologists devised elaborate methods of officer selection based less on objective tests than on qualitative observations of expressive movements and of behaviour in situations involving stress. In some of the tasks candidates had to drill recruits, give instruction or short lectures, or carry out complex orders requiring quickness of uptake, physical agility, or endurance, or improvization in emergencies. Their reactions were observed and interpreted by trained psychologists. No good evidence of the validity of such methods was ever collected, and it is only too likely that the tasks were too artificial or the judgments too subjective to be of much value. Nevertheless, during the war, British psychologists in War Office Selection Boards, and American psychologists in the Office of Strategic Services,[2] developed similar techniques, which combined objective tests of abilities, questionnaires and projection tests of personality, with interviews by military officers and psychiatrists, and with observations of behaviour at certain group exercises. The W.O.S.B. technique has frequently been described. Groups of about eight candidates for commissions were studied over a 2- to 3-day period by a senior army officer, a military testing officer, a psychiatrist, and a psychologist, who at the end pooled their information before deciding on the suitability of each candidate. The exercises, which were watched by the testing officer and sometimes by the other staff, were designed, not to bring out particular traits (leadership, co-operativeness, initiative, etc.), but to be analogous to some of the common social situations of army life, and to afford opportunities for observing how each candidate behaved in a small group. In a typical ' leaderless-group ' test, for instance, the group is assigned some task such as moving a heavy object over a set of obstacles, and is left to work out its own solution. Some candidates behave merely as passengers, others try to dominate the rest, while some seem naturally to come to the fore, though acting in the group's rather than their

[1] Burt, C. L., ' The Factorial Analysis of Emotional Traits '. *Char. & Person.*, 1939, 7, 238–254, 285–299.

[2] Cf. Vernon and Parry. Also, Office of Strategic Services Staff. *Assessment of Men.* New York : Rinehart, 1948.

own interests. Note that this is not an objective test of any quality. It falls rather under the indirect or expressive methods of Chap. IV, since the candidates would usually assume that their ingenuity rather than their social response was being tested. And, along with the other exercises and interviews, it yields, not scores or measurements, but subjective ratings by the observer of the candidate's personality as a whole. Hence it depends enormously on the skill and experience of the observers. Other weaknesses have been pointed out by the writer elsewhere, for example, the obvious dependence of the candidate's behaviour on *his* interpretation of the procedure and his preconceived notions of the sort of personality that he should try to display. Thus the agreement between different observers, or between ratings given on two or more occasions, is nothing like so high as that of time-sampling ; it is usually around ·6 to ·7. Nevertheless this is somewhat higher than the reliability of judgments based on interview alone, or of ratings based on general acquaintance and on casual, as contrasted with directed, observation. Various follow-up studies of candidates selected by these' procedures have given quite low correlations with the officers' subsequent success at a training unit or in the field. There are, however, extreme difficulties in securing a reliable criterion of ' success ', and validation is necessarily confined to the highly-selected candidates who have actually been chosen ; i.e. there is no way of proving how unsuccessful the rejected candidates would have been. One can at least state that the method is superior to the older methods based on interview alone. Moreover, it has the tremendous advantage of appearing to be fair to the army, thus stimulating the supply of candidates and improving the confidence of senior officers in their subordinates.

It is because of this high ' face validity ', and the acceptability to candidates and to users, not because of their proven value, that group observational procedures have had such a vogue since the war. They are still used, in somewhat abbreviated form, by all three Services for officer selection. The most important adaptation was in selecting high-grade civil servants for the administrative class and foreign service (where the ordinary interview plus academic examination method of selection was obviously inappropriate for assessing men and women whose careers had been interrupted by war service).[1] Here the analogous exercises were designed chiefly to bring out desirable qualities of intellect, for example : free discussions on a given topic among a group of candidates, giving a short lecture, studying a brief and expounding it to a committee, and acting as chairman to a committee. Judgments based on these situations were supplemented by the study of objective test and examination results, background data and references, and by interviews. It was possible to demonstrate quite high validity for the procedure as a whole when the selected candidates were followed up after 2 years in the Civil Service (cf. p. 29). Correlations of around ·6 were almost as high as the correlation between the Civil Service's own judgments of suitability after 1 and after 2 years. In other words, the systematic 2- to 3-day procedure was nearly as accurate in forecasting success as was casual observation of the whole of the first year's work. But it should be stressed that the exercises, although quite time-consuming, supplied only about a quarter or a third of the material on which the final choices were made. Moreover, the staff were exceptionally experienced and very stable in composition. It certainly does not follow that any *ad hoc* adaptations of the ' house-party ' method, either by psychologists or laymen, will be equally successful. Both the Army and the Civil Service have departed from their original procedures, on grounds of economy, and satisfactory validation of their present watered-down methods is not yet available.

Munro Fraser [2] describes numerous applications to the selection of industrial executives, where an appointments committee, including a psychologist, spends half or a full day on a group of candidates. He reports general satisfaction with the products of the method, but this is no substitute for scientific validation. Candidates for the ministry, for teacher training, and for youth leaders, have been similarly dealt with.

[1] Cf. Wilson, N. A. B., ' The Work of the Civil Service Selection Board '. *Occup. Psychol.*, 1948, 22, 204–212. Vernon, P. E., ' The Validation of Civil Service Selection Board Procedures '. *Occup. Psychol.*, 1950, 24, 75–95.

[2] Fraser, J. M., ' New-Type Selection Boards in Industry '. *Occup. Psychol.*, 1947, 21, 170–178.

In one or two education areas, groups of 11-year-old children who are borderline candidates for grammar school places have been collected at a convenient centre for a day, and observed at a variety of tasks not unlike the Army leaderless-group tests—group games, constructional, imaginative, and dramatic activities. The teachers and psychologists who watch them apparently reach an agreed judgment quite readily as to which children show most initiative, co-operation, and other desirable personality qualities ; but again there is no evidence yet as to how far this predicts anything relevant to grammar school success. Here, too, there is some danger of children behaving unnaturally, through a sense of the importance of the occasion, or as a result of coaching by schools or parents. One would have thought that a week or a month's trial period in an actual grammar school, with a teacher specially trained to observe their social and intellectual adjustments, would be more diagnostic ; or indeed that a system of intermediate schools before a final decision is reached at 13 years would be even more effective.

In conclusion : these group procedures do not constitute personality tests. They are likely to be somewhat superior to the conventional interview method of assessing people, because they provide a more prolonged and varied set of situations in which to observe and interpret. But they are just as dependent as the interview on the skill, experience, and impartiality of the observer, and they should be applied with all the more caution because they engender in the observers an undue measure of confidence in the accuracy of their judgments. One might expect them to be superior also to the observation of behaviour at performance or other tests, described in Chap. IV, because they bring out social reactions of the candidates to their fellows, instead of only to the tester. But this is a dubious, and as yet unsubstantiated, advantage since it also means that the situation is more complex, less standardized, more apt to stimulate self-consciousness and playing a part.

VII

Ratings and Judgments of Personality

THE object of the rating method is to draw on the knowledge that a person's associates have acquired about him, and to turn this into numerical estimates of his standing on various personality traits. Let us look first at the acquisition of such knowledge. As soon as we meet a person we jump to conclusions about him. We interpret his features and expressive movements, and any actions we see or words we hear, and arrive at a kind of picture or *schema* of his personality as a whole. Our further contacts, observations, and conversations, help to fill in and extend, sometimes to modify, this *schema*. But when we are asked to rate him and give him, say, a high mark for Sociability or a low mark for Dependability, it is not so much because we have observed any particular pieces of behaviour which are representative of these traits, as because we generalize from our total impressions. Sometimes certain observations stand out in our minds and influence our judgments : he may have failed to carry out some commission, so we call him undependable. But usually a whole conglomeration of more or less unanalysed recollections and emotional reactions is bound up in any judgment. Earlier conclusions about him considerably affect later observations ; once the *schema* has been formed we tend to interpret what we see of him to fit in with it. Thus the *schema* is not an objective portrait or summary of the person. Although it may embody visual images and verbal descriptions, it also involves an emotional attitude or sentiment towards him. Landis [1] has studied the reasons given by raters for their judgments, and pointed out that good or bad reasons have little effect on accuracy. They tend to be rationalizations, in the psychoanalytic sense, of whose real origins the rater is largely unaware.

Our own theories of human nature and the meanings we attach to various traits also affect our judgments. In the

[1] Landis, C., 'The Justification of Judgments'. *J. Personnel Res.*, 1925, 4, 7–19.

8

course of our lifetime, our analysis of self, our contacts with other people, and the books and newspapers we read or the cinema films and plays that we see, all help to build up in us a set of stereotypes or stock personalities—the typical athlete, the aesthete, the absent-minded professor, the pedantic civil servant, etc. We are very apt to fit each new acquaintance into one or other of these categories. Actions which fail to conform are often not noticed. Hence our *schemas* remain primitive and far too simple to cover the complexities of the personalities we actually meet. (An enlightening discussion of the development of conceptions of people among children and poorly educated adults is given by Watts.[1] The interplay between our linguistic education and our understanding of people deserves much more study.)

The result, as mentioned in Chap. I, is the halo phenomenon. Either our general liking or disliking affects our judgments of what should be distinct traits ; or our *schema* embodies so strong an impression of one personality type or trait—say joviality, devotion to work, selfishness, or their opposites—that we interpret all other behaviour and rate other traits to accord with this. The subjectivity of judgments of personality is apparent whether these judgments are expressed in a free description (witness the varied interpretations of Napoleon's or Hitler's personalities by different authors), or as ratings. Although the latter are given in more standardized form, and the rater is usually warned to avoid halo, yet discrepancies between raters are probably as great as, or greater than, between biographers because of ambiguities in the interpretation of traits to be rated, and variations in standards of judgment. Ratings are therefore best regarded as samples of the ' reputation ' of the subject in the eyes of the rater. They are most inadequate as sole criteria of a person's traits, or as the sole source of data for the scientific study of personality. Yet at the same time they cover a much wider range of more natural behaviour than any practicable battery of personality tests or time-samples, and they have the tremendous advantage of being applicable without taking up the time of the subjects— even without their knowing anything about it. In an extensive research by the writer on a small group of students, the average

[1] Watts, A. F., *The Language and Mental Development of Children.* London : Harrap, 1944.

validity coefficient of sets of associates' ratings, when compared with trait-composites, was $+ \cdot 60$, whereas most of the better objective tests yielded coefficients between $\cdot 30$ and $\cdot 45$. Undoubtedly, then, ratings are useful, and they should be included in any approach to the assessment of people, provided that certain precautions are observed. Indeed they have probably been more widely used (in the form of school reports and record cards, merit ratings in industry, etc.) and more thoroughly studied than any other psychometric technique except the intelligence test.

It should be noted that ratings overlap with many of the more objective methods described in previous chapters, and particularly with the expressive methods of Chap. IV. There we saw that measurements of the speed, extent, pressure, etc., of expressive behaviour were seldom as diagnostic as judgments of the behaviour by an impartial observer. (Nevertheless there is much to justify the argument [1] that a properly weighted combination of measurements from such tests as Porteus Mazes, the Luria apparatus, or some form of dotting or stress test, would be more accurate than subjective interpretation.) Time-sampling and group observational methods are kinds of rating, and the former—when applicable—is superior to the latter just because it leaves so little to the judgment of the observer. Some researches based on ratings such as Webb's, Burt's, and Newcomb's [2] have required the judges to observe their subjects systematically over a considerable period ; and several rating devices mentioned below try to make the judges rate more from direct observation than from generalized recollections. These steps should help to make their *schemas* fuller and more impartial, though they certainly do not eliminate all halo, stereotypy, and bias.

RATING TECHNIQUES

1. *Ranking and Paired Comparisons.* A school teacher may arrange her class, or an officer his platoon, in order of merit for

[1] Upheld, for example, by Eysenck, H. J., *The Scientific Study of Personality*. London : Routledge, 1952.

[2] Webb, E., ' Character and Intelligence '. *Brit. J. Psychol. Monogr. Suppl.*, 1915, No. 3. Burt, C. L., ' The Factorial Study of Temperamental Traits '. *Brit. J. Psychol. Statist. Sec.*, 1948, 1, 178–203. Newcomb, T. M., ' The Consistency of Certain Extrovert-Introvert Behavior Patterns in 51 Problem Boys '. *Teachers College Contr. Educ.*, 1929, No. 382.

a trait. This is hardly applicable when the number of cases exceeds, say, twenty because of the difficulty of distinguishing among the bulk of middling people. But it has the advantage of avoiding the vagaries of absolute standards (cf. below). It is best to put each name on a separate card and let the rater sort them out. If a printed list is given, judges are apt to rank people at the top too high, those at the bottom too low.

In the paired comparison method the rater is given every possible pair of names and asked to say which of the two is higher. The results can be expressed finally as a ranking or a scaled score.[1] For most purposes this is an unnecessary refinement. It is usual to convert rankings into normally distributed scores, for example by means of Hull's or Symond's [2] tables. If this is done it is quite simple to combine or average rankings provided by different raters, each of whom may have judged a somewhat different list.[3] (For example, the Mathematics, French, and English teachers may each have ranked some, but not all, of a group of children.)

2. *Numerical Ratings.* It is an old parlour game to give people marks for traits. Dr. Johnson is said to have been annoyed at getting 0 out of 20 for Good Temper and Manners from Mrs. Thrale, though he also received 20/20 for Morality. Obviously it is impossible to distinguish as many as twenty grades, or to give any consistent meaning to percentage marks and the like. Experiments by Symonds and others show that five, or at most seven, grades is the largest number that the average rater can cope with. These may be denoted 5, 4, 3, 2, 1, or +2, +1, 0, −1, −2, or turned into letters, A to E, or verbal labels :

Strongly present, Present, Average, Lacking, Strongly Lacking, and so on. A smaller number of grades than five (e.g. Yes, Doubtful, No, or +, 0, −) is rather wasteful of the rater's powers of discrimination, but is nevertheless often used where

[1] Cf. Guilford, J. P., *Psychometric Methods.* New York : McGraw-Hill, 1936.

[2] Hull, C. L., *Aptitude Testing.* Yonkers, N.Y. : World Book Co., 1928. Symonds, see Bibliography.

[3] Note that it is essential that each person should be rated or ranked by the same *number* of judges. If 4 judges rate some, and only 2 judges others, the spread or scatter of ratings among the former will necessarily be smaller than among the latter.

there are many questions to be answered or traits to be rated, or when the rater has little detailed knowledge of the subjects or ' ratees '.

The outstanding defect of this type of scale is the variations in standards and distributions adopted by different raters. (Just the same difficulty arises in the marking of English essays or essay-type examinations, which is, of course, a form of rating.) The psychologist would naturally prefer the ratings of any large group of subjects to conform fairly closely to a normal distribution, say :

A	B	C	D	E
7	24	38	24	7%

Most raters tend to be too generous ; indeed they seem to regard C or Average as a term of abuse ; and most avoid using the extremes. Thus the distribution often reduces to something like this :

A	B	C	D	E
3	60	30	7	0%

But unfortunately no two raters distort in the same way, and this means that their judgments cannot be compared or combined. If one rater scarcely ever awards an A, his A's represent a much higher standing on the trait than do those of another rater who frequently gives them. The writer would go so far as to say that the ratings given on record cards by primary school teachers from numerous different schools are of practically no value to the secondary school teacher of the same pupils, because the latter cannot know what distributions the different raters adopted. The same is true for different supervisors in industry, or different officers commanding groups of soldiers. Again, it is impossible to combine the results of several sets of ratings of overlapping groups of people when distributions vary (just as different sets of examination marks cannot properly be combined unless scaled to a common standard).[1] Sometimes, therefore, raters or markers are presented with

[1] Cf. Vernon, P. E., *The Measurement of Abilities*. London : University of London Press, 1940.

an ideal distribution which they are advised to adhere to, such as :

A	B	C	D	E
10	20	40	20	10

This is a very simple pattern, which approximates closely enough to normality. But they seldom conform to this unless they are trained to do so, and are frequently checked. It may be preferable, then, to force them to use relative rather than absolute ratings, that is, to get them to pick out the best 10% and worst 10% of their group of ratees, then 20% of B's and 20% of D's. (The same method can be applied to other forms of distribution.) They will naturally object that their groups are almost all higher, or lower, than the general run. This may well be true when, for example, ratings are collected from different primary schools that feed one grammar school, or from different streams within any one school. If the groups are quite small they are especially apt to vary in merit, so that it is unfair to reduce them all to the same mean and standard deviation. It is sometimes possible to adjust the ratings to allow for such group differences, as when essay examination marks are scaled against objective attainment tests.[1] But the difficulty is such a serious one in the field of personality, that we must conclude that ratings should generally be used only within groups all of whose members are known to two or more raters. There is no really satisfactory way of comparing ratings by different judges of different groups, unless the groups are large enough and similar enough for relative ratings to be fair. Obviously this greatly restricts the practical usefulness of ratings.

3. *Man-to-Man Scales.* Various devices have been introduced in an attempt to pin raters down to more consistent standards. Thus in rating Leadership among American Army officers in 1917–18, each rater was told to think of an officer, A, whom he regarded as highest in this trait, then another, E, who was lowest, another half-way between, and a B and a D. These names were retained as a private yardstick, so that in rating any new officer, X, the rater would judge which of the five X most closely resembled. Similar scales were to be constructed

[1] Cf. McClelland, W., *Selection for Secondary Education.* London : University of London Press, 1942.

for other traits. Since different raters still have different scales, it is doubtful whether this is of much value. Its application to the marking of handwriting specimens or children's compositions or drawings by means of quality scales, where all markers use the same standard set of specimens, is a different matter.

4. *Verbal and Graphic Scales.* The substitution of such terms as : Excellent, Good, Average, Poor, Bad, for letters or numbers is of little help ; though a clever choice of terms will sometimes help to counteract the tendency to undue generosity or the tendency to avoid extremes. For example : Excellent, Very Good, Good, Fair, Weak, may produce a better distribution. But an extension of this idea, proposed by Freyd,[1] has been very widely adopted. In the graphic scale, each step is defined as concretely as possible, so that the rater no longer has to think quantitatively or bother about standards. In addition the ambiguity of vague trait-names like leadership, industriousness, etc., is avoided to a considerable extent ; verbs describing behaviour are substituted for nouns and adjectives. Here is an example from the American Council on Education scale for rating college students [2] :

Does X need constant prodding, or does he go ahead with his work without being told ?

Needs much prodding in doing ordinary assignments	Needs occasional prodding	Does ordinary assignments of his own accord	Completes suggested supplementary work	Seeks and sets for himself additional tasks

The rater merely puts a tick or cross at whatever point on the line that he thinks appropriate, but the experimenter can measure off this position as accurately as he wishes. Similar scales were used during the war for assessing the suitability of officer candidates, or the efficiency of serving men and officers, and are still considered the most satisfactory type. Generally they embody several questions with only three steps or grades

[1] Freyd, M., ' The Graphic Rating Scale '. *J. Educ. Psychol.*, 1923, 14, 83–102.

[2] Cf. Bradshaw, F. F., ' The American Council on Education Rating Scale '. *Arch. Psychol.*, 1930, 18, No. 119.

(ocasionally two or four), these being couched as far as possible in Service language. For example :

> A.1. Hard conditions tended to get him down.
>   2. He accepted bad conditions cheerfully enough.
>   3. He helped to keep up the men's spirits when conditions were bad.
>
> B.1. He has a flair for improvising (tools, materials, etc.) in an unexpected difficulty.
>   2. He is reasonably good at making the best use of what is to hand when things go wrong.
>   3. He is lost without the usual tools, materials, etc.

The grading on any one question would naturally be too coarse, but with half a dozen to two dozen or so questions, each covering some different aspect of efficiency, a total score can be derived, and these scores tend to show good distributions. Another advantage of such scales is that inexperienced raters find them easy to understand and apply. Even though the number of questions looks formidable they can actually be answered quite quickly. A minor objection is that they use up a lot of paper. Major ones are that some raters continue to be much more generous than others, and that correlations between different raters of the same subjects are still quite low.

5. *Analytic Scales.* Our last example illustrates the device of breaking up a general trait into a number of more specific components, which are separately rated and the scores combined. Such components should, of course, be relatively independent of one another, in order to cover the whole scope of the trait as efficiently as possible. However, halo is usually so strong that most of the items within such a scale tend to be rated in the same direction. Components regarded as more important can, of course, be given higher weight in the total score, though actually this makes so little difference that it is seldom worth while. One would expect such scales to be more objective, and to be more consistently answered by different raters, because they avoid indefinite and equivocal trait-names. But the evidence is not very favourable. In several studies, the correlations between total scores given by two raters have been around the same ·5 level which is normally found for

general-trait ratings. (Similarly in the marking of essays, analytic schemes are often found to be no more reliable than impressionistic).

A number of detailed scales, or third-person questionnaires (i.e. personality questionnaires to be filled in by a rater) have been published. Marston's scale of twenty items indicative of extraversion-introversion in children, and Bridges's scales for the social and emotional maturity of pre-school children, are good examples.[1] Laird's C-3 test of introversion, Willoughby's Emotional Maturity scale, and Heidbreder's questionnaires on introversion and inferiority attitudes,[2] have given rather poor results—perhaps because they are designed for adults, whose emotional traits are less overtly expressed than those of children.

The writer would suggest, then, that breaking down a trait into a small number of 3-point sub-scales may be worth while, because most raters find this easy to answer, and because it will usually yield a good distribution of total scores ; but that the inclusion of more than half a dozen items or aspects of a trait is likely to be a waste of time. If several traits, presumed to be distinct, are to be rated at the same time, each should be covered by three or four items, and the complete scale tried out on a typical sample of raters and ratees. If every item is now inter-correlated with every other, the coefficients will show whether they do group together as expected, whether some of the items overlap so much that they are better combined or reformulated, or whether some items presumed to represent Trait A actually overlap more closely with Trait B items, and so on. Either by means of factorial analysis, or by simply studying average inter-correlations, a much improved composite scale can thus be constructed.

6. *Standardized and ' Derived ' Scales.* We generally assume, without justification, that the various steps on a graphic, verbal,

---

[1] Marston, L. R., ' The Emotions of Young Children '. *Univ. Iowa Stud. Child Welfare*, 1925, 3. Bridges, K. M. B., *The Social and Emotional Development of the Pre-School Child.* London : Kegan Paul, 1931.

[2] Laird, D. A., *Personal Inventory, C-3.* Hamilton, N.Y. : Hamilton Republican, 1925. Willoughby, R. R., ' A Scale of Emotional Maturity '. *J. Soc. Psychol.*, 1932, 3, 3–36. Scale published by Stanford University Press, 1931. Heidbreder, E., ' Measuring Introversion and Extroversion '. *J. Abn. Soc. Psychol.*, 1926, 21, 120–134.. Heidbreder, E., ' The Normal Inferiority Complex '. *J. Abn. Soc. Psychol.*, 1927, 22, 243–258.

or numerical scale are equidistant, i.e. that A is as much superior to B as B is to C, etc. One technique of achieving equivalent units is to apply Thurstone's method of attitude scaling to a long series of statements. As shown in Chap. IX, this enables us to assign a rational numerical value to each of the statements we select, and at the same time to eliminate ambiguous or unsatisfactory statements. The following are three statements, standardized on a 0 to 8 scale, for assessing the efficiency of travelling salesmen [1] :

> (6·9) He is making exceptional progress.
> (3·2) He is somewhat in a rut on some of his brand talks.
> (5·6) He tends to keep comfortably ahead of his work
>   schedule.

Any of the statements that are thought to apply to the ratee are checked, and their average scale value gives his score. Willoughby's Emotional Maturity scale [2] is similar.

A different form of scaling is represented by the *Vineland Social Maturity scale*.[3] This contains 117 items such as :

Reaches for familiar persons	(4 months.)
Dries own hands.	(2½ years.)
Is trusted with money.	(5½ years.)
Makes telephone calls.	(10½ years.)
Provides for the future.	(25 years.)

Each item has been proved to be typical of the average (American) person of the age indicated. The scale is applied by a trained examiner who obtains the required information in an interview with a parent or someone else who knows the subject well. He checks the items that apply, and works out a Social Age and Quotient in the same manner as a Binet Mental Age and I.Q. The subjective element is greatly reduced since the

[1] Richardson, M. W., and Kuder, G. F., ' Making a Rating Scale that Measures '. *Personnel J.*, 1933, 12, 36–40.

[2] *Op cit.*

[3] Doll, E. A., *Vineland Social Maturity Scale*. Vineland, N.J. : Training School, Educational Test Bureau, 1936. Cf. Doll, E. A., ' Preliminary Standardization of the Vineland Social Maturity Scale '. *Amer. J. Orthopsychiat.*, 1936, 6, 283–293. It appears to be suitable for application in Britain ; cf. Kellmer Pringle, M. L., ' Social Maturity and Social Competence '. *Educ. Rev.*, 1951, 3, 113–128, 183–195.

examiner, by skilful questioning, can discriminate fact from interpretation in the informant's statements. It is claimed that different examiners, even interviewing different informants, arrive at Social Ages with as good a reliability as ·90. The resulting S.Q.s tend to correlate rather highly with I.Q.s, but there are good grounds for thinking that they also represent some aspect of social competence and personality maturity which is particularly relevant in certifying mentally defective subjects. A similar scale for assessing altruism among children is described by Turner.[1]

The Haggerty-Olson-Wickman *Behavior Rating Schedules* [2] represent another interesting development. A series of graphic scales for rating thirty-five common traits was applied by teachers to a group of children who had previously been very carefully assessed by psychologists for personality maladjustment. By analysing the numbers of well and poorly adjusted children who received each particular rating, a maladjustment index was derived for that rating. The Schedule could now be applied to any fresh child, and the total indices calculated for all his ratings in order to show his maladjustment. This has the advantage that the teachers are not asked to assess personality disorders as such, but only some of the more acceptable social, emotional, and other traits. Thus biases and misinterpretations of traits should be greatly reduced. Nevertheless there is still considerable subjectivity, since the maladjustment scores obtained from ratings by two teachers usually correlate only to about ·60. As Olson points out, the same set of ratings could be standardized against other criteria ; a series of scoring keys could be built up in the manner of the Strong Interest Blank (cf. p. 164). It would be of interest to try out this technique in grammar school selection, where it is known that ordinary personality ratings by primary school teachers are of little value (cf. p. 25). If teachers were asked to check a series of concrete statements (similar in form to the Army rating scales, p. 108) about the work and behaviour of their pupils, also about health and home environment, it might well be

[1] Turner, W. D., ' Altruism and its Measurement in Children '. *J. Abn. Soc. Psychol.*, 1948, 43, 502–516.

[2] Published by World Book Co., Yonkers, N.Y., 1930. Cf. Olson, W. C., *Problem Tendencies in Children.* Minneapolis : University of Minnesota Press, 1930.

found empirically that some of the statements differentiated pupils who later had successful and unsuccessful grammar school careers. Only a proportion of the statements might be diagnostic, but a really valuable measure might be constructed from these. Such a research would be lengthy and would have to be done on very large numbers, rated by many teachers, in order to yield a reliable scoring key.

Somewhat similar is A. H. J. Baines's [1] method of deriving gradings of the efficiency of civil servants. A number of supervisors of, say, clerical officers, rate these officers on a dozen aspects of their work, on 3-step scales, and also give a final general (5-step) grading. Correlations are calculated for the sub-scales with one another and with the final grading, and these show which sub-scales most closely predict general efficiency. A total score is then based on the general grading plus the best sub-scales, suitably weighted. Note that the supervisors are not asked which qualities or aspects they think relevant; by their own use of the scale they show the ones to which they attach most importance.

The most sophisticated development of derived rating scales is the *Forced Choice* type, which is employed, for example, in U.S. Army officer report forms. Such scales contain several blocks of items, like the following :

> A go-getter who always does a good job.
> Cool under all circumstances.
> Doesn't listen to suggestions.
> Drives instead of leads.

The rater is instructed to pick out the item in each block which is most characteristic and that which is least characteristic of the individual he is rating. The two favourable items are known, from previous trials, to be equally popular among raters but to differ in their discriminatory power ; one correlates well, the other badly, with some criterion—say a set of exceptionally thorough efficiency ratings. Similarly the two unpopular items differ. Thus a scoring key is available which, by contrasting the valid and non-valid items, reduces the liability of the ratings to bias and halo. It is too early to say whether the advantages of this technique outweigh the obvious

[1] Cf. Anstey, E., ' Staff Reporting in a Government Department '. *Occup. Psychol.*, 1950, 24, 200–229.

disadvantage that most raters find it highly irritating.[1] Probably it has greater promise in the field of self-rating questionnaires.

7. *Voting and Guess-Who Techniques.* Ratings of pupils by one another on ordinary rating scales are of little or no value. Children are even less familiar than educated adults with the meaning of traits, less able to think of traits quantitatively, less able to observe objectively ; and their suggestibility or contrasuggestibility to the teacher or psychologist who asks for the ratings may entirely distort the results. The idea of voting, however, goes down more readily, and by the age of 9 years or so they can pick out the two or three in their class who they think are highest or lowest in various respects. Hartshorne and May drew up a series of short character sketches, e.g. of a very selfish, moderately selfish, an average, and an unselfish child. Each member of the class was asked to guess whom these represented. With so large a number of raters, a pupil's score for selfishness is readily obtained from the number of times each sketch is assigned to him, and the scores show satisfactory reliability. Here is an example from a scale used in a British research on emotional stability with 10 to 12 year olds [2] :

> These three people are always happy and enjoying themselves. It is impossible to annoy them. They never change.
>
> (1)........................   (2)........................   (3)........................
>
> Here are three people who are very changeable. You can never depend on them. They are offended and annoyed very easily.
>
> (1)........................   (2)........................   (3)........................

[1] Cf. Travers, R. M. W., ' A Critical Review of the Validity and Rationale of the Forced-Choice Technique '. *Psychol. Bull.*, 1951, 48, 62–70. Baier, D. E., ' Reply to Travers' " A Critical Review of the Validity and Rationale of the Forced-Choice Technique'" '. *Psychol. Bull.*, 1951, 48, 421–434. Recent work indicates that the most reliable results are obtained with blocks of all-favourable items.

[2] Connor, D. V., *The Effect of Temperamental Traits upon Intelligence Test Performance.* Ph.D. Thesis, University of London, 1952.

Very similar are the well-known sociometric techniques of Moreno,[1] where each child writes the names of other pupils he would like to sit next to, or to play with, and so on. The results are generally used to present a picture of the social structure of the group rather than to assess the popularity or other traits of individuals. During the war the so-called nominations method was often applied, particularly in America, for gauging the suitability of a recruit, in the eyes of his fellows, for a commission. Among relatively uneducated or unsophisticated adults this very simple form of rating is as appropriate as it is among school children. Obviously such techniques may yield extremely biased judgments ; the reputation of a pupil in the eyes of his class-mates may seldom accord with that held by his teachers. Nevertheless it may possess useful validity. Thus in MacArthur's study of persistence (cf. p. 14), pupils' ratings agreed rather more highly than teachers' with the composite results of persistence tests. And follow-up results in the Services indicate that the summed opinions of a recruit's fellows tend to have better predictive value than the recommendation of a commanding officer.[2]

8. *Ratings Within Persons.* This refers to the rating or ranking of a number of traits according to their prominence within an individual, as contrasted with the ordinary procedure of rating a number of individuals on a trait. In some ways it is easier to judge whether a person is most outstanding for, say, Sociability, Instability, etc., than to arrange numerous individuals according to degrees of Sociability. Either the traits may be ranked, or, if they number a dozen or more, they can be sorted on a 5-, 7-, or 9-step scale ; (which are the 10% most outstanding traits in X, which the next 20% most characteristic, and so on ?) This method is most useful when the number of traits is large, the number of individuals small, or when none of the available raters is acquainted witn more than a few individuals. Burt and Stephenson [3] have shown how the results can be analysed statistically by calculating

[1] Moreno, J. L., ' Who Shall Survive ? ' *Nerv. Ment. Dis. Monogr.*, 1934, No. 58.

[2] Cf. Jenkins, Bibliography.

[3] Burt, C. L., ' Correlations Between Persons '. *Brit. J. Psychol.*, 1937, 28, 59–96. Stephenson, W., ' The Inverted Factor Technique '. *Brit. J. Psychol.*, 1936, 26, 344–361.

correlations between different persons (Stephenson's ' Q-technique '), as distinct from correlations between different tests or trait-ratings (' R-technique ').

DEVICES FOR IMPROVING RATINGS

A number of steps have been shown to increase the reliability of ratings, i.e. the agreement between different raters, though little is known regarding their effects on validity. We have considered already : (1) the superiority of relative to absolute ratings ; (2) of graphic to numerical or letter scales ; (3) the possible advantages of breaking down traits into components.

(4). Choose only straightforward, unambiguous traits and define them concretely, avoiding as far as possible terms suggestive of approval or disapproval. Hollingworth and others have published lists of relatively equivocal and unequivocal traits, though obviously much depends on how they are defined. An interesting study by Stephenson [1] showed how it is possible to analyse what a trait means to raters. He got 10 teachers to judge the Reliability of 100 children, and factor-analysed the correlations between the 10 sets of judgments. About half the teachers agreed quite closely with one another, while the other half agreed with each other but less closely with the first group. Clearly there were two different conceptions of Reliability. The first group appeared to base their ratings chiefly on placid, submissive behaviour, whereas the second type looked for more active and direct evidence of the trait. Clearly, better definition was called for.

(5). When several traits are to be rated, rate all individuals on one trait at a time, not each individual on all traits (unless using within-persons technique). This is supposed to produce greater independence between traits, i.e. less halo.

(6). However, if a rating form is being used for each individual, containing numerous traits or items, then the items should be arranged on the form so that the relatively desirable and undesirable extremes alternate in random fashion. Otherwise the rater is liable to go down the page checking the desirable (or undesirable) answers or grades throughout.

[1] Stephenson, W., ' Introduction to Inverted Factor Analysis, with Some Applications to Studies in Orexis '. *J. Educ. Psychol.*, 1936, 27, 353–367.

(7). Warn the raters of the nature of halo and encourage them to avoid it. One way of eliminating it is to sum the ratings of each individual on all traits and to regard this as a measure of halo or general popularity, which can then be subtracted from the separate trait-ratings, or he'd constant by partial correlation or factor analysis. Since, however, different traits of which society approves certainly do overlap to some extent, this will tend to over-correct. Nevertheless, in a research by the writer, this device did improve the validity of sets of ratings when compared with trait-composites. An alternative would be to get raters to estimate their personal liking for or dislike of each ratee, in addition to assessing his traits, and to remove the influence of this from the total ratings. Though this greatly oversimplifies the nature of halo, it would be of some help. Hartshorne and May, and Chi,[1] suggest that halo differs among different judges, hence we could estimate the true overlapping between traits by correlating A's rating of Trait 1 with B's rating of Trait 2, and so on. The differences between such correlations and the inter-correlations of A's (or B's) ratings of all traits, would provide a measure of halo. The flaw in the argument is that A's and B's biases are only too likely to overlap, especially if they are both people with a similar relation to the ratees, say teachers. And even raters with such different outlooks as teachers, parents, and pupils are liable to be similarly influenced by liking, or by common confusions about the meanings of traits. In other words, the correlation between Traits 1 and 2, when rated by several judges, is made up of :

> genuine overlapping between the behaviour included in the traits, plus confusions and biases common to all, or to any pair of, raters.

It is reduced by confusions and biases which affect individual raters only. This is why, in Chap. I, little credence was attached to factorial studies of ratings. They throw more light on the linguistic problem of how people interpret traits than they do on the structure or organization of personality traits as such.

(8) Nevertheless it is certainly an advantage in any experimental or practical application of ratings, to obtain independent judgments from 2 or more judges, since this helps to cancel out

[1] Chi, P. L., ' Statistical Analysis of Personality Ratings '. *J. Exper. Educ.*, 1937, 5, 229–245.

individual prejudices. There is little point in having more than 4 or 5, unless the rating scale is very coarse (as in voting among pupils). By inter-correlating the sets of judgments and applying the Spearman-Brown prophecy formula, it is easy to determine how many judges are needed in order that their combined rating may reach an acceptable level of reliability, say ·9. The writer would suggest, however, that diversity of judges is more important than number. The ideal would be to have 2 or more of each type of judge, for example, 2 teachers, 2 psychologist-observers, 2 relatives, and a group of pupils and to aim for high agreement between the judges within type, but lower correlations (representing different viewpoints between types.

(9). Raters should be trained in the use of the scale, and if they are required to use it frequently—for industrial, educational or other purposes—their distributions, reliability, etc. should be checked periodically. Normally they can be assured that the ratees will not know what they say about them, so that they can be completely candid. But their attitudes to the person requiring the ratings should also be considered, and their full co-operation sought. In fact, much the same difficulties occur here as with self-ratings and personality questionnaires (cf. Chap. VIII). For example, raters are likely to be defensive about attributing undesirable traits to their friends. During the war it was noticed that instructor officers at a training school would willingly agree that some of their cadets were weak in efficiency, social adjustment, intelligence, etc. But similar officers in command of units to which these cadets were posted would give much higher ratings because, consciously or unconsciously, they resented the suggestion that their own unit could contain any inefficient people.

(10). It is usually stated that raters should have had plenty of opportunity to observe the kind of behaviour they are rating, and should be well acquainted with the ratees. Obviously there is some truth in this : an interviewer who merely talks to a prospective employee for half an hour can hardly assess his practical skills or the dependability of his character. But the tendency for an individual to express his personality in everything he does, also the tendency for closer acquaintanceship to lead to more rigid and biased opinions and greater halo, should not be forgotten. Thus the evidence, so far as it goes, actually

9

suggests that an impartial observer and interviewer (particularly if he has applied performance tests or analogous exercises which provoke significant behaviour) can give at least as reliable and valid ratings as a close friend. Ferguson [1] compared ratings of travelling salesmen by managers who were acquainted with them to varying degrees, and did obtain better ratings from the better acquainted ; but all of them, presumably, would be fairly distant in their relations to the ratees. Slawson [2] found that a period of observation before rating improved the reliability of judgments to some extent. But Knight [3] showed that intimacy or length of acquaintanceship led to more over-rating and greater halo. Presumably a more superficial knowledge is also more detached. In Newcomb's [4] research at a boys' summer camp, careful records were kept of actual behaviour, and these were used for checking the accuracy of raters who had observed some, but not other, kinds of behaviour. The validity of the ratings on observed traits was represented by correlations of ·54 and ·45, while for traits which had not been observed but were inferred the correlations were ·89 and ·40. The latter figures are somewhat lower, but to a statistically insignificant extent.

JUDGING ABILITY [5]

It is dangerous to generalize about the goodness of different types of raters, since there is seldom any criterion of accuracy except other ratings. If rater A coincides more closely with B, C, and D than does rater B with A, C and D, this shows that the *conformity* of A's judgments is higher, not that his intuitive skill is superior. Moreover, there appear to be large variations, depending on the particular traits to be judged or the manner in which the judgments are given, and on whether the ratees

[1] Ferguson, L. W., ' The Value of Acquaintance Ratings in Criterion Research '. *Amer. Psychologist*, 1948, 3, 290.

[2] Slawson, J., ' The Reliability of Judgment of Personal Traits '. *J. Appl. Psychol.*, 1922, 6, 161–171.

[3] Knight, F. B., ' The Effect of the " Acquaintance Factor " upon Personal Judgments '. *J. Educ. Psychol.*, 1923, 14, 129–142.

[4] *Op cit.*, p. 95.

[5] An excellent review of this field is given by R. Taft in an as yet unpublished thesis (University of California, 1950). The generalizations listed here are partly based on his intensive experimental investigation.

are new acquaintances or old friends.[1]   Nevertheless, there is fairly strong evidence that ' good ' judges are not so much outgoing, socially intelligent people as rational, analytic, in some respects introverted. (Adams [2] found that the good judges of self tend to be extraverted ; for the extravert is more detached about his own personality, but he may be too interested in others to judge them impartially.) The good rater tends also to be above average in intelligence and in personality maturity, and integration. Though in some situations artistic inclinations seem helpful, there is stronger evidence that natural scientists are superior to social science or arts students. They are superior also to psychologists, except in so far as the judgments involve knowledge of technical terminology. There is no support for the belief in feminine superiority. Raters are generally more successful in judging people of similar age, sex, and cultural background to themselves. Hollingworth and others provide some evidence that people who are high in a desirable trait tend to rate it better, and that the reverse holds for undesirable traits. Thus the most ' snobbish ' are not good at rating ' snobbishness '. Finally, the degree of confidence that a rater expresses in his judgments is a very poor criterion of their accuracy.

People vary also in their judg-ability, i.e. the extent to which several raters agree about them, and in the extent to which ratings of their different traits are influenced by, or free from, halo. The former is sometimes considered to show their openness vs. enigmaticness, the latter their mediocrity vs. individuality. But there is little evidence to confirm such suppositions.

OTHER METHODS OF EXPRESSING JUDGMENTS OF PERSONALITY

In view of the difficulties of getting useful ratings in education or industry—where few raters are likely to know large numbers, and where thorough training is seldom possible—we should enquire into the value of less formal methods, such as the testimonial and the free personality sketch. The ordinary

[1] Cf. Vernon, P. E., ' Some Characteristics of the Good Judge of Personality '. *J. Soc. Psychol.*, 1933, 4, 42–58.

[2] Adams, H. F., ' The Good Judge of Personality '. *J. Abn. Soc. Psychol.*, 1927, 22, 172–181.

testimonial or reference is notoriously superficial and unreliable, especially when given to the individual himself to pass on to prospective employers. The trust placed in more confidential references generally depends on the employer's knowledge of, and respect for, the writer. Actually only one careful experiment seems to have been carried out, and this gave rather promising results.[1] Confidential references are obtained for candidates for the higher Civil Service from 5 persons, representing their schools, universities, employers, and private acquaintances. Sets of reports on 268 candidates were graded by 13 Civil Service Selection Board staff members, without any further information about the candidates. The average inter-correlation between the grades was ·67, and their average correlation with the Final Board decision was ·43. Thus predictions based on testimonials were just about as good as those based on examination results and objective tests of abilities.

If the confidential testimonial has been somewhat under-rated, the case-study and personality sketch written by a psychologist or psychiatrist has perhaps been over-valued. It is based chiefly on interview, supplemented by observation of behaviour at tests or, in the case of mental patients, in the wards, and by information from relatives and acquaintances.[2] The value of such a study is sometimes judged by its comprehensiveness, and by the consistency of the personality structure that it reveals. But this provides no guarantee that it is not distorted by the writer's subjective interpretation of the complex mass of evidence. We have already referred to discrepancies between different psychologists or psychiatrists in discussing the interview (Chap. II). An experiment was carried out at a War Office Selection Board,[3] where pairs of psychiatrists interviewed candidates independently and observed them at analogous exercises, finally assessing their suitability for commissions. Their mean inter-correlation of ·65 was distinctly lower than the ·86 obtained by military officers who merely observed the exercises. In the Civil Service Selection Board follow-up, the psychologist's final judgment correlated as highly as ·87 with the Final Board decision, and his

---

[1] Cf. Vernon, P. E., ' The Validation of Civil Service Selection Board Procedures '. *Occup. Psychol.*, 1950, 24, 75–95.

[2] For a useful account, and references, cf. Strang, Bibliography.

[3] Cf. Vernon and Parry, Bibliography.

validity coefficient with efficiency gradings after 2 years was ·49. But these figures were no higher than those of the non-psychological staff members. On the other hand, the studies of vocational guidance conducted by the National Institute of Industrial Psychology (cf. p. 29) show that psychologists' judgments based on a free synthesis of interview and other material possess good, though certainly not perfect, validity.

The following conclusions seem to emerge regarding the best way of obtaining useful information from associates about a candidate for employment, or from teachers about a pupil being considered for promotion to secondary schooling, etc. A set of ratings should be asked for, probably in the graphic or questionnaire form described on pp. 107–9. The number of questions, say ten to twenty with three answers each, should be kept as few as possible, consistent with covering most of the relevant aspects of personality. If the various questions can be validated and keyed against an external criterion of later success, in the manner of the Haggerty-Olson-Wickman or forced-choice scales, so much the better. But the main object of the ratings will usually be to force the judge to consider the subject from as many angles, and as systematically and objectively, as possible. Thereafter he should be asked to write a free personality description, testimonial, or case-study, explaining and commenting on his ratings, mentioning supporting evidence, and filling in what seem to him the main gaps.

VIII

Self-Ratings and Personality Questionnaires

AN individual's written account of his past behaviour, feelings and wishes obviously constitutes an important source of information about his personality. G. Allport [1] points out the value of diaries, creative writings, and other personal documents in the ' clinical ' study of the individual personality ; and psychiatrists and clinical psychologists often require their patients to write autobiographies. The interpretation of such material is inevitably as subjective as that of oral interview responses, and it cannot readily be treated quantitatively. It was hoped, therefore, that self-ratings and the answers to standard questions would overcome these difficulties.

Ratings by the individual of his own traits may be obtained by the same techniques as are used in rating others. It is commonly found that they deviate even more from associates' ratings than associates' do from one another, and that most people overrate themselves considerably on desirable traits, i.e. they possess a favourable halo towards their own personalities. Allport finds that university students tend to make themselves as interesting as possible, for example—overrating their radicalism, introversion, and emotionality ; and Husén [2] shows that the qualities valued by self-raters vary with their education and social background. But just as associates' ratings may be improved by analytic scales and third-person questionnaires, so self-ratings have developed into the innumerable personality inventories and paper-and-pencil tests.

These questionnaires contain anywhere from 10 to 223 items (or even more in multiple scales), thus covering a wide range of presumed manifestations of some trait—say introversion-extraversion. The individual's score is based on the total

---

[1] Allport, G. W., *The Use of Personal Documents in Psychological Science.* New York : Social Science Research Council, 1942.

[2] Husén, T., ' The Popular Conception of Personality as Revealed in Self-Ratings '. *Essays in Psychology Dedicated to D. Katz.* Stockholm, 1951.

questions, usually unweighted, which he answers in the intro-verted direction. The questions tend to be highly personal and embarrassing, and we shall see later that so much depends on the testee's attitude to the test and his interpretation of the questions, that the results are of very dubious value.

The test items are generally made up in the first place (or borrowed from other tests) to accord with the author's con-ception of the trait. Thereafter they are always pruned or standardized by one of the stock item-analysis techniques [1]; for a small number of good items is more easily answered and is likely to discriminate better than a long and miscellaneous test.[2]

(*a*) Internal consistency techniques : these show whether all the items correlate with the testees' total scores, i.e. whether they all measure the same presumed trait reliably. Note that reliability is used now in the sense of consistency of a testee's answers to different questions, not (as in the case of associates' ratings) as meaning agreement with anybody else's judgments.

(*b*) Factor analysis of inter-item correlations again shows whether all items are measuring the same variable, or whether they should be sub-divided into two or more sets measuring distinct traits. Guttman's ' scale analysis ' [3] has occasionally been used to give an even stricter check on the homogeneity or unidimensionality of the items.

(*c*) Items are analysed against some external criterion. They are retained or dropped, or scoring weights are determined, by their success in differentiating, say, neurotic patients from normals. The forced-choice technique (cf. p. 112) is promising in this field, but has so-far seldom been applied.[4]

---

[1] Cf. Vernon, P. E., ' Indices of Item Consistency and Validity '. *Brit. J. Psychol. Statist. Sec.*, 1948, 1, 152–166.

[2] Popular weeklies sometimes publish short questionnaires claiming to show whether the reader is an easy person to get on with, or possesses other traits. Almost certainly these have not been item-analysed, standardized or validated in any scientific way.

[3] Guttman, L., ' On Festinger's Evaluation of Scale Analysis '. *Psychol. Bull.*, 1947, 44, 451–465.

[4] In a recent investigation by Gordon, an ordinary and a forced-choice questionnaire for measuring Ascendancy, Hypersensitivity, Responsibility and Sociability were compared with associates' ratings. The mean ' validity ' coefficients were ·34 for the former and ·56 for the latter. Gordon, L. V., ' Validities of the Forced-Choice and Questionnaire Methods of Personality Measurement '. *J. Appl. Psychol.*, 1951, 35, 407–412.

(*d*) Several persons besides the author judge the suitability of each item. An extension of this is the application of the Thurstone attitude-scaling technique (cf. Chap. IX).

Most of the hundred or more tests that have been published are modifications or extensions of three prototypes : Woodworth's *Personal Data Sheet*, Freyd-Heidbreder's *Introversion-Extraversion* test, and Allport's *A-S* (*Ascendance-Submission*) *Reaction Study*. Instead of trying to give a comprehensive list, we shall outline these, and mention briefly others which have been widely used, or which embody special points of technique.

TESTS OF PSYCHONEUROTIC TENDENCY AND EMOTIONAL INSTABILITY

The 116 items in Woodworth's [1] test were originally derived from medical psychologists' descriptions of the symptoms of neurotic patients. The following are some representative examples :

> Do you usually feel well and strong ?
> Do you ever walk in your sleep ?
> Have you ever had fits of dizziness ?
> Did you have a happy childhood ?
> Do you know of anybody who is trying to do you harm ?
> Does it make you uneasy to cross a bridge over a river ?
> Have you ever been afraid of going insane ?
> Have any of your family had a drug habit ?

Each question is followed by ' Yes, No ', one of which is to be checked. Mathews, Cady,[2] and others have adapted the test for use with children, and Burt [3] publishes a British version which, however, he recommends as an interview aid rather than as a quantitative test. Laird's [4] *Personal Inventory B-2*

---

[1] Woodworth, R. S., *Personal Data Sheet*. Chicago : Stoelting, 1920.

[2] Mathews, E., ' A Study of Emotional Stability in Children '. *J. Delinq.*, 1923, 8, 1–40. Cady, V. M., ' The Estimation of Juvenile Incorrigibility '. *J. Delinq. Monogr.*, 1923, No. 2.

[3] Burt, C. L., *The Subnormal Mind*. Oxford University Press, 1935.

[4] Laird, D. A., ' Detecting Abnormal Behavior '. *J. Abn. Soc. Psychol.*, 1925, 20, 128–141. Inventories published by The Hamilton Republican, Hamilton, N.J., 1925.

contains similar items, but with multiple-choice (graphic) responses, e.g. :

Have you (during the past few weeks) been afraid of responsibility ?	avoided it	accepted when forced upon me	did not mind it	liked it	welcomed it

The most widely used pre-war test, Thurstone's [1] *Personality Schedule*, contains 228 items collected from Woodworth, Laird, and other sources. Percentile norms are available for college students. Many other shorter and simpler tests were devised during the war, and used with some success in screening recruits who might be liable to neurotic breakdown. These included the National Defence Research Council's inventory (*NDRC Short Format*), the Neuropsychiatric Screening Adjunct (*NSA*), and the *Cornell Index*,[2] in America ; also the *Maudsley Medical Questionnaire*,[3] and the *Sutton Booklet* or Bennett-Slater [4] test in Britain. The latter is a composite test, in ten sections, whose items are cleverly disguised. Three sections deal with symptoms of anxiety, hysteria, and depression ; but in about half the questions a negative, instead of a positive, response indicates neurotic tendencies, so that the testee who wants to create a good impression cannot merely check ' No ' throughout. Four sections contain lists of various types of annoying situations :

(1) Frustration of self-assertion, e.g. ' Somebody tells you how to do your job '.
(2) Personal inadequacy, e.g. ' You forget what you're looking for '.
(3) Dirt or untidiness, e.g. ' An unmade bed '.
(4) Noise, e.g. ' The sound of hammering '.

[1] Thurstone, L. L., and Thurstone, T. G., 'A Neurotic Inventory'. *J. Soc. Psychol.*, 1930, , 13–30. Test published by University of Chicago Press, 1929.

[2] Cf. Office of Scientific Research and Development, *Human Factors in Military Efficiency*. Washington, D.C. : National Defence Research Council, 1946. Stouffer, S. A., *et. al.*, *Studies in Social Psychology in World War II*, Vol. IV. *Measurement and Prediction*. Princeton, N.J. : Princeton University Press, 1950. Weider, A., Mittelmann, B., *et. al.*, ' The Cornell Selectee Index '. *J. Amer. Med. Assoc.*, 1944, 124, 224–228. Test published by Psychological Corporation, New York, 1948.

[3] Cf. Eysenck, Bibliography.

[4] Bennett, E., and Slater, P., ' Some Tests for the Discrimination of Neurotic from Normal Subjects'. *Brit. J. Med. Psychol.*, 1945, 20, 271–282.

Evidence is given to show that neurotics check items of types (2) and (4) as annoying much more often than normals do, whereas (1) and (3) affect normals and neurotics alike. Thus scores are based, unknown to the testee, on the differences between these sections. Finally, three sections are adapted from Pressey's Cross-Out test (cf. p. 175). They contain lists of words where the testee crosses out anything :

    (1) For which people should be blamed, e.g. ' Flirting, Speeding '.
    (2) Which he has worried about, e.g. ' Loneliness, Falling '.
    (3) In which he is interested, e.g. ' Football, Comedians '.

Neurotics are likely to give many answers to (1) and (2), but relatively few to (3).

INTROVERSION AND ASCENDANCE TESTS

Freyd-Heidbreder Test.[1] Freyd collected fifty-four items descriptive of the introvert type from Jung's writings, of which the following are samples :

Blushes frequently ; is self-conscious.
Day-dreams.
Prefers to read a thing rather than experience it.
Shrinks when facing a crisis.
Is reticent and retiring ; does not talk spontaneously.
Is slow in movement.
Keeps in the background on social occasions.

Heidbreder turned these into a self-rating test, where the testee checks each item +, ? or —. Laird's[2] *Personal Inventory C-2* and various other adaptations are available. Other tests such as Neymann-Kohlstedt's and Root's (described and used in England by Wyatt and Langdon),[3] were constructed so

[1] Freyd, M., ' Introverts and Extroverts '. *Psychol. Rev.*, 1924, 31, 74–87. Heidbreder, E., ' Measuring Introversion and Extroversion '. *J. Abn. Soc. Psychol.*, 1926, 21, 120–134.
[2] *Op cit.*
[3] Neymann, C. A., and Kohlstedt, K. D., ' A New Diagnostic Test for Introversion-Extroversion '. *J. Abn. Soc. Psychol.*, 1929, 23, 482–487. Root, A. R., ' A Short Test of Introversion-Extroversion '. *Personnel J.*, 1931, 10, 250–253. Wyatt, S., and Langdon, J. N., ' Fatigue and Boredom in Repetitive Work '. *Industr. Hlth. Res. Board Rep.*, No. 77. London : H.M. Stat. Office, 1937.

that items discriminated between schizophrenic and manic-depressive patients. The assumption that these psychotic groups represent the extremes of normal introversion and extraversion is very dubious ; in fact, Eysenck offers an experimental disproof (cf. p. 36). Hence this type and the Freyd-Heidbreder type of test give very poor correlations with one another.

A similar scale for schizothymia-cyclothymia, based on Kretschmer's work, is published by Scholl.[1]

Allport's A-S Reaction Study.[2] Here the items were made up to represent concrete manifestations of dominatingness (ascendance) or submissiveness, and were standardized by comparing the answers of students who had been rated by associates as highly ascendant or submissive. The following are examples ; the numbers show the weighted scores for ascendance :

A salesman takes manifest trouble to show you a quantity of merchandise ; you are not entirely suited ; do you find it difficult to say ' No ' ?	Yes, as a rule . . −1 Sometimes . . 0 No . . +1

If you hold an opinion the reverse of that which a lecturer has expressed in class, do you usually volunteer your opinion ?	In class . . . +3 After class . . 0 Not at all . . −3

An alternative form is available for women, and an adaptation for children has been prepared.

TESTS OF OTHER TRAITS

A test for Inferiority Feelings, based on Adler's writings, has been compiled by Heidbreder,[3] along the same lines as her introversion test. Bernreuter[4] published a test of

[1] Scholl, R., ' Untersuchungen über die teilinhaltliche Beachtung von Farbe und Form bei Erwachsenen und Kindern '. *Zs. f. Psychol.*, 1927, 101, 225–280.

[2] Allport, G. W., ' A Test for Ascendance-Submission '. *J. Abn. Soc. Psychol.*, 1928, 23, 118–136. Allport, F. H., and Allport, G. W., *A-S Reaction Study.* Boston : Houghton Mifflin, 1928.

[3] Heidbreder, E., ' The Normal Inferiority Complex '. *J. Abn. Soc. Psychol.*, 1927, 22, 243–258.

[4] Bernreuter, R. G., ' The Measurement of Self-Sufficiency '. *J. Abn. Soc. Psychol.*, 1933, 28, 291–300.

Self-sufficiency vs. Dependence on Others. Maslow [1] has developed tests of Security-Insecurity and of Self-esteem or Dominance feeling (the latter for women only), on the basis of clinical studies of well and poorly adjusted students. Jasper, and Chant and Myers [2] have tests of Depression-Elation, the latter being scaled by Thurstone's technique. Its items range from :

> Everything in the world is against me (Score 0·9) to, Life could not be better for me (10·7).

Willoughby's *E-M* (*Emotional Maturity*) *Scale* [3] contains similarly standardized items, e.g. :

> S develops affective difficulty in the presence of a necessity for precise and realistic thinking, e.g. mathematics. —— (Score 2)
>
> S organizes and orders his efforts in pursuing his objectives, evidently regarding systematic method as a means of achieving them. —— (7)

This is intended primarily for third-person application, e.g. for ratings of a patient by a psychiatrist, but can also be used for self-rating (at a sophisticated level).

Wang's [4] Persistence test contains items which, in the opinion of 75 judges, should differentiate the persistent and non-persistent person. Cason [5] originated the Annoyances

---

[1] Maslow, A. H., *et. al.*, ' A Clinically Derived Test for Measuring Psychological Security-Insecurity '. *J. Gen. Psychol.*, 1945, 33, 21–41. Maslow, A. H., ' A Test for Dominance-Feeling (Self-Esteem) in College Women '. *J. Soc. Psychol.*, 1940, 12, 255–270. *Social Personality Inventory for College Women.* Stanford, Cal. : Stanford University Press, 1942.

[2] Jasper, H. H., ' The Measurement of Depression-Elation and its Relation to a Measure of Extraversion-Introversion. *J. Abn. Soc. Psychol.*, 1930, 25, 307–318. Chant, S. N. F., and Myers, C. R., ' An Approach to the Measurement of Mental Health '. *Amer. J. Orthopsychiat.*, 1936, 6, 134–140.

[3] Willoughby, R. R., ' A Scale of Emotional Maturity '. *J. Soc. Psychol.*, 1932, 3, 3–36. Test published by Stanford University Press, 1931, now out of print.

[4] Wang, C. K. A., ' A Scale for Measuring Persistence '. *J. Soc. Psychol.*, 1932, 3, 79–90.

[5] Cason, H., ' An Annoyance Test and Some Research Problems '. *J. Abn. Soc. Psychol.*, 1930, 25, 224–236.

test (adapted for the Bennett-Slater questionnaire, p. 125). It lists 217 situations which the testee rates from 3 (extremely annoying) to 0 (not annoying). The average score can be used as measure of Irritability.

Wallen's [1] test of Food Aversions consists of twenty foods which are ticked for liking or disliking. Normal adults dislike an average of one or less, whereas neurotics average three to five aversions. Eysenck has found the test effective in this country also.

MULTIPLE TESTS

Tests such as Woodworth's or Thurstone's obviously contain a wide range of symptoms drawn from many different neurotic or psychotic conditions. It would be theoretically possible for several testees to give neurotic answers to entirely different sets of, say, twenty items, and yet get the same score and be labelled equally neurotic or unstable. Attempts have been made to classify the Thurstone Schedule items,[2] e.g. under Extravert-Introvert, Physical Disorders, Fantasy, etc., but these tend to inter-correlate too highly to be accepted as distinct. In Laird's B-2 Inventory the items are classified as Psychasthenoid, Schizophrenoid, and Neurasthenoid.

Cattell [3] published a questionnaire with separate sets of items for seven syndromes—Neurasthenia, Anxiety Neurosis, Anxiety Hysteria, Conversion Hysteria, Obsessive-Compulsive, Epileptoid, and Paranoid. Better known is Hathaway and McKinley's *Minnesota Multiphasic Personality Inventory (MMPI)*,[4] which is widely used in mental hospitals in this country as well as America. Its 550 statements are more varied than usual, including some dealing with interests and social attitudes. They are generally presented individually, on separate cards,

[1] Wallen, R., ' Food Aversions of Normal and Neurotic Males '. *J. Abn. Soc. Psychol.*, 1945, 40, 77–81.

[2] Cf. Willoughby, R. R., ' Some Properties of the Thurstone Personality Schedule and a Suggested Revision '. *J. Soc. Psychol.*, 1932, 3, 401–424.

[3] Cattell, R. B., *A Guide to Mental Testing*. London : University of London Press, 1936.

[4] Hathaway, S. R., and McKinley, J. C., ' A Multiphasic Personality Schedule (Minnesota). I. Construction of the Schedule.' *J. Psychol.*, 1940, 10, 249–254. Inventory published by Psychological Corporation, New York, 1942.

and sorted by the patients into ' True, False, and Cannot Say ' boxes. It may take anywhere from 30 minutes to several hours to complete. On the basis of the responses of 500 normal adults (16 to 55 years) and 800 miscellaneous patients, a series of empirical scoring keys has been developed, so that a profile is obtained showing relative scores on : Hypochondriasis, Depression, Hysteria, Psychopathic Deviate, Masculinity-Feminity, Paranoia, Psychasthenia, Schizophrenia, and Hypomania. Note that the significance attached to an item depends, not on its manifest content, but on its correlation with an external criterion. Other keys can be and are being developed by various authors, e.g. for differentiating academically unsuccessful from successful students.[1] Four additional scores provide checks on self over-evaluation, malingering, and other sources of unreliability. The authors do not claim that the profile will provide an automatic differential diagnosis of patients. The MMPI is a clinical instrument which requires considerable skill in interpretation, and even then is likely to agree with the psychiatric diagnosis only in 60% of cases (according to critics the figure is less than 50%). It is more successful in differentiating abnormal persons in general from normal. While experienced testers can acquire a remarkably detailed insight into a personality from the pattern of scores, this approach is open to all the weaknesses mentioned in Chaps. I and II.

Another test with a psychiatric background is the *Humm-Wadsworth Temperament Scale*.[2] It aims to measure seven ' components ' distinguished by Rosanoff : Normal, Hysteroid, Manic Cycloid, Depressive Cycloid, Autistic Schizoid, Paranoid, and Epileptoid. Scoring keys were based on the responses of groups of patients, criminals, and normals known to be strong or weak on these components. Some of the 318 items score for more than one component, while others are not scored at all, since they did not differentiate between any of the groups ; but they were left in the final form of the test for the sound reason that the value of an item may be affected by its context.

---

[1] Cf. Gough, H. G., ' Factors Relating to the Academic Achievement of High-School Students '. *J. Educ. Psychol.*, 1949, 40, 65–78.

[2] Humm, D. G., and Wadsworth, G. W., ' The Humm-Wadsworth Temperament Scale '. *Amer. J. Psychiat.*, 1935, 92, 163–200. Scale published by Humm Personnel Service, Los Angeles, Cal., 1940.

This has the disadvantage of making the test rather long, the average time for answering being 55 minutes. Another interesting feature is that the proportions of Yes's and No's to the test as a whole provides a check on the testee's conscientiousness. Negativistic persons tend to give an undue number of No's, highly suggestible people too many Yes's. Humm insists that it is the pattern or profile of scores on all the components, considered in the light of these checks, which enable the well-trained tester to diagnose personality trends. He has applied the test widely in business and industry and quotes striking instances of correct detection of dishonesty or character weakness among employees. Other writers, however, quote only moderate or poor validities.[1]

The *Bernreuter Personality Inventory* [2] has achieved enormous popularity in America, with little justification. It claims to measure four traits—Neurotic tendency, Introversion-Extraversion, Dominance-Submissiveness, and Self-Sufficiency. Each of its 125 items (mostly taken over from Thurstone, Heidbreder and Allport, etc.) is scored for each trait. For example the responses to : ' Do you day-dream frequently ? ' are scored :

	Neurotic	Introversion	Dominance	Self-Sufficiency
Yes . .	+5	+3	−1	+1
No . .	−4	−4	+1	−1
Doubtful .	−2	0	+2	+2

These weights were obtained empirically by contrasting the responses of high and low scorers on four established scales—Thurstone's, Laird's C-2, Allport's, and Bernreuter's own Self-Sufficiency test. In this instance the external criteria for item-validation are highly fallible, and the resulting inventory scores show odd features. Several experiments have demonstrated that Neurotic and Introverted are almost identical, correlating to +·93, and that Dominance is nearly the reverse of both, its

---

[1] Cf. Dorcus, R. M., ' A Brief Study of the Humm-Wadsworth Temperament Scale and the Guilford-Martin Personnel Inventory in an Industrial Situation '. *J. Appl. Psychol.*, 1944, 28, 302–307. Guilford, J. P., and Lacey, J. I., *Printed Classification Tests*. Army Air Forces Aviat. Psychol. Prog. Res. Rep. No. 5. Washington, D.C. : U.S. Government Printing Office, 1947.

[2] Bernreuter, R. G., ' The Theory and Construction of the Personality Inventory '. *J. Soc. Psychol.*, 1933, 4, 387–405. Inventory published by Stanford University Press, 1931

correlations being −·81 and −·67. Self-Sufficiency is relatively distinct, though overlapping moderately with Dominance ; its correlations are −·41, −·32, and +·58. Flanagan [1] applied factor analysis to these scores and showed that the test was in effect measuring two, not four things. The first, a compound of Neurotic, Introverted and low Dominant, and Self-Sufficient scores, seems to represent general Lack of Self-Confidence. A second and smaller factor may be denoted as Sociability. Flanagan constructed a fresh set of keys so that responses could be scored for these two factors.

Bell's Adjustment Inventory [2] is another test widely used at high school and college level. Its 160 items are grouped under four headings—Home, Health, Social, and Emotional Adjustment.

Boyd's Personality Questionnaire [3] is the only one to have been used at all extensively among British university students. Its 120 items are classified under twenty headings or traits, including the following :

Trait	Sample Question
Obsessional Carefulness	Do you often go over a job again and again to make it just right ?
Worry, Anxiety	Do you brood long over humiliating or unhappy experiences ?
Suspiciousness	Do you sometimes suspect that people are talking about you ?
Self-consciousness	Are you greatly interested in what goes on in your own mind ?

Testees are not told about these traits, and the questions are so arranged that they are unlikely to guess that six deal with carefulness, six with worry, etc. Each question is answered Yes, Yes ?, 0, No ? or No, or omitted ; and is scored 4 to 0. Thus there is a possible range of 24 to 0 for each trait. Naturally the traits overlap considerably, and a factor analysis by the writer of the scores of 100 students

[1] Flanagan, J. C., *Factor Analysis in the Study of Personality.* Stanford, Cal. : Stanford University Press, 1935.

[2] Bell, H. M., *Adjustment Inventory.* Stanford, Cal. : Stanford University Press, 1934.

[3] Boyd, W., 'A New Personality Test '. *Scot. Educ. J.*, 1939, Sept. 1st–15th, 998–999, 1014–1016, 1024–1025.

indicated that they could be boiled down to three or four distinct tendencies :

(1) Self-depreciatory and psychoneurotic tendency—a general factor particularly strong in the scores for Depression, Instability, Worry, Lack of Self-Control, Shrinking Responsibility, and Lack of Confidence.

(2) ' Care-freeness ', most marked in Shrinking Responsibility, Suggestibility, Inability to Concentrate, Lack of Definite Interests, and in low scores on Worry, Self-Consciousness, Emotional Thinking, Dissociation, and Tenseness.

(3) ' Scrupulousness ', most marked in Obsessional Carefulness, Acting Readily without Pressure, Suspiciousness, Self-Control, and Low Instability, Emotional Thinking, and Inability to Concentrate.

(4) A sex difference factor.

These results indicate the dangers of taking questions at their face value. Even when multiple tests are devised to measure traits distinguished by factor analysis, the resulting scores tend to be far from distinct. An example of this is provided by the :

Guilford-Martin Temperament Profile Chart.[1] In several publications Guilford has analysed correlations between typical items from extraversion-introversion tests, and claimed to break down this trait into separate components. Two of his tests attempt to measure such factors, namely :

Inventory of Factors STDCR	*Inventory of Factors GAMIN*
Social Introversion	General Pressure for Overt Activity
Thinking Introversion	Ascendancy in Social Situations
Depression	Masculinity of Attitudes and Interests
Cycloid Disposition	Inferiority Feelings
Rhathymia (Carefreeness)	Nervous Tenseness and Instability

Actually the correlations between these sub-scores are so high that, in the absence of validation against external criteria, they all seem to measure much the same introversion-neuroticism

[1] Guilford, J. P., and Guilford, R. B., ' Personality Factors *S*, *E*, and *M*, and their Measurement '. *J. Psychol.*, 1936, 2, 109–127. Martin, H. G., ' The Construction of the Guilford-Martin Inventory of Factors G–A–M–I–N '. *J. Appl. Psychol.*, 1945, 29, 298–300. The three inventories published by Sheridan Supply Co., Beverly Hills, Cal., 1940–1943.

factor as does the Bernreuter Inventory.[1] A third test included
in Guilford's Profile Chart is his *Personality Inventory I.* This
aims to pick out trouble-makers and paranoid individuals in
business and industry by means of three groups of items
measuring : Objectivity, Agreeableness, and Co-operativeness.
It has been shown to correlate moderately with ratings of
employees,[2] but whether it would work equally well as a
selection test, when testees are on the defensive, is not known.

Cattell's 16 *P.F. Test.*[3] Perhaps the most ambitious questionnaire is the one constructed by Cattell to cover the twelve
' source traits ' of his personality factor analysis, together with
four additional traits (radical-conservative, self-sufficiency,
will-control, and nervous tension). There are two parallel
forms, each containing 187 items. They are designed for college
student level, but a children's edition is being prepared. The
amount of overlapping among the sixteen scores is not stated,
and no evidence of validity is so far available.

QUESTIONNAIRES FOR CHILDREN

The reactions of children, particularly under 14 years, to
personal questions are even more unpredictable than those of
adults, and we would strongly deprecate the use of such tests
except in experiments conducted by trained psychologists. In
an attempt to reduce introspectiveness, contrasuggestibility, or
other undesirable attitudes, some American questionnaires
have adopted third-person questions, similar to those of Guess-
Who ratings.

Maller's Character Sketches [4] contains 200 short descriptions ;
the testee has to say whether or not he feels or acts like the
person described. For example :

—— This person insists on having his own way and likes to
command and rule everybody.

—— This person finds it difficult to forget unpleasant
memories and can't help thinking about them.

---

[1] Cf. Lovell, C., ' A Study of the Factor Structure of Thirteen Personality
Variables '. *Educ. Psychol. Measmt.*, 1945, 5, 335–350.

[2] Cf. Dorcus, *op. cit.*, p. 131.

[3] Cattell, R. B., *et. al.*, *The 16 Personality Factor Questionnaire*. Champaign, Ill. : Institute of Personality and Ability Testing, 1950.

[4] Maller, J. B., *Character Sketches*, 1932 ; *Personality Sketches*, 1936.
New York : Teachers College, Columbia University, Bureau of Publications.

Each item is repeated in reverse form, elsewhere in the test, as a check on consistency ; e.g. :

—— This person never insists on having his own way and does not like to command and rule everybody.

All questions have been shown to differentiate significantly between groups of 308 delinquent or problem cases and 310 normal pupils. They are classified under the following six headings, which are admitted to overlap to a moderate extent :

Desirable character traits	Personal adjustment (freedom from anxiety)
Self-control and integration	Mental health (freedom from psychotic or neurotic symptoms)
Social adjustment (extraversion)	Readiness to confide in others

A later edition, *Personality Sketches*, consists of 100 items, presented on cards, so that no written response is required.

Pintner's *Aspects of Personality* [1] contains thirty-five items for measuring each of three traits—ascendance-submission, extraversion-introversion, and emotionality. It is sufficiently simply worded to be applicable from about 10 to 15 years.

Sanders,[2] in Australia, has developed a test for individual application to 9- to 13-year-old boys, containing third-person items dealing with Physical and Economic Insecurity, Social Under-evaluation, and Non-Social Tendencies. The two latter sections are highly correlated. He finds that delinquents tend to give high scores on all sections, and that anxious or neurotic boys surpass normals on the second and third.

Several other inventories and questionnaires, either for American adolescents or for the long-suffering college student, are listed and critically reviewed in Buros's Year books.

BIOGRAPHICAL INVENTORIES

Hollingworth, in the 1920s, studied the predictive value of responses to application blanks by candidates for employment,

---

[1] Pintner, R., and Forlano, G., ' Validation of Personality Tests by Outstanding Characteristics of Pupils '. *J. Educ. Psychol.*, 1939, 30, 25–32. Test published by World Book Co., Yonkers, N.Y., 1938.

[2] Sanders, C., ' Insecurity and Social Maladjustment in Children '. *Brit. J. Educ. Psychol.*, 1948, 18, 148–155.

and found that a weighted score derived from the most valid questions might correlate well with subsequent success. Such validation necessitates very large numbers, thus this technique was useful in selecting pilots, officers, or other large groups in the Second World War.[1] Inventories were devised containing a hundred or more multiple-choice questions which covered a wide range of mainly factual information—educational and occupational career, financial status, skills and trade experience, home background, marital record, athletic and leisure activities, health, etc. The relevance of each answer was determined by giving the inventory to groups of, say, successful and failing pilots, and a purely empirical scoring key was developed. The same inventory, with a different key, could be used for navigators or other groups. Note that this type of questionnaire does not set out to measure any specified trait or traits. But it was certainly the most useful of all the personality measures tried out in the U.S. Army Air Force. Unfortunately it is applicable only when the job requirements and the type of applicant remain constant over a long period, and it would probably work only with adults of good intelligence. It might well be tried in the selection of university students.

DISCUSSION OF PAPER-AND-PENCIL PERSONALITY TESTS

The weaknesses of the questionnaires described above seem so obvious that their use in countries other than America has been confined almost entirely to a few tentative experimental investigations. But in America they have not only been used in hundreds of studies with pupils and students, but are (or at least used to be) applied regularly in mental hospitals, clinics, and schools, for detecting problem cases and neurotics, and for educational or vocational guidance. They are so easily made up and given to large numbers that it seems to be forgotten that a count of emotional responses is a very different matter from a count of right answers to intelligence or educational tests. However, since the publication of a highly critical article by

[1] Cf. Guilford and Lacey, *op. cit.*, p. 131. Vernon and Parry, Bibliography. Stuit, D. B. (edit.), *Personnel Research and Test Development in the Bureau of Naval Personnel.* Princeton, N.J.: Princeton University Press, 1947.

Ellis, there are signs of greater caution, and of some realization of the importance of the testees' attitudes to the tests.

The majority of the questions deal with personal matters which one might discuss with a sympathetic and trusted friend, or a psychoanalyst, but would certainly hesitate to commit to writing for some relatively unknown tester to read. Many experiments have in fact shown that when people do not have to give their names they admit to larger numbers of symptoms of maladjustment.[1] Interesting studies by Smith, and Sletto,[2] compared items set in a positive or socially acceptable form with similar ones in negative form, e.g. :

> Feels people speak well of him and like him.
> Feels people criticize him and dislike him.

It was found, (*a*) that more people admitted that the positive form did not apply than that the negative form did apply ; (*b*) that the correlation between scores on the two types was not high ; (*c*) that the negative type showed higher internal consistency. Presumably this means that negative items all tend to arouse a suspicious, hostile, or defensive attitude. Hence testees answer them all alike, regardless of their real meaning. Positive items, however, are considered more calmly, and so evoke a greater diversity of response and lower consistency. Thus the common application of the internal consistency technique of item analysis tends to produce a piling up of negative items.[3]

Many tests, such as Allport's A-S, try to draw on recollections of objective behaviour rather than on feelings, and it has been shown that answers to such items tend to be more stable or less likely to alter if the test is repeated (although their internal consistency may be lower). But affective reactions naturally enter into these just as, in the case of external ratings, halo continues to operate however objectively the traits are defined. Although the name of the trait or traits at which a test is aimed

[1] Cf. Ellis, Bibliography.

[2] Smith, R. B., ' The Development of an Inventory for the Measurement of Inferiority Feelings at the High School Level '. *Arch. Psychol.*, 1932, 22, No. 144. Sletto, R. F., ' A Critical Study of the Criterion of Internal Consistency in Personality Scale Construction '. *Amer. Sociol. Rev.*, 1936, 1, 61–68.

[3] Cf. Willoughby, R. R., and Morse, M. E., ' Spontaneous Reactions to a Personality Inventory '. *Amer. J. C.thopsychiat.*, 1936, 6, 562–575.

is usually withheld, and some non-committal title like Inventory or A-S Study is given, it is obvious that testees will make their own guesses as to the object of the test, and will answer each question not so much at its face value as in accordance with their own interpretation of the object, and with how much they are willing to reveal.

This explains why, on the one hand, different tests of nominally the same trait, given on different occasions, often show remarkably poor agreement, whereas on the other hand tests of nominally different traits given in the same experiment (particularly if combined together into a multiple test) tend to show much too high correlations. In fifty-five studies listed by Ellis, the median correlation between tests claiming to measure the same trait was ·40. The present writer found a figure not much lower, namely ·34, in fifty-eight studies where introversion, psychoneurotic tendency and submission-ascendance were inter-correlated. The far higher overlapping in the Bernreuter and other multiple tests has already been pointed out.[1] This strong general factor which runs through the responses to extremely diverse questions in any one testing situation surely reflects the testee's halo and general attitude to this situation.

It is not only the subject's willingness to co-operate that affects his responses, but also his unconscious resistances. People literally do not know themselves well enough to answer many of the questions correctly ; their responses are only too likely to be rationalizations or unwitting self-deceptions. Alexander [2] has compared questionnaires with psychoanalytic techniques, pointing out that the psychoanalyst would never expect to get valid information from direct questions or introspections, where conscious criticism is at its maximum. Another important factor is suggestion. The well-known experiments on testimony show how liable to falsification are our recollections of emotionally toned experiences, and how easily suggestive questioning may lead us to accept experiences as our own which never really occurred. Thus while most testees may be expected,

[1] A relevant finding by the Research Branch, Information and Education Division of the U.S. Army, was that its NSA test of 15 items dealing with psychosomatic symptoms was as effective in screening neurotic recruits as a multiple test of over 100 items, which were carefully compiled to cover all the main aspects of maladjustment.

[2] Alexander, F., ' Evaluation of Statistical and Analytical Methods in Psychiatry and Psychology '. *Amer. J. Orthopsychiat.*, 1934, 4, 433–448.

wittingly or unwittingly, to disguise their emotional weaknesses in answering personality questionnaires, others of a more suggestible type may greatly exaggerate. This was brought out in a study by Hollingworth,[1] who applied the Woodworth inventory to groups of soldiers in a mental hospital shortly before the 1918 armistice, and to other similar groups shortly after. The average incidence of neurotic symptoms was about twice as great in the former, presumably on account of their conscious or unconscious fear of being returned to active service.

Yet another factor appears to raise scores in the well-educated and academically minded. It is a remarkable fact that university students and professional people obtain much higher average psychoneurotic and introverted scores than do the relatively uncultured ; not infrequently they are found to be as unstable as neurotic and psychotic mental hospital patients. (There is a slight tendency also for the better students to be more introverted and neurotic, though the evidence on this point is somewhat contradictory.) Conceivably such persons are more neurotic than the less educated classes, but it is just as likely that they are also more self-analytic, more used to verbalizing their emotional experiences, more willing to admit to themselves and to the tester the possession of the symptoms which the tests describe. Thus the explanation of the high consistency and overlapping of questionnaire tests probably lies in these various distorting attitude factors. High scorers are not necessarily the most neurotic, introverted, submissive, lacking in confidence, nor given to fantasy, shrinking responsibility, instability, and inferiority feelings ; they may be the more sophisticated and introspective, or the more suggestible, or the more willing to co-operate with the tester.

The influence of temporary mood—optimism, worry, etc.— might also be thought to affect test responses. An experiment with the Bernreuter test by Johnson [2] showed that this does occur, though only to a very slight extent. Objections are often raised, again, to the rigid limitation of testees' responses to Yes, No, or at most to five steps for each item. It is true that this worries many educated testees, whose natural reactions to the

[1] Hollingworth, H. L., *The Psychology of Functional Neuroses.* New York : Appleton, 1920.
[2] Johnson, W. B., ' The Effect of Mood on Personality Traits as Measured by Bernreuter '. *J. Soc. Psychol.*, 1934, 5, 515–522.

questions are infinitely varied. Eisenberg [1] carried out an introspective study of what different subjects meant when they selected a given response to a typical question, and showed that there were enormous variations. However, this is less serious than it sounds since variations in interpretation will tend to be random, and to cancel one another out when total scores are considered. It is when all the variations take the same direction, as when the ' tough-minded ' or the resentful testee underestimates his instability throughout, that they upset the test results.

A much less obvious distortion enters whenever testees are allowed to omit questions, to answer by question mark, or to give various grades of response. Some people are much more cautious or non-committal than others. For example, in the Boyd questionnaire it was found by the writer that the proportions of extreme responses (definite Yes's and No's as contrasted with Yes ?, 0, or No ?) ranged from 17% to 98%. Cronbach [2] calls this factor ' response-set ' and shows that it is fairly persistent or general from one test to another. (It occurs also, of course, in associates' ratings and in the markings of examinations, where some markers adopt a much wider spread than others.) In ability tests, as we have seen, it may give some indication of impulsiveness-caution, but its psychological significance in personality questionnaires is very dubious. For the most part it is a quite irrelevant feature of the testees' interpretations of the test instructions, which nevertheless operates to raise all high, or lower all low scores. Such tests as MMPI and Humm-Wadsworth try to provide checks, and recognize that abnormal sets may invalidate all test scores. Cronbach recommends the use of forced-choice items in order to eliminate it.

VALIDITY

However, the constructors of questionnaires can justifiably answer that speculations about testees' attitudes and interpretations do not concern them, provided that the tests work.

[1] Eisenberg, P., ' Individual Interpretation of Psychoneurotic Inventory Items '. *J. Gen. Psychol.*, 1941, 25, 19–40.

[2] Cronbach, L. J., ' Further Evidence on Response Sets and Test Design '. *Educ. Psychol. Measmt.*, 1950, 10, 3–31.

The important thing is whether they correlate with other evidence of the traits. There is no need for us to survey validation studies in detail, since this has been done by Ellis. He outlines the results of 380 relevant investigations and concludes that, with two exceptions, these are generally unfavourable to personality questionnaires. Perhaps his standards of ' favourable ' are unduly high. Thus he regards a correlation of ·4 as only ' questionably positive '. We would agree that this level of validity is too low for making predictions about individuals, but it does indicate that questionnaires have some value, especially if combined with other kinds of tests. In just over half of the following 217 investigations the results were positive or questionably positive :

Comparisons of the scores of behaviour prob-
    lem children and of delinquents with
    normal children :   (24 out of 48)
Comparisons of neurotic and psychotic
    adults with normals :   (45 out of 75)
Correlations with ratings by associates on the
    traits at which the tests are aimed :   (22 out of 44)
Correlations with other tests of the same
    traits :   (27 out of 55)

The fourth category consists entirely of comparisons with other questionnaires ; thus it indicates weak reliability rather than moderate validity. However, in the present writer's research, the mean correlation of five questionnaires with trait composites (chiefly made up of ratings and objective tests) was ·45.

More striking than the average result is the wide range of success and failure of questionnaires, even in similar investigations. This does not seem to be mainly due to differences in the value of different questionnaires, although Ellis does show that the Bell and Bernreuter Inventories, the Thurstone Schedule, and Woodworth questionnaire tend to be the least successful. More probably it is a matter of the subjects' attitudes. Two studies of the Thurstone Schedule among college students provide an interesting contrast. Hanna [1] gave it to 179 students who applied for psychological or vocational guidance at a college clinic, who, therefore, presumably thought that it

[1] Hanna, J. V., ' Clinical Procedure as a Method of Validating a Measure of Psychoneurotic Tendency '. *J. Abn. Soc. Psychol.*, 1934, **28**, 435–445.

would help them if they answered it really frankly. Independent estimates of their emotional stability were made by clinical psychologists and good agreement was found with the Schedule scores (corresponding to a correlation of over ·5). Moran,[1] on the other hand, showed that 41 students who were classified as maladjusted scored scarcely any higher than 146 well-adjusted students. But here the Schedule (in abridged form) was taken along with various tests of abilities at the beginning of the college year, so that many students may have thought that the authorities would be influenced by the kind of picture they drew of themselves.

Two exceptions were mentioned to Ellis's general condemnation. The first is the Minnesota Multiphasic Inventory. A considerable majority of studies have shown significant differences between various abnormal groups and normals, though the validity of the test for differentiating among different abnormal types is less well attested. Usually, of course, the test is administered individually, and patients are more likely to answer as they would to oral questioning by a psychiatrist. Secondly, there is no doubt that such inventories as the NDRC, NSA, Cornell and others were of value in screening abnormal recruits during the war. The great majority of seventy-one studies showed significant agreement with subsequent psychiatric diagnoses. Harris's [2] study of 2081 naval recruits who answered NDRC and Cornell (in about 6 minutes) is representative. Of these 297, or 14·3%, scored above a certain borderline, and 52 of them were discharged after psychiatric interview or as a result of referrals during 10 weeks' training ; another 16, not ' caught ' by the tests were also discharged. Thus three-quarters of the discharges were diagnosed, and 11·7% of acceptable recruits were incorrectly picked out. Similar tests were applied experimentally, but not regularly, in the British Services. On the whole they were less successful. Thus Eysenck found some correlation between the Maudsley Medical Questionnaire and neuroticism among recruits, but this was smaller than that of the body-sway suggestibility, leg persistence, dark vision, and other objective tests.

[1] Moran, T. F., ' A Brief Study of the Validity of a Neurotic Inventory '. *J. Appl. Psychol.*, 1935, 19, 180–188.
[2] Harris, D. H., ' Questionnaire and Interview in Neuropsychiatric Screening '. *J. Appl. Psychol.*, 1946, 30, 644–648.

Ellis and Conrad point out that such tests always produced large numbers of 'false positives', i.e. normals with high neuroticism scores. Nevertheless, they did save a considerable amount of psychiatric interviewing time by picking out most of the potential neurotics. Much of their good validity could be attributed to 'criterion contamination', that is, to the fact that they asked questions similar to those asked orally in a psychiatric interview ; indeed often the psychiatrists would know, and be influenced by, the test scores. Thus the results were far less favourable in thirty-six studies where tests were checked against objective criteria such as failure in training. For example, several tests tried out on USAAF pilots gave very small or zero correlations with learning to fly. No satisfactory investigations of their value in predicting breakdown in combat appear to have been carried out.

In so far as questionnaires do work better in military than civilian contexts, it is probably due to the tremendous heterogeneity of samples of recruits, and to better motivation. Recruits may be more candid, either because of military discipline, or because they may assume that scores indicating abnormality will be to their advantage. Further, the better tests were carefully constructed from items each of which had been proved to differentiate abnormals from normals, in contrast to the haphazard collection of items in most civilian tests, described at the beginning of this chapter, plus the misleading internal consistency check.[1] It is noteworthy that the civilian tests which on the whole give the best results such as Allport A-S, MMPI, Humm-Wadsworth, and Character Sketches, also consist of empirically validated items.

We may conclude then that, despite their extreme weaknesses and dangers, paper-and-pencil personality tests and questionnaires should not be entirely condemned. Well-constructed ones, given under suitable motivating conditions, can be of value both for experimental research, and in clinical or other applied psychological work.

[1] Cf. the useful discussion by Stuit, *op. cit.*, p. 136.

IX

Measurement of Attitudes and Interests

THE techniques which, as we have seen, work rather badly in the measurement of emotional traits, are considerably more successful in measuring social attitudes, opinions, and interests; for example, radicalism vs. conservatism, nationalism, favourableness or unfavourableness to religion, to birth control, or to coeducation, liking for particular school subjects or occupations, etc. The term 'attitude' has been used by psychologists in a great many senses, and there is no agreed definition.[1] But in this context it generally implies a personality disposition or drive which determines behaviour towards, or opinions and beliefs about, a certain type of person, object, situation, institution or concept. It includes both McDougall's 'sentiments' and the medical psychologist's 'complexes', though it is not necessarily thought to arise either from innate instincts or from repressed wishes. Often our attitudes are adopted ready-made, as it were, from our parents, teachers, or friends, though usually modified by our own experiences.

Note that, as in the case of personality traits, attitudes may be expressed either through behaviour or through verbal statements, and that not infrequently these may seem to be inconsistent or contradictory. Katz and Allport[2] point out also that our publicly admitted attitudes may differ considerably from our deeper and more private feelings. A man's pro- or anti-semitism, for example, is exceedingly complex, and could not be assessed satisfactorily merely by asking him if he liked Jews, nor only by observing such actions as his willingness to patronize Jewish shops. It would be desirable to sample both representative acts and opinions. Actually the majority of attitude tests sample verbal expressions only, and the extent

---

[1] Cf. Allport, G. W., 'Attitudes'. *A Handbook of Social Psychology* (edit. C. Murchison). Worcester, Mass. : Clark University Press, 1935.

[2] Katz, D., and Allport, F. H., *Students' Attitudes.* Syracuse, N.Y., Craftsman Press, 1931.

to which they penetrate to the ' private ' level is doubtful.
But they are none the less useful provided that these limitations
are realized, and that they are not assumed to be predictive of
behaviour without further evidence. And we shall see that
quite an amount of evidence has been collected showing that
they do correlate with behaviour, at least to a moderate
extent.

The notion of broad sampling is important in attitude
measurement, both because any single verbal statement may
give an inaccurate index of a person's more general attitude,
and because of the need to avoid stereotyped value judgments. If a man is asked straight out how religious he is,
how tolerant to foreigners, etc., his answer will inevitably
be biased by what he regards as socially respectable. Thus
it is better to break down the attitude into a number of
more concrete manifestations, and ask what he did in particular
situations, or what he thinks about specific points (just as
in analytic rating scales). For example, how often does
he go to what church services, what religious books has he
read recently, does he accept such-and-such beliefs ? It
does not matter if some of the items seem only doubtfully
relevant to, or partially dependent on, the general attitude.
Statistical analysis will show whether they are too remote to
be included.

Whatever kind of test is adopted, the conception of attitude
measurement necessarily involves a unidimensional variable,
that is a definite object or issue towards which some people are
more favourable than others. This requirement has given rise
to considerable criticism ; it is said that peoples' attitudes on
any topic show an infinite variety of qualitative differences, and
that they cannot be arranged along a single scale without
distortion. For example, liberals do not merely hold views
intermediate between those of socialists and conservatives.
But the answer to this is that, if other important dimensions
exist, they should be measured separately. Thus if liberals
do differ both from socialists and conservatives in favouring
greater freedom for the individual (or any other doctrine),
then an appropriate test should be devised. As in the wider
sphere of personality, factor analysis is of the greatest assistance
in showing what attitudes are sufficiently unidimensional to be
suitable for measurement, which are distinctive and which

overlap so much that they are better combined.[1] On many issues, shades of opinion are indeed too varied and unpolarized to be readily measurable. For example, in one research in London on the value of school visits (to museums, factories, etc.) it was not found possible to produce a satisfactory test of children's attitudes. They almost all liked visits, and though many recognized various drawbacks, there was no single clear continuum from pro- to anti-. This is very apt to occur among children ; adults' attitudes are generally more crystallized. The most pervasive factors running through the political, social, and religious opinions of adults are two bipolar tendencies which contrast : (*a*) progressive or radical with conservative, and (*b*) authoritarian or ' tough-minded ' with tolerant attitudes. But numerous sub-factors have been described in the literature. For example, Cattell claims that most attitudes can be grouped under McDougall's list of instincts.

PUBLISHED ATTITUDE TESTS

Many readers may be more concerned with techniques of attitude test construction, which they can apply to their own social, educational, or other researches, than with published tests. However, a few of the better known tests will be described or listed for illustration.

Thurstone's Scales.[2] Thurstone and his collaborators have produced a whole series of scales of attitudes to the Church, war, negroes, communism, capital punishment, etc. There are many other scales similar in form : Peterson's Attitude to War, Remmers's[3] generalized scales for measuring attitudes to any school subject, or any social institution, etc. (The latter are of

[1] Cf. McNemar, Bibliography ; Cattell, R. B., *Description and Measurement of Personality*. London : Harrap, 1946. Vernon, P.E., ' A Study of War Attitudes '. *Brit. J. Med. Psychol.*, 1942, 19, 271–291. Eysenck, H. J., ' Social Attitudes '. *Current Trends in British Psychology* (edit. C. A. Mace and P. E. Vernon). London : Methuen, 1953.

[2] Thurstone, L. L., *et. al.*, *Scales for the Measurement of Social Attitudes*. Chicago : University of Chicago Press, 1930. Also, Thurstone and Chave, Bibliography.

[3] Peterson, R. C., *Scales for Attitude Toward War*. Chicago : University of Chicago Press, 1930. Remmers, H. H., *et. al.*, *Attitude Scales*. Lafayette, Ind. : Purdue University, Division of Educational Reference, 1934. Remmers, H. H., and Silance, E. B., ' Generalized Attitude Scales '. *J. Soc. Psychol.*, 1934, 5, 298–312.

very dubious value.) In Britain, Jordan [1] has published a scale for children's attitude to French, and numerous other scales on various educational and social questions are contained in student M.A. and Ph.D. theses.[2] Each of these consists of about twenty statements graded on a 1 to 11 scale from highly favourable to highly unfavourable, but printed in random order.

The following examples are from Jordan's scale :

> I think that it takes so long to learn a foreign language that the attempt is not worth while (2·0);
> I like to listen to French talks on the wireless, because I think it will improve my knowledge of the language (9·5);
> I only borrow French books occasionally from the school or public library (7·6).

The testee ticks the statements with which he agrees and the median or mean scale value of these gives his attitude score.

Multiple-choice Tests of Radicalism-Conservatism and Other Attitudes. Lentz's [3] C-R Opinionaire contains fifty statements such as :

> The metric system of weights and measures should be adopted instead of our present system.
> Even in an ideal world there should be protective tariffs.
> Conscience is an infallible guide.
> Armistice Day should be celebrated with less martial spirit.

Each of these is answered $+$ for agreement or $-$ for disagreement. They are not graded as in Thurstone-type scales ; instead the testee's score consists of the number of statements he answers in the conservative direction (i.e. No in the first and fourth examples, Yes in the second and third). Alternatively the multiple-choice or 'cafeteria' question may

[1] Jordan, D., ' The Attitude of Central School Pupils to Certain School Subjects, and the Correlation between Attitude and Attainment '. *Brit. J. Educ. Psychol.*, 1941, 11, 28–44.

[2] Cf. Blackwell, A. M., *A List of Researches in Education and Educational Psychology.* London : Newnes, 1950.

[3] Lentz, T. F., *et. al.*, *C-R Opinionaire.* St. Louis, Mo. : Washington University, Character Research Institute, 1935.

be used, as in this example, abbreviated from Vetter's [1]
questionnaire :

> What are your views on HEREDITARY WEALTH ?
> 1. All wealth should revert to the State at death.
> 2. Taxes should confiscate the bulk, leaving only enough
>   for support of dependents.
> 3. Inheritances should be taxed on a rapidly graded scale,
>   up to about 50% for large fortunes.
> 4. Very large fortunes should pay a reasonable inheritance
>   tax, but not so high as to become confiscatory.
> 5. Individual thrift and initiative should not be damped
>   by any inheritance taxation.

Here the score is based on the grade of responses to several such
questions.

Likert [2] has published tests of Internationalism, Imperialism,
and Attitude to Negroes, and all tests with multiple-choice
answers are sometimes referred to as Likert-type, as contrasted
with Thurstone-type. In point of fact, Likert did not originate
a new type of question, but only a technique of weighting the
graded responses to any question according to their centroids or
z-values. This technique has not been generally adopted
because the simpler method of weighting the responses 5, 4, 3,
2, 1 or +1, 0, −1, etc. gives practically the same results.

Eysenck's [3] test of anti-semitism combines the Thurstone and
multiple-choice types. Thus the following two statements have
graded responses : Strongly Agree, Agree, Undecided, Disagree,
Strongly Disagree.

> The Jews have too much power and influence in this
> country (6·9).
>
> The Jews have survived persecution because of the many
> admirable qualities they show (1·0).

The first is much more strongly anti-semitic than the second,
and possesses a higher Thurstone scale-value. This is allowed

---

[1] Vetter, G. B., ' The Measurement of Social and Political Attitudes and
the Related Personality Factors '. *J. Abn. Soc. Psychol.*, 1930, 25, 149–189.

[2] Likert, R., ' A Technique for the Measurement of Attitudes '. *Arch.
Psychol.*, 1932, 22, No. 140.

[3] Eysenck, H. J., and Crown, S., ' An Experimental Study in Opinion-
Attitude Methodology '. *Int. J. Opinion Attitude Res.*, 1949, 3, 47–86.

for by weighting the five responses to the two statements :
2, 3, 4, 5, 6, and 8, 6, 4, 2, 0 respectively (a high score represents pro-semitism).

Other tests deserving special mention include Neumann, Kulp and Davidson's Test of Internationalism, Hartshorne and May's ethical attitude scales, Rundquist and Sletto's studies of the morale of unemployed men, and the extensive series of scales applied in the American Army by Stouffer and others.[1] An interesting scale recently constructed by Shoben [2] contains eighty-five items representing domineering, possessive, rejective, or other undesirable parental attitudes regarding child-upbringing, which have been proved to differentiate mothers of problem children from mothers of normal children, e.g. :

> A child should be seen and not heard. Strongly Agree, Mildly Agree, Mildly Disagree, Strongly Disagree.
> Parents cannot help it if their children are naughty.
> A parent should see to it that his child plays only with the right kind of child.

ATTITUDE TEST CONSTRUCTION :
CHOICE AND WORDING OF STATEMENTS

No amount of statistical treatment will compensate for poverty in the initial choice of statements. The scope or content of the attitude should be defined in detail, and as many differences as possible tabulated between people thought to be strong or weak, pro- or anti-. Preference should be given to differences in behaviour, although, as our illustrations show, many tests are based almost entirely on beliefs and judgments. Thurstone advocates collecting statements about the issue from conversations with people, student essays, newspaper editorials, etc., in order to avoid the narrowness or lack of variety of items thought out solely by the author. If the test is intended

[1] Neumann, G. B., Kulp, D. H., and Davidson, H., *Test of International Attitudes*. New York : Teachers College, Bureau of Publications, 1926. Hartshorne and May, Bibliography. Rundquist, E. A., and Sletto, R. F., *Personality in the Depression*. Minneapolis : University of Minnesota Press, 1936. Stouffer, S. A., *et. al.*, *The American Soldier. Studies in Social Psychology in World War II*. Princeton, N.J. : Princeton University Press, 1949–1950.

[2] Shoben, E. J., ' The Assessment of Parental Attitudes to Child Adjustment '. *Genet. Psychol. Monogr.*, 1949, 39, 101–148.

II

for school pupils, samples of their opinions in their own words should be collected. Each statement or question must also be formulated in such a way as to seem natural and credible to the kind of people for whom the test is intended, so that it may be readily acceptable to, or rejectable by, them. In a multiple-choice test, it must be conceivable that at least a few people will agree with the most pro-, and others with the most anti-, answers.

Wang [1] gives a useful list of rules for wording statements or questions. They should be short, simple, and unambiguous. The following is bad, since it could be taken as representing support for, or opposition to, birth control :

Birth control legislation is a disgrace to our civilization.

Double-barrelled statements are always ineffective, since some testees may pay attention to one clause, others to the other. As in the case of personality questionnaires, some of the more intelligent and critical testees are likely to object to their attitudes being straight-jacketed by the form of the item, and will want to qualify every response. This can be reduced by careful wording, and by allowing additional space at the bottom of the test blank for spontaneous comments, in which they can let off steam ; but best of all by having a trial run. That is, the test should be discussed freely with a small group of typical testees and suggestions welcomed for reducing ambiguities. That the distortion or simplification of shades of opinion in attitude measurement is less serious than many critics think is shown by an experiment by Stouffer.[2] He obtained from 238

[1] Wang, C. K. A., ' Suggested Criteria for Writing Attitude Statements '. *J. Soc. Psychol.*, 1932, 3, 367–373.

[2] Stouffer, S. A., ' Experimental Comparison of the Statistical and a Case History Technique of Attitude Research '. *Publ. Amer. Sociol. Soc.*, 1931, 25, 154–156. This experiment could be interpreted the other way round ; i.e. it shows that spontaneous expressions of attitude can be used to give a reasonably reliable index of the attitude, when assessed by experienced and impartial judges. James and Tenen raise a number of legitimate criticisms of questionnaires, particularly when applied to children, and advocate assessing attitudes by free interview. But they give no indication as to how the type of interviewer bias to which Rice drew attention (cf. p. 21) is to be controlled. James, H. E. O., and Tenen, C., ' How Adolescents Think of People '. *Brit. J. Psychol.*, 1950, 41, 145–172. Further evidence on the unreliability of attitude assessments even by skilled interviewers is given by Wedell, C., and Smith, K. U., ' Consistency of Interview Methods in Appraisal of Attitudes '. *J. Appl. Psychol.*, 1951, 35, 392–396.

students anonymous accounts of their own experiences and opinions about alcohol and prohibition. These completely unforced expressions of attitude were rated by four independent judges for their favourableness or unfavourableness to prohibition, their average agreement being shown by a correlation of ·86. The combined ratings correlated ·81 with the scores of the same students on an ordinary test of Attitude to Prohibition.

By the ' acceptability ' of items is meant the proportion of a typical group of testees who agree with the item, or who check each response to it. This acceptability must be estimated at least roughly in advance, since the levels vary markedly in different types of test. In a Thurstone-type test, statements must range from very high to very low, or strong pro- to strong anti-, and include a good proportion of moderate or neutral shades. In a test like Vetter's the statement may be non-committal or neutral, while the responses should range down to about 10% acceptability in either direction. But in most multiple-choice tests (Lentz's, Likert's, Eysenck's, etc.) the statements are around 85 to 65% and 35 to 15%. For if very extreme items are included, almost all the responses will be No or Disagree ; while if they are too middling, they cannot reveal any definite variations in attitude.

Rundquist and Sletto [1] have demonstrated clearly that, in a test which asks for socially approved or disapproved opinions, questions which state the disapproved view are not always answered in the same way as apparently identical questions stating the approved view. For instance, if 40% of a group accepts as True :

> The Government's policy is subservient to big business interests,

it will not usually be found that all the same testees, or even the same proportion, will answer No or False to :

> The Government's policy is independent of big business interests.

Much as in personality questionnaires, the unpopular question or item seems to arouse more emotion and to be answered less

[1] *Op cit.*, p. 149.

rationally than the same item stated in the reverse way. These authors recommend including both types, since they touch off different aspects of the attitude.

Eysenck and Crown [1] carry the argument further by pointing out that acceptability depends not only on positive or negative strength, but also on social stereotypes. For example, these two statements have almost the same Thurstone scale-values:

> The Jews have too much power and influence in this country.
> Jews lack physical courage.

But the former was agreed to by 38% of a group of 250 normal adults, the latter by only 24%. For there is a common stereotype that Jews are mercenary, but not that they are cowardly. One would deduce from these findings that it is desirable to include a large number of varied items in an attitude test in order to cancel out the effects of such specific stereotypes.

ITEM ANALYSIS AND SCALING

In constructing a test one should start with at least twice as many items as one is likely to require for the final form. The various techniques for picking the best of these, and ensuring their relevance to a unidimensional attitude, were listed briefly on p. 123. The simplest is to ask a group of judges to assess each item, and to eliminate those which are criticized by a substantial proportion. Judges can help also in defining the scope of a complex attitude; for example, the consensus of their opinions can be taken regarding the proportions of political, religious, sociological, and other items to include in a test for general radicalism. Thurstone's [2] scaling technique is an extension of this, whose main object is to place each item on a scale of equivalent units, according to its favourableness or unfavourableness. It is based on the psychophysical method of equal-appearing intervals. Thurstone usually employs several hundred judges, though reasonably accurate results can be obtained with as few as twenty-five. Each is given a set of items, typed on separate slips, and asked to sort them into eleven piles, the left-most pile, No. 1, containing items considered most favourable, and the right-most pile, No. 11, the

[1] *Op cit.*, p. 148.   [2] Cf. Thurstone and Chave, Bibliography.

most unfavourable. The other piles are intermediate and
should be approximately equally spaced in degree of favourableness, in each judge's opinion. It is easier, perhaps, to have
nine piles ; then the judges can first sort into three large piles
and later sub-divide each one. The numbers of items assigned
to each pile can be uneven, but no one pile should contain as
many as a quarter of the total.

A cumulative frequency graph is then plotted for each item
(cf. Fig. 5). Say there are 40 judges : 1 puts an item in pile 1,

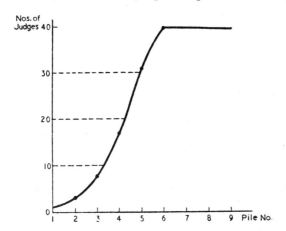

Fig. 5.—The Scaling of an Attitude Statement.

2 more making 3 in pile 2 ; 8 calls it 3 or higher, and so on. No
one puts it lower than No. 6. The median and quartile positions
are then read off to the first decimal place.[1] Thus the position
opposite the twentieth judge is 4·2, and this is taken as the
scale value of the item. The quartiles fall at 4·9 and 3·3, and
the difference between them, namely 1·6, gives Q—a measure
of the agreement between the judges. If their opinions of its

[1] A scale value will be less than 1 if more than 50% of judges place it in
the first pile. Its median position is then found by extrapolation. The
same applies to statements placed by more than 50% in the last pile.
More often one or other of the quartiles falls outside the graph, in which
case Q is read off from the median and the other quartile instead of from
both quartiles.

scale value vary widely, it is obviously unsatisfactory and should be eliminated. On a 9-point scale, Q should seldom exceed 2·0, and an average of less than 1·5 should be aimed at.

To make up the final scale, about twenty to thirty statements are selected which are : (a) fairly evenly spaced throughout the scale. Thus there might be three items having each value 1+, 2+ . . . 8+ ; (b) low in Q ; (c) heterogeneous in content. The tester must still use his subjective judgment to ensure that the scale contains a variety of expressions of attitude. Thurstone does not mention this point, but he describes an ' index of similarity ' or ' irrelevance ', which would tend to reduce heterogeneity. It is based on the responses to the statements of a large group of testees, and resembles a correlation between each statement and every other. Actually, few attitude testers have ever adopted this.

It might be thought that the judges' own attitudes would affect the results of their scaling, but experiments prove that this is not so. Possibly it is unwise to apply scales sorted by adults to children, since the meanings they read into the items may differ. The Thurstone method is laborious, but it does yield scales which ' go down ' well with most subjects. The fact that they need check only a few statements, instead of having to give a Yes, No, or graded response to every item, is an advantage. A major defect in many scales is that the scores are insufficiently reliable. This may be due to vagueness or multidimensionality in the attitude itself, or to the small number of items that subjects check. It is desirable, therefore, to try out a new scale on a group of one or two hundred people, and to calculate their scores separately on the odd-numbered and even-numbered items. These two scores should correlate to at least ·74 if the scale as a whole is to have a corrected split-half reliability of ·85. Note that Thurstone scale units, although equal-*appearing*, are not absolute. It is not legitimate to compare an individual's score on two or more scales (except via percentiles); nor can any one score, say 5, be designated as a neutral attitude. The Guttman type of scale is the most successful in establishing the point where favourable changes over to unfavourable.[1]

[1] Cf. Guttman, L., ' On Festinger's Evaluation of Scale Analysis '. *Psychol. Bull.*, 1947, 44, 451–465.

MULTIPLE-CHOICE SCALES

A separate group of external judges is not needed for multiple-choice scales, unless they be of the type proposed by Eysenck. Instead, item selection is based on the responses of a group of 200 or so testees to a preliminary draft of the test. The simplest technique is to tabulate separately the responses of subjects with the highest, middle, and lowest thirds of scores on the test as a whole. By combining these, the distribution of responses for each item in the total group is obtained. As already mentioned, preference should be given to items whose distribution is not too bunched. Thus with 5-response items :

Response	1	2	3	4	5
Percent Frequency :	18	42	27	9	4
Is better than :	37	55	7	1	0

By contrasting the upper and lower groups, the most consistent items can be found, e.g. :

Response	1	2	3	4	5
Percent Freq. in Top Third :	30	45	21	4	0
Percent Freq. in Bottom Third :	15	28	39	15	3

The statistical significance of the difference in mean response can be determined. Here the means are 1·99 and 2·63, and if there are, say, 70 in each group, the Critical Ratio of 4·1 is highly significant. Alternately, a split may be taken at the response which cuts off as nearly as possible half the combined groups—in this case between Responses 2 and 3, as this cuts off 118/200. Then the difference between the two percentages above the split, 75−43=32, would be regarded as sufficiently large. A percentage difference of less than 15 would usually indicate too little agreement with the test as a whole.[1]

The group can be rescored on the selected items, or, better, the revised test given to a fresh group, and the split-half reliability determined as before. With about a dozen items this will usually be quite high ; and if not, the necessary number of items can readily be calculated. Eysenck claims that his mixed

---

[1] Note that this technique automatically favours items of middling acceptability. Cf. Vernon, P. E., ' Indices of Item Consistency and Validity '. *Brit. J. Psychol. Statist. Sec.*, 1948, 1, 152–166.

type gives even better coefficients. Here Thurstone sorting *and* item analysis are applied. The responses to items with different scale values may be scored according to the following table, adapted from Eysenck and Crown's article.

Scale Value	Responses ++	+	0	−	−−
8·3+	8	6	4	2	0
7·7+	7	6	4	2	1
7·1+	7	5	4	3	1
6·5+	6	5	4	3	2
5·9+	5	5	4	3	3
5·3+	5	4	4	4	3
4·7+	5	4	4	4	5
4·1+	3	4	4	4	5
3·5+	3	3	4	5	5
2·9+	2	3	4	5	6
2·3+	1	3	4	5	7
1·7+	1	2	4	6	7
1·6+	0	2	4	6	8

Factor analysis can be applied to test items, as well as to different attitude tests, in order to ensure reasonable reliability and unidimensionality [1] ; but this is seldom done because of the vast number of correlations when there are many items to analyse. Stouffer [2] and his associates advance strong arguments for Guttman's scalogram analysis technique. This is especially useful for constructing very short unidimensional and reliable scales. But we will not describe it, since it seems to offer little practical advantage to compensate for its laboriousness. One of its weaknesses is that the initial choice of suitable items for scaling depends entirely on the test-constructor's skill. Edwards and Kilpatrick [3] therefore advocate, first choosing a suitable range of items by Thurstone sorting, then pruning by ordinary item-analysis, and making a final selection by scalogram technique.

[1] Cf. Eysenck, H. J., ' Primary Social Attitudes : I. The Organization and Measurement of Social Attitudes '. *Int. J. Opinion Attitude Res.*, 1947, 1, 49–84.

[2] *Op cit.*, p. 149.

[3] Edwards, A. L., and Kilpatrick, F. P., ' A Technique for the Construction of Attitude Scales '. *J. Appl. Psychol.*, 1948, 32, 374–384.

In duplicating or printing opinionaire or Thurstone-type tests, pro- and anti- statements should be arranged in random order. In multiple-choice tests, the most pro- response is sometimes put first, sometimes last. This is desirable in order to prevent testees checking Yes (or Strongly Agree, No, etc.) throughout without considering each item carefully, also so as to reduce ' space errors '. (In any multiple-choice test there is a tendency to tick the topmost or left-most response rather than responses printed on the right, or at the bottom, of a set.)

DISCUSSION

It is probably a mistake to aim at extremely high reliability in attitude scales, since this may be obtained at the expense of validity.[1] It will usually arise when the items are too homogeneous in content, or very numerous. Under these circumstances the testee can hardly fail to realize that they all refer to his own radicalism, or other attitude, and he will be more likely to answer each item according to his stereotype, or according to what he thinks is socially approved.

The attitude of the subjects to the test and tester is just as important as it is with personality questionnaires, though distortion of responses is likely to be less serious because the subject-matter of most attitude tests is less disturbing. One would not expect to get results of any value from school-children until they reach Mental and Educational Ages of at least 12 years. But it is certainly possible to construct scales that get across to adults of lowish ability, witness the extensive practical use made of them with all grades of American recruits during the war.

No one appears to have tried to validate attitude tests by the trait composite method. Such evidence as correlations with associates' ratings or with indices of behaviour is useful, but inconclusive, since these criteria are imperfect for the reasons already given. As mentioned in Chap. VI, there is little correlation between ethical attitude tests and honest conduct. However, many tests have been shown to differentiate significantly

[1] Cf. Kirkpatrick, C., ' Assumptions and Methods in Attitude Measurements '. *Amer. Sociol. Rev.*, 1936, 1, 75–88. See also McNemar's detailed analysis of the weaknesses of different types of scales.

(albeit with a good deal of overlapping) between groups which would be expected to possess contrasting attitudes. For example, Eysenck finds good discrimination on his radicalism scale between people who vote Conservative, Liberal, and Labour. On Thurstone's Church scale the average scores of Roman Catholic students was 2·90, of Jewish students, 5·44. Watson's test of fair-mindedness (cf. below) shows social psychology students in an eastern American university to be less prejudiced than middle-west parsons. Likert finds large differences in attitudes to negroes between southern and north-eastern colleges. Adorno and Frenkel-Brunswick, also Allport and Kramer [1] have traced out extremely interesting and psychologically plausible, differences between subjects with high and low scores on tests of racial and religious prejudice (ethnocentrism). The consistent way in which strong prejudice connects with factors of upbringing and with the personality as a whole is very convincing. Many scales have been used successfully in investigations of the effects of propaganda or of various types of instruction.[2]

STUDIES OF GROUP ATTITUDES

Actually it is hardly necessary, in studying differences between attitudes of groups to use tests which yield reliable individual scores ; less elaborate techniques are often adequate.[3] An enormous amount of work is done in social and applied psychology on group attitudes which falls outside the scope of the psychology of personality. Examples are children's interests in different school subjects or leisure pursuits at different ages, employees' views on sources of satisfaction and dissatisfaction in their work, the innumerable surveys conducted by Gallup polls, Mass Observation, and like organizations, not to speak of newspaper competitions which determine their readers' most popular film-star or novel, and voting in Parliamentary

---

[1] Adorno, T. W., and Frenkel-Brunswick, E., *et. al.*, *The Authoritarian Personality*. New York : Harper, 1950. Allport, G. W., and Kramer, B. M., ' Some Roots of Prejudice '. *J. Psychol.*, 1946, 22, 9–39.

[2] Cf. Lichtenstein, A., ' Can Attitudes be Taught ? ' *Johns Hopkins Univ. Stud. Educ.*, 1934, No. 21.

[3] Cf. Vernon, P. E., ' The Assessment of Psychological Qualities by Verbal Methods '. *Industr. Hlth. Res. Board Rep.*, No. 83. London : H.M. Stat. Office, 1938.

elections. These normally rely on one or two questions only as indices of majority attitudes, and compensate for the consequent loss of reliability by the large number of voters. Nevertheless, the validity or practical significance of the results is often unsatisfactory, partly because of the difficulties of getting really representative samples, and partly because of doubts as to the proper interpretation of responses. Unless the questions are extremely straightforward, the respondents may read different meanings into them from those expected by the investigators.[1] Eysenck points out that the proportion of a population favouring a given issue may appear to range almost anywhere from about 10% to 90%, depending on the kind of question asked and the extent to which it touches off common sterotypes (cf. p. 152). Cantril [2] provides a useful summary of the large body of research into wording of questions, effects of interviewer bias, sampling and other errors in opinion-polling ; and McNemar gives a detailed critique of polling methods. McNemar concludes that the results of such polls would be considerably more accurate if more use was made of properly constructed scales and tests, though these could be shorter and simpler than those required for measuring individual attitudes.

INDIRECT TESTS OF ATTITUDES

We have already suggested that the questions or statements in attitude tests should not be too direct. A number of tests which are still more carefully disguised have been suggested.[3] Probably it is because of the obvious difficulties of validation that they have seldom been used for any practical purpose. G. B. Watson's [4] early test of fairmindedness is an ingenious example. Testees are told that it is a ' Survey of Public Opinion ', but their prejudice or fairmindedness in political,

---

[1] An amusing example of this is quoted by McNemar. In one American survey a remarkable proportion of negroes were found to be opposed to government control of profits. Closer questioning showed that they believed that God alone should control prophets.

[2] Cantril, H., *et. al.*, *Gauging Public Opinion*. Princeton, N.J. : Princeton University Press, 1944.

[3] A useful survey is provided by Campbell, see Bibliography.

[4] Watson, G. B., ' The Measurement of Fair-mindedness '. *Teachers College Contr. Educ.*, 1925, No. 176.

social, and religious matters is brought out in six varied sub-tests. One of these contains such statements as :

All, Most, Many, Few, No Roman Catholics are super-stitious.

An ' All ' or a ' None ' answer is taken to show religious prejudice ; the less extreme answers are accepted as a sign of tolerance. In another sub-test a statement is presented :

In the United States 3% of the people own 60% of the wealth.

This is followed by several conclusions that might be drawn, including the following :

The great incomes should be more heavily taxed.
Such a concentration of capital is inevitable if industry is to be effectively developed.
No conclusion stated here can fairly be drawn.

The testee who checks the first of these as a legitimate inference gets a mark for socialistic prejudice ; the second—capitalistic. Only if he checks the last does he obtain a mark for fair-mindedness. Other tests which measure the influence of bias on logical reasoning are Morgan's, and the Watson-Glaser *Tests of Critical Thinking*.[1] Watson's use of extreme vs. moderate opinions is amplified in Thouless's [2] study of degrees of certainty in religious beliefs. He shows that the distribution of responses to multiple-choice questions on religious topics, which are highly charged with prejudice, tend to be bimodal, since so few individuals take up moderate views. He suggests, too, that this might provide a measure of irrational thinking. As in the case of personality questionnaires, however, it is difficult to prove that this ' response set ', or extremeness tendency, is psychologically meaningful.

[1] Morgan, J. J. B., and Morton, J. T., ' The Distortion of Syllogistic Reasoning Produced by Personal Convictions '. *J. Soc. Psychol.*, 1944, 20, 39–59. Glaser, E. M., ' An Experiment in the Development of Critical Thinking '. *Teachers College Contr. Educ.*, 1941, No. 843.

[2] Thouless, R. H., ' The Tendency to Certainty in Religious Belief '. *Brit. J. Psychol.*, 1935, 26, 16–31.

Distortions of perception and memory have also been employed, e.g. by Horowitz, and Cattell.[1] Thus an Aussage test (cf. p. 88) may be given with suggestive questions that allow scope for colour prejudice to enter. Thematic apperception (cf. p. 181), doll play, and some other projective techniques have similarly been applied with material liable to touch off various attitudes. These do not yield any quantitative scores, but assessments of the subjects' responses correlate fairly closely with attitude scale scores. Perhaps the most promising of recent tests are Hammond's,[2] which take the form of information tests. A typical item is :

The average weekly wage of workers in the U.S. in 1948 was : (*a*) \$40, (*b*) \$60.

The true answer happens to be \$50. Hence the choice of (*a*) indicates socialist, (*b*) capitalist, attitudes. Finally Travers [3] and others have shown that a person's estimates of the proportion of people who hold a given attitude correlates positively with his self-expressed attitude. For example, the radical is much more likely than the conservative to overestimate the proportions of radicals in the population.

INTERESTS

Interests are very much the same as attitudes, though their definition is also a matter of controversy.[4] Their subject-matter is usually more concrete. We are interested in or like athletics, music, model aeroplanes, etc., whereas we have favourable or other attitudes to religion, foreigners, etc. But an interest is just as complex as amalgam of subjective feelings and objective behaviour tendencies, and interests are at least as manifold and as difficult to reduce to a few unidimensional variables. The best-known test, Strong's Vocational Interest

---

[1] Horowitz, E. L., ' The Development of Attitude Toward the Negro '. *Arch. Psychol.*, 1936, 28, No. 194. Cattell, R. B., *et. al.*, ' The Objective Measurement of Attitudes '. *Brit. J. Psychol.*, 1949, 40, 81–90.

[2] Hammond, K. R., ' Measuring Attitudes by Error-Choice : An Indirect Method '. *J. Abn. Soc. Psychol.*, 1948, 43, 38–48.

[3] Travers, R. M. W., ' A Study in Judging the Opinions of Groups '. *Arch. Psychol.*, 1941, 37, No. 266.

[4] Cf. Berlyne, D. E., ' " Interest " as a Psychological Concept '. *Brit. J. Psychol.*, 1949, 39, 184–195.

Blank, solves the problem of what to measure by taking different occupations as the criterion. Obviously the number of these is limitless, and many occupational interests overlap, positively or negatively. Other testers have therefore adopted *a priori* classifications of a limited number of more general types of interest. Factorial analysis is beginning to provide a more objective answer.[1]

Allport and Vernon's *Study of Values* is based on the classification proposed by Spranger in his ' Types of Men '.[2] It is designed to test an individual's relative standing on six main types of value or general interest : theoretical or scientific, economic or utilitarian, aesthetic or artistic, social or humanitarian, political or power-seeking, and religious or spiritual. It employs the forced-choice technique. The testee is told to rank his order of preference to the four answers to such questions as :

> If you could influence the educational policies of the public schools of some city, would you undertake :
>
> (*a*) to promote the study and performance of drama ;
> (*b*) to develop co-operativeness and the spirit of service ;
> (*c*) to provide additional laboratory facilities ;
> (*d*) to promote school savings banks for education in thrift.

If he puts (*c*) top he scores 3 for theoretical values, and if he puts (*a*) bottom he scores 0 for aesthetic values, and so on. By summing the answers to all the questions a range of marks from 0 to 60 is possible on each value. Note that, as in an attitude test, the questions are rather indirect expressions of the values, couched in terms of behaviour. Testees are not told the object of the test since one does not wish to get merely their own impressions of how religious, artistic, etc., they are. The items have been analysed in the manner described above, and shown to yield reasonably consistent scores.

[1] Cf. Vernon, P. E., ' Classifying High-Grade Occupational Interests '. *J. Abn. Soc. Psychol.*, 1949, 44, 85–96.
[2] Allport, G. W., Vernon, P. E., and Lindzey, G., *Study of Values* (Rev. ed.). Boston : Houghton Mifflin, 1951. Vernon, P. E., and Allport, G. W., ' A Test for Personal Values. *J. Abn. Soc. Psychol.*, 1931, 26, 231–248. Spranger, E., *Types of Men*. Halle : Niemeyer, 1928.

The *Kuder Preference Record* [1] is similar, but aims to measure nine more specifically occupational interests, at high school, college, and adult level : Mechanical, Computational, Scientific, Persuasive (salesmanship, etc.), Artistic, Literary, Musical, Social Science, and Clerical. (Other editions include Outdoor, Sociable, Practical, Theoretical, Smooth Personal Relations, and Dominant interests, together with a verification or check score.) It is widely employed by American vocational guidance centres, and is noteworthy for its ingenious rapid-scoring device. The testee pricks his preferences through a series of sheets ; and when these are unfolded the numbers of pricks in printed circles, corresponding to each interest type, are counted up.

Strong's *Vocational Interest Blank.* [2] The occupational interests claimed by a person undergoing vocational guidance tend to fluctuate, and are often based on entirely mistaken notions of what the occupations entail. Freyd and others, at the Carnegie Institute of Technology, [3] and later Strong at Stanford University, hit on the method of recording the testee's immediate likes and dislikes for a large number of miscellaneous items, and then deducing his true interests from the total pattern of his responses. Strong's Blank contains some 420 items, including lists of :

Occupations, e.g. actor, advertizer . . . Y.M.C.A. worker.

Amusements, e.g. golf, tennis, chess, pet canaries.

Subjects of study, e.g. algebra, arithmetic . . . zoology.

Miscellaneous activities, e.g. repairing a clock, arguments, saving money.

Types of people, e.g. optimists, pessimists, foreigners, cripples, socialists.

Famous people, e.g. Caruso, Edison, Henry Ford, etc., etc.

Each item is followed by L I D (like, indifferent, dislike), or other simple responses, one of which is to be checked. There is no time limit, but rapid answering is advised, and the test

[1] Kuder, G. F., *Kuder Preference Record.* Chicago : Science Research Associates, 1942.

[2] Strong, E. K., *Vocational Interest Blank.* Stanford, Cal. : Stanford University Press, 1927. *Vocational Interests of Men and Women.* Stanford, Cal. : Stanford University Press, 1943.

[3] Cf. Fryer, Bibliography.

should not take more than about 35 minutes. The scoring is purely empirical, being derived from the actual responses of very large groups of individuals concerned in particular occupations (artists, architects, doctors, farmers, real estate salesmen, psychologists, etc.). Several techniques of constructing scoring keys have been suggested. Strong finds the following simple one effective. Take as an example the item : Actor L I D, and its scoring for interest in Personnel Management. The percentages of a group of personnel managers, and of members of other vocations in general, who check the responses are :

	L	I	D
Personnel Managers	49	38	13
All others	38	35	27
Difference	+11	+8	−14

That is, personnel managers are slightly more apt than most to say that they like this occupation. The differences are transposed into somewhat smaller figures, and the final marks for the item are +2, +1, and −3 respectively. Similarly the scores are determined for each of the 1200 or so possible responses for each occupational group. An individual's score for an interest is the sum of his + and − marks, which thus indicate the resemblance of his pattern of interests to the typical patterns of personnel managers, or artists, etc. Scoring a single blank by hand against forty occupations takes several hours ; it is therefore usually done by machine, at considerable expense. If the testee's score falls within the range of scores given by 75% of the personnel managers (or other) group, he is given an A-rating for that occupation ; if it is within the range of the lowest 25% he is given a B-rating ; if it is lower than the score of any of the original personnel managers, a C-rating. A candidate for guidance is advised to enter only those occupations for which he receives an A-rating.

Keys for some forty-nine different occupations are available. Another blank is published for measuring women's interests in twenty-six occupations, and a new test has recently been constructed by Clark [1] for differentiating interests in civilian and naval skilled trades. The same technique has been applied

[1] Clark, K. E., ' A Vocational Interest Test at the Skilled Trades Level '. *J. Appl. Psychol.*, 1949, 33, 291–303.

by Garretson [1] to measuring the academic, technical, or commercial interests of secondary schoolboys. None of these tests would be of any use in Britain, unless restandardized, since it is unlikely that the likes and dislikes of Californian and British vocational groups would be sufficiently similar. Many of the present items, also, might arouse ridicule (e.g. Acting as yell-leader, Pursuing bandits in sheriff's posse, People with gold teeth, Men who use perfume). The *Study of Values* and *Kuder Preference Record* are also too American in phraseology. Some adaptations of the former have been used here experimentally, but are not published. A test of the Strong type was constructed for Army recruits during the war, with a view to allocating them to one of six main types of employment.[2] The mechanical scores were shown to have considerable predictive value in picking men for mechanical jobs, but the test never came into general use, both because the scoring was too lengthy and because the keys were not very reliable. Strong considers it desirable to have standardization groups of about 500 in each occupation for which a key is being prepared. We found also that interest tests tend to be less effective among average or dull adults than at professional and business levels ; education and intelligence have a considerable influence on the responses. For example, the Likes checked by a skilled instrument mechanic tend to bear a closer resemblance to those checked by an equally intelligent clerk than to those of a lower-grade mechanical worker. None the less, a test covering a few main types of high-grade occupational interests would be extremely useful in this country, though its preparation and standardization would be a herculean task.

A weakness which applies to all the tests in this (as in the previous) chapter is that they are extremely open to faking. Several experiments have shown that subjects can raise or lower their scores significantly if they wish to make themselves out as possessing certain interests. Thus, none of these tests is very suitable for educational or vocational selection, where an incentive to fake may operate. But this does not detract from their value in vocational guidance or other situations where the

---

[1] Garretson, O. K., ' Relationships between Expressed Preference and Curricular Abilities of Ninth Grade Boys '. *Teachers College Contr. Educ.*, 1930, No. 396.

[2] Cf. Vernon and Parry, Bibliography.

subjects realize the desirability of truthfulness. Some psychologists would criticize the extreme empiricism of a test which takes no account of the meaning the questions have for the subject. Their doubts may be heightened by an experiment carried out by Burnham and Crawford,[1] who obtained a set of purely chance scores on the Bernreuter Inventory and the Strong Blank by throwing dice to decide each response. On applying the keys it was found that the dice had obtained scores characteristic of a psychoneurotic boy scout master or journalist !

Nevertheless all the interests tests mentioned do work.[2] Correlations around ·5 are found between *Study of Values* scores and associates' ratings on these values, which is fairly high considering the difficulty of explaining the values to the raters. Large differences are obtained in values profiles between student groups taking different courses (engineering, arts, theological, etc.), and correlations of up to ·45 with some of the Strong interests,[3] in spite of the totally different techniques of the two tests. Strong has shown that the repeat reliability coefficients of interest scores in adults are remarkably high, approximating ·80 even over a 20-year period. Naturally scores are somewhat less stable in adolescents. Persons tested before taking up their careers, who are not told the results, do tend spontaneously to enter vocations consonant with these results ; and those who later forsake a vocation are found to score lower than those who stay in it. The test may also be useful for predicting occupational success, as in Kelly and Fiske's research (cf. p. 26).

OTHER METHODS OF ASSESSING INTERESTS

Many vocational psychologists make use of a blank like Strong's, or else a much briefer list, and by going over the testee's responses in an interview build up a fairly complete

[1] Burnham, P. S., and Crawford, A. B., ' The Vocational Interests and Personality Test Scores of a Pair of Dice '. *J. Educ. Psychol.*, 1935, 26, 508–512.

[2] Cf. Berdie, Bibliography.

[3] Cf. Duffy, E., and Crissy, W. J. E., ' Evaluative Attitudes as Related to Vocational Interests and Academic Achievement '. *J. Abn. Soc. Psychol.*, 1940, 35, 226–245.

picture of his interests. This, of course, does not constitute a test, and subjective interpretation plays a large part. It might be thought that by classifying items under a few major types, and simply adding the numbers of responses under each type, a useful set of objective scores, or an interest profile, could be obtained. Thorndike[1] has studied adult interests by such a test, covering thirty-five topics or fields ; and recently Guilford, Shneidmann, and Zimmermann[2] have published their GSZ Interest test, which includes twenty items for measuring each of eighteen main types of vocational and leisure interests. But this method fails to work well because people are found to vary so enormously in their standards of marking Like or Dislike. Some interpret Like far more broadly than others and check three-quarters or more of the items in this way, whereas others are more selective and check less than a quarter. To some extent this may reflect genuine breadth or narrowness of interests, but often it is merely an irrelevant ' response set '. This is the reason why both the *Study of Values* and the *Kuder Preference Record* force the testee to indicate relative preferences. In so far as he scores high on one value or interest, he must obtain lower scores on some other interest or interests. Though no direct allowance is made for response set in the Strong Blank, the scoring keys probably compensate for most of it automatically.[3]

Strong[4] has investigated the items checked by men of various ages from 15 to 55 years, and on this basis developed a scoring key for what he calls Interest Maturity. Similarly Furfey and

[1] Thorndike, E. L., ' The Value of Reported Likes and Dislikes for Various Experiences and Activities as Indications of Personal Traits '. *J. Appl. Psychol.*, 1936, 20, 285–313.

[2] *GSZ Interest Survey*. Beverly Hills, Cal. : Sheridan Supply Co., 1948. Cf. Guilford, J. P., Shneidmann, E. S., and Zimmermann, W. S., ' The Guilford-Shneidmann-Zimmermann Interest Survey '. *J. Consult. Psychol.*, 1949, 13, 302–306. Incidentally these authors show that hobbies often give very poor indications of occupational interests.

[3] Tyler, L. E. (private communication) has pointed out to the writer that most subjects tick a vast majority of Likes, hence in fact most of the differences between different interest scores are based on the Dislikes that they choose. Tests of the Strong type do not work well with children, nor with many adults, because they have not developed sufficiently clear-cut patterns of Dislikes.

[4] Strong, E. K., *Change of Interests with Age*. Stanford, Cal. : Stanford University Press, 1931.

Weber [1] constructed tests of emotional maturity or developmental age for children, which included lists of interests, games, books, etc., common among boys from 8 to 18 years, together with Pressey X-O items (cf. p. 175). It was claimed, for example, that delinquents tend to give responses typical of normal children younger than themselves. Probably, however, fashions in interests vary too much for such tests to have much permanent value.

Wyman [2] devised an indirect test of interests for Terman's studies of gifted children, which was based on free word association responses. Groups of children were taken who, according to teachers' ratings, were keenly or weakly interested in ' intellectual, social, or activity ' interests. Their responses to a list of stimulus words were tabulated, and differential scores developed for each response. Thus when any new child takes the test, his responses can be scored for resemblance to those of the intellectual, social, and activity groups. The technique is exceedingly laborious, and the resulting interest measures were found to have low validity (probably because the three standardization groups of 130 each were too small). Thus the correlations between the scores of fresh groups and teachers' ratings were only ·54, ·35, and ·20. Moreover, the correlations of the three interest scores with one another ranged from ·68 to ·80, suggesting that the original criteria for selecting the groups were far too much affected by halo. The sets of children were not really distinct, as were Strong's occupational groups or Kent-Rosanoff's mental patients and normals (cf. p. 174). Nevertheless Wyman's technique deserves mention because of its objectivity. It would be very difficult to guess the associations that score highly, or to fake one's results. Other objective tests of interests have already been discussed in Chap. VI.

MASCULINITY-FEMININITY TESTS

Strong provides an additional scoring key based on the differential likes and dislikes of men and women. As already

[1] Furfey, P. H., ' Developmental Age '. *Amer. J. Psychiat.*, 1928, 3, 149–157. Weber, C. O., ' Further Tests of the Wells Emotional Age Scale '. *J. Abn. Soc. Psychol.*, 1932, 27, 65–78.

[2] Wyman, J. B., ' Tests of Intellectual, Social, and Activity Interests '. *Genetic Studies of Genius*, Vol. I., by L. M. Terman. Stanford, Cal. : Stanford University Press, 1925.

mentioned (p. 130) a similarly constructed key is available for the Minnesota Multiphasic Inventory. Sex differences occur in many other psychological qualities and abilities, for example in knowledge of meanings of words drawn from different fields of interest. Thus Slater's [1] *Selective Vocabulary Test* contains forty words answered better by males, and forty by females. It can be applied from 13 years up. The most elaborate test is the *Attitude-Interest Analysis (M-F) Test* of Terman and Miles,[2] containing seven sub-tests :

Word Association (all items have multiple-choice responses); Inkblot Associations ; General Information ; Emotional and Ethical Attitudes ; Interests ; Opinions ; Introvertive Responses.

Considerable overlapping of the sexes occurs on the test as a whole, but mean scores are about $+50$ for men and -70 for women on a scale from $+200$ (extreme masculine) to -200 (extreme feminine). Homosexuals do not necessarily score like the opposite sex, and a tentative additional scoring key for inversion is provided. Athletes of both sexes tend to obtain more masculine, and artists more feminine, scores than average ; and numerous other plausible group differences are described. Thus, although the test, like the Strong Blank, may be criticized for its blind empiricism and lack of any coherent underlying psychological theory, it does seem to be a useful research instrument. The three tests—Strong, MMPI, and M-F—overlap to a reasonable extent. Shepler [3] finds an average intercorrelation of ·58 in single-sex groups.

[1] Slater, P., *Selective Vocabulary Test*. London : Harrap, 1944.

[2] Terman, L. M., and Miles, C. C., *Attitude-Interest Analysis Test*. New York : Psychological Corporation, 1933. *Sex and Personality*. New York : McGraw-Hill, 1936.

[3] Shepler, B. F., ' A Comparison of Masculinity-Feminity Measures '. *J. Consult. Psychol.*, 1951, 15, 484–486.

X

Projection Techniques

IN Freudian theory, ' projection ' is the mechanism whereby
the Ego defends itself from unwelcome or repressed wishes
and ideas by attributing them to others, or by projecting them
on to the external world. The aggressive paranoiac, for
example, thinks that everyone is attacking or plotting against
him. Few of the numerous tests which are commonly grouped
under this heading directly involve Freudian projection ;
rather they provide a vehicle through which the subject
expresses his personality structure. (Cattell [1] points out how
heterogeneous they are, and suggests that ' dynamism ' tests
might be a better term.) Thus they are closely linked with the
expression of personality through movement, which we considered in Chap. IV. Indeed Bell's useful and comprehensive
summary classifies expressive movement and graphology as
projective techniques. In this chapter, however, most of the
techniques reveal personality through its effects on a subject's
perception of some stimulus, and on the mental associations,
imaginative or creative activities thereby aroused, rather than
through bodily characteristics or activities. Moreover, they
take account of what we called content, in addition to style, of
expression.

Frank [2] has pointed out that they originate from psychoanalytic techniques of dream analysis and free association
on the one hand, and from Gestalt psychology, with its emphasis
on the whole as more than the sum of its parts, on the other.
The dream is ' the royal road to the Unconscious ' ; and the
creative productions of writers and artists have often been
claimed by psychoanalysts to reveal underlying personality
trends and conflicts. At the same time, no single trait, mechanism, or complex manifests itself in isolation from the rest of

---

[1] Cattell, R. B., ' Projection and the Design of Projective Tests of
Personality '. *Char. & Person.*, 1944, 12, 177–194.
[2] Frank, L. K., ' Projective Methods for the Study of Personality '.
J. Psychol., 1939, 8, 389–413.

the personality structure ; equally no single feature of a person's fantasies, nor of his responses to a projection test, should be considered in isolation. Projection testing arose indeed partly as a revolt against the search for tests of particular traits, because it seemed to yield insights into the structure of the personality as a whole. In effect this means that these methods are not tests at all. They do not set out to measure specified variables, any more than the psychoanalyst, say, aims to measure the strength of his patient's Oedipus Complex. We shall see, also, that subjective interpretation by the ' tester ' enters to a great extent, and that attempts to render the methods more objective—with which this chapter is largely concerned—have proved disappointing. Another important difference from orthodox testing is that the stimulus situation and the subject's responses are as unconstricted or ' unstructured ' as possible. This allows maximum scope for individual differences, and it helps to reduce the self-consciousness and the critical attitudes which are so prominent in answering personality questionnaires. Usually certain instructions are standardized, or certain material is employed, with a view to stimulating the subject's fantasies ; and these do limit the situation sufficiently to make possible comparisons between one subject and another (thus dreams, artistic productions, and completely free play are not, in fact, very suitable for projection testing). But the subject's spontaneous reactions are observed and recorded in full ; he is not forced to choose between multiple responses made up by the tester, nor does the tester attend only to a few specified categories of behaviour.

Within the limitation just mentioned, an enormous variety of techniques can be, and have been, employed. Indeed there has been a plethora of new ones in recent years, and our survey will be confined to those which are best established. In addition to Bell's book, an article by Sargent may be recommended as giving an excellent description and classification.[1]

---

[1] Bell and Sargent, see Bibliography.   Useful accounts of selected techniques such as Sentence Completion, Drawing, and Finger-painting, Mosaics and Bender-Gestalt, together with a discussion of the theory and applications of projective testing, are contained in : Abt, L. E., and Bellak, L., *Projective Psychology*. New York : Knopf, 1950.

FREE WORD ASSOCIATION

Though relatively little used nowadays, this was not only the first projection test, but also one of the earliest methods for exploring mental differences—being developed by Galton in 1879. Usually a list of 50 to 100 stimulus words is read out by the tester ; to each word the subject responds with the first word that comes to mind. He is told *not* to search about for particularly apt associations. Many of the associations are superficial verbal habits—opposites, rhymes, genus-species, etc. (Jung's ' objective ' type) ; e.g. black-white, father-mother. But a few stimuli may touch on emotional complexes and lead to personal (Jung's ' subjective ' or ' egocentric ') responses. Often these are accompanied by signs of embarrassment, blocking, or laughter, and by a slow reaction time (2 seconds or more) or complete failure to respond. These so-called complex indicators draw attention, as it were, to a sore spot in the personality, which repays fuller exploration. Some testers go through the list a second time and ask the subject to reproduce his original responses. Failures of reproduction are also considered significant.

The first systematic studies of the diagnostic possibilities of the test among psychoneurotic patients were carried out by Jung.[1] He also experimented with the psychogalvanic reflex, whose deflections provide another sign of tension (though they do not, as Whately Smith [2] claimed, closely parallel lengthened reaction times). More fruitful is the Luria technique of recording voluntary and involuntary muscular accompaniments (cf. p. 54).

Jung's list of 100 words is often used, since it contains stimuli likely to evoke many common complexes ; Rapaport, Gill, and Schafer provide an alternative. Kent and Rosanoff's [3] list was selected for a different purpose and avoids words likely to ' call up personal experiences '. Cattell [4] gives a list suitable

[1] Jung, C. G., *Studies in Word Association*. London : Heinemann, 1918.
[2] Smith, W. W., *The Measurement of Emotion*. London : Kegan Paul, 1922.
[3] Kent, G. H., and Rosanoff, A. J., ' A Study of Association in Insanity'. *Amer. J. Insanity*, 1910–1911, 67, 37–96, 317–390.
[4] Cattell, R. B., *A Guide to Mental Testing*. London : University London Press, 1936.

for application to children, and another by Boyd (unpublished) is used at several Scottish Child Guidance Clinics. ' Chain ' or continuous association tests are sometimes preferred, where the subject is instructed to say everything that comes to mind in connection with a given stimulus word or words. Meltzer,[1] for example, studied children's attitudes to their parents by getting them to ' think aloud ', first about some innocuous words like ' table ' and ' ball ', then ' father ' and ' mother '. He recorded the first ten associations to the latter.

The clinical or qualitative applications of free association by the psychoanalyst or psychiatrist lie outside our scope. The simplest method of scoring responses is by counting the numbers that fall under various types. Many classifications have been proposed, but Wells and Murphy [2] show that there are considerable discrepancies when the same responses are classified by different testers, and that there seems to be no correlation between the types to which a subject is prone and his personality traits or his neurotic or psychotic syndrome. The same conclusion probably holds for the diagnostic scheme elaborated by Rapaport, *et al.* Other measures which have been widely investigated include the average or median reaction time, or its dispersion, the total number of complex indicators, and the average psychogalvanic response. None of these seems to correlate consistently with tests or ratings of emotionality or other personality traits. A few more suggestive findings deserve mention. Cantril [3] showed that persons with high scores on the *Study of Values* test react more quickly to stimulus words connected with their values (cf. also Moore and Gilliland's use of ' aggressive ' words, p. 90). Fisher and Marrow [4] found that depressed or elated moods, induced in their subjects by hypnotic suggestion, affected the content and

[1] Meltzer, H., ' Children's Attitudes to Parents '. *Amer. J. Orthopsychiat.*, 1935, 5, 244–265.

[2] Wells, F. L., ' Association Type and Personality '. *Psychol. Rev.*, 1919, 26, 371–376. Murphy, G., ' Types of Word-Association in Dementia Praecox, Manic-Depressives, and Normal Persons '. *Amer. J. Psychiat.*, 1923, 2, 539–571.

[3] Cantril, H., ' General and Specific Attitudes '. *Psychol. Monogr.*, 1932, 42, No. 192.

[4] Fisher, V. E., and Marrow, A. J., ' Experimental Study of Moods '. *Char. & Person.*, 1934, 2, 201–208.

the speed of response. Meltzer [1] was able to classify children's chain associations fairly reliably under such headings as pleasant vs. unpleasant tone, attachment to parents, level of socialization, and then to study the kinds of homes in which healthy and unhealthy attitudes appeared.

An entirely different approach to the quantification of word associations was put forward by Kent and Rosanoff [2] in 1910–11. (This was the prototype of the empirical method of standardization, later adopted by Haggerty, Olson, and Wickman ; by Bernreuter, Strong, and others in different contexts.) They tabulated all the responses of 1000 miscellaneous normal persons to their special 100-word list, and noted the frequency of each response. When a new subject takes the same test, the frequency values of all his responses are summed to give a measure of what is called his idiosyncrasy (a low score) or commonality (a high score). Alternative simpler forms of scoring are to count the number of common responses (i.e. the modal or most frequent responses of the standardization group), or the number of individual responses (those not listed in the tables owing to the infrequency of their appearance). Such tables are, of course, useful only among people similar in language and background to the standardization group ; they quickly get out of date, and would certainly be unsuitable in Britain. Woodrow and Lowell [3] prepared a new set for children, incidentally using a written instead of oral form of the test. O'Connor's [4] tables were based on the responses of 2000 U.S. industrial workers. Probably the best plan for anyone using the test now is to score individual responses by reference to his own group of subjects, that is, to count for each subject the number of responses given by no other subject.

The empirically scored word association test does have some value as a measure of mental abnormality; for Kent and Rosanoff showed that the average member of their standardization group gave 7% of individual responses, whereas 247 mental hospital patients gave an average of 27%. The present writer also obtained fair correlations between individual responses and other measures of emotionality in a group of normal students.

[1] *Op cit.*   [2] *Op cit.*
[3] Woodrow, H., and Lowell, F., ' Children's Association Frequency Tables '. *Psychol. Monogr.*, 1916, 22, No. 97.
[4] O'Connor, J., *Born That Way*. Baltimore : Williams & Wilkins, 1928.

Many individual responses, low commonality, slow reaction time and other complex indicators all overlap to some extent, but their psychological significance is most obscure. Some writers have identified idiosyncrasy with ' autistic thinking ', others with introversion or with emotionality, some with intelligence or originality, others with lack of intelligence, and so on. But for the most part the relations with other tests and ratings are so inconsistent that the Kent-Rosanoff technique appears nowadays to have been abandoned, even by psychiatrists. Additional reasons for this are the lack of satisfactory scoring tables, and the length of time required for giving the test and scoring.

Other applications of empirical techniques are Wyman's standardization against interest groups (cf. p. 168), and Kelly and Krey's [1] even less successful attempt to measure children's character traits through word associations.

PRESSEY X-O OR CROSS-OUT TESTS

Like free association, Pressey's [2] tests were devised, not as a measure of any particular trait, but as an exploratory instrument, to be applied in group form, for revealing the stimuli that evoke emotional responses. Form A, for adults, contains four sub-tests, each with twenty-five rows of five words. In the first sub-test the subject crosses out all words that are unpleasant to him and encircles the most unpleasant in each row. In the second, each set of five is preceded by a word in capitals : the subject crosses out the words associated with this stimulus and encircles the most closely associated. In the third, things regarded as wrong are crossed out and encircled, and in the fourth, things about which the subject has worried or felt nervous. Form B, for children, contains three similar sub-tests, calling for reactions of wrong, worry, and like or interest, respectively. Collins [3] adapted this and published it for British use, and Bennett and Slater included it in their Sutton

[1] Kelley, T. L., and Krey, A. C., *Tests and Methods in the Social Sciences.* New York : Scribner, 1934.

[2] Pressey, S. L., ' A Group Scale for Investigating the Emotions '. *J. Abn. Soc. Psychol.*, 1921, 16, 55–64. Tests published by Stoelting, Chicago, 1919.

[3] Collins, M., ' British Norms for the Pressey X-O Tests '. *Brit J. Psychol.*, 1927, 18, 121–133.

Booklet (cf. p. 125). A later edition, known as Pressey's Interest-Attitude Test [1] includes a section on personal characteristics that the testee admires.

Apart from their possible clinical uses, X-O tests have been scored in a number of ways. Pressey regarded the total words crossed out as measure of ' affectivity ' or ' richness in emotional associations '. There is no confirmation of this, but scores on dislikes, worries, and blameworthy actions tend to be high in neurotics and delinquents.[2] In Form A, Sub-test 1, Pressey chose the five words in each line so that one should refer to disgust tendencies, one to fears, one to sex, one to suspicions, and one unemotional or a joker ; e.g. :

drunk   choke   flirt   unfair   white

Similarly in the fourth sub-test, the words are supposed to represent special types of abnormality—paranoiac, neurotic, schizoid, melancholic, and hypochondriacal ; e.g. :

injustice   noise   self-consciousness   discouragement   germs

There is no evidence that scores based on the numbers of responses under each of these headings are diagnostic.[3]

Empirical scoring, analogous to Kent and Rosanoff's, has been applied to the encircled words to yield a measure of ' idiosyncrasy ' or abnormality. Pressey's own lists of the words most commonly encircled in each line were based on small and unrepresentative groups, and the scores are defective in reliability. Collins listed the commonest responses among 1500 11- to 14-year-old British children, and found somewhat higher idiosyncrasy scores among delinquents than normals. But, like the free association measure, it fails to give appreciable and consistent correlations with other measures of emotional

[1] Pressey, S. L., and Pressey, L. C., ' Development of the Interest-Attitude Tests '. *J. Appl. Psychol.*, 1933, 17, 1–16. Test published by Psychological Corporation, New York, 1933.

[2] Cf. Courthial, A., ' Emotional Differences of Delinquent and Non-Delinquent Girls of Normal Intelligence '. *Arch. Psychol.*, 1931, 20, No. 133. Himmelweit, H. T., and Petrie, A., ' The Measurement of Personality in Children '. *Brit. J. Educ. Psychol.*, 1951, 21, 9–29. Bennett, E., and Slater, P., ' Some Tests for the Discrimination of Neurotic from Normal Subjects '. *Brit. J. Med. Psychol.*, 1945, 20, 271–282.

[3] Cf. Flugel, J. C., and Radclyffe, E. J. D., ' The Pressey Cross-Out Test Compared with a Questionnaire '. *Brit. J. Med. Psychol.*, 1928, 8, 112–131.

traits,[1] and has now dropped out of use. The Interest-Attitude test is more promising, since it consists of words that boys and girls tend to answer differently according to age, and was standardized on 4000 cases aged 11 years upwards. Thus it yields a measure of emotional maturity. Pressey quotes high correlations with ratings of this trait, but there seems to be no further confirmation. Durea [2] has prepared a scoring key which shows some success in differentiating delinquent from normal children.

OTHER WORD ASSOCIATION TESTS

Word-Connection. Another controlled association test for adults was devised by Maller and Malamud, and adapted for British use by Crown.[3] Crown's list consists of fifty stimulus words each followed by two responses, one commonly given by normals, one by neurotics ; e.g. :

SINK   wash
drown

Subjects are given this as a printed group test, and tick what seem to them the best associations. Their scores are the numbers of neurotic choices. Moderate correlations have been obtained with neuroticism in several researches. But scores appear to be affected by education or socio-economic level, since normal groups average anywhere from 6·8 (hospital staff) to 13·9 (unskilled labourers) ; neurotic groups average 14·7. The test is very quick and simple to give, and is perhaps one of the more promising derivatives of word association.

Incomplete Sentences Tests. One of the difficulties of ordinary free association is that the single-word responses provide so

[1] Cf. Bridges, J. W., and Bridges, K. M. B., ' A Psychological Study of Juvenile Delinquency by Group Methods '. *Genet. Psychol. Monogr.*, 1926, 1, 407–506. Flemming, E. G., ' The Predictive Value of Certain Tests of Emotional Stability as Applied to College Freshmen '. *Arch. Psychol.*, 1928, 15, No. 96.

[2] Durea, M. A., ' Personality Characteristics of Juvenile Delinquents '. *Child Develpm.*, 1937, 8, 115–128, 257–262.

[3] Maller, J. B., *Controlled Association Test.* Teachers College, Columbia University, Bureau of Publications, 1934. Malamud, D. I., ' Value of the Maller Controlled Association Test as a Screening Device '. *J. Psychol.*, 1946, 21, 37–43. Crown, S., ' The Word Connection List as a Diagnostic Test : Norms and Validation '. *Brit. J. Psychol.*, 1952, 43, 103–112.

little material to analyse. The very form of the test encourages subjects to give non-diagnostic associations. Payne [1] suggested presenting short phrases in printed form, such as :

| Other people............................... | I failed.. |
| If only...................................... | My father.................................. |

The subject is instructed to write a few words—the first that occur to him—after each. This has the great advantage of being applicable as a group test, and although subjects often do give superficial responses, and can fairly readily fake if they wish to, it usually yields a wealth of emotionally toned material. Numerous lists, ranging from 20 to 100 phrases, have been published, among the best known being Rohde and Hildreth's Shor's and Rotter's.[2] Himmelweit and Petrie [3] find similar tests suitable for use with children of 9 to 14 years. Ordinary single-word stimuli, but with written sentence responses, were also used in British Army officer selection during the war.

The responses can, of course, be interpreted clinically, but in addition several methods of reasonably objective scoring have been proposed. The simplest is based on the proportion of unpleasantly toned ideas to pleasant. Rotter classifies responses as unhealthy or showing conflict, neutral, and positive or healthy, and lists specimens of each so that others can follow his scheme. He claims correlations around ·70 with emotional maladjustment. Shor looks for recurrent themes, signs of resistance or evasion, unusual or atypical associations, and other variables ; while Rohde tries to assess the strength of various needs. The more elaborate methods are certainly less reliable and there is less evidence of their validity.[4] It will be remembered that this was the most successful of the projection

[1] Payne, A. F., *Sentence Completions*. New York : New York Guidance Clinic, 1928.

[2] Rohde, A. R., and Hildreth, G., *Rohde-Hildreth Sentence Completion Blank*. New York : Psychological Corporation, 1940. Shor, J., 'Report on a Verbal Projective Technique '. *J. Clin. Psychol.*, 1946, 2, 279–282. Rotter, J. B., *et. al.*, ' Validation of the Rotter Incomplete Sentences Blank for College Students '. *J. Consult. Psychol.*, 1949, 13, 348–356.

[3] *Op cit.*, p. 176.

[4] Cf. Symonds, P. M., ' The Sentence Completion Test as a Projective Technique '. *J. Abn. Soc. Psychol.*, 1947, 42, 320–329.

tests used in Kelly and Fiske's research on selecting clinical psychologists (p. 26).

Raven's *Controlled Projection Test*.[1] This should be mentioned briefly because, although it does not attempt to measure anything and has received no experimental validation, it does provide a method of exploration suitable for children from 6 years and for adults. In the individual form the subject does a free drawing and is simultaneously told an incomplete story about someone similar to himself, and asked a number of questions : what did he (or she) think about so-and-so, what did he do next, etc. ? The dual task is supposed to produce more spontaneous responses and more identification with the person described, though there is no evidence for this. In the group form the subjects look at a picture containing a person with whom they can identify themselves, and answer questions about him in writing. No principles of interpretation are suggested, but sample drawings and responses for different ages are reproduced. Foulds [2] lists typical, and often very different, responses for normal and delinquent boys ; and Kaldegg [3] has applied the method in an extensive study of differences in family and other attitudes among English and German children and students.

Self-Description. Candidates for commissions in the British Army and for the higher Civil Service are asked to write two short descriptions of themselves, first as seen by a good friend, secondly by a candid critic. These are interpreted by the psychologist or psychiatrist in conjunction with material gathered during the interview and with other projection test responses. No evidence regarding its value is available.

Several writers have made use of more free forms of verbal fantasy than Raven, presenting, for example, skeleton stories

[1] Raven, J. C., *Controlled Projection Test.* London : Lewis, 1952.

[2] Foulds, G. A., ' Characteristic Projection Test Responses of a Group of Defective Delinquents '. *Brit. J. Psychol.*, 1950, 40, 124–127.

[3] Kaldegg, A., ' Responses of German and English Secondary School Boys to a Projection Test '. *Brit. J. Psychol.*, 1948, 39, 30–53. ' A Study of German and English Teacher-Training Students by means of Projective Techniques '. *Ibid.* 1951, 42, 56–113.

or beginnings of stories and getting children or adults to elaborate or complete these.[1] These are usually analysed along the same lines as responses to the Thematic Apperception test (*q.v.*).

Griffiths [2] describes the wealth of material obtainable from 5-year-old children by free story-telling, drawings, accounts of dreams, reactions to simple inkblots, and interviews. She was more concerned with emotional development and imagination in this age group than with personality diagnosis.

Literary Productions. It is a truism that the creative writer, painter, musician, scientist, or philosopher expresses his personality in the style and content of his productions. But discussions of this topic are almost wholly subjective and speculative. Kretschmer's pyknic (cyclothyme) and asthenic (schizothyme) writers, etc., are claimed to show distinctive styles. William James's tough and tender-minded philosophers represent a similar dichotomy. Eysenck and Gilmour,[3] however, classified 107 philosophers as materialists or idealists on the basis of a short attitude-type test, but found no relationship between these views and any aspect of extraversion-introversion as measured by Guilford's questionnaire. Wolff and Arnheim's matching experiments (cf. p. 49 f.) have shown some consistency between literary style and other expressive characteristics. In one investigation, the present writer found it possible to match essays produced anonymously by 18 students with sketches of their personalities based on observation during an hour's testing session, with moderate success. F. Allport, Walker, and Lathers [4] carried out a larger study of several essays written by a group of students, demonstrating that their style was generally consistent throughout. This style often seemed to throw light on the personalities of the writers, but they did not try to verify this. Probably the uncontrolled literary

---

[1] E.g. Murray, H. A., ' Techniques for a Systematic Investigation of Fantasy '. *J. Psychol.*, 1936, 3, 115–143. Sargent, H., ' An Experimental Application of Projective Principles to a Paper and Pencil Personality Test '. *Psychol. Monogr.*, 1944, 57, No. 265.

[2] Griffiths, R., *A Study of Imagination in Early Childhood.* London : Kegan Paul, 1935.

[3] Eysenck, H. J., and Gilmour, J. S. L., ' The Psychology of Philosophers : A Factorial Study '. *Char. & Person.*, 1944, 12, 290–298.

[4] Allport, F. H., Walker, L., and Lathers, E., ' Written Composition and Characteristics of Personality '. *Arch. Psychol.*, 1934, 26, No. 173.

production is far too complex to provide a basis for any scientific approach to personality diagnosis.

THEMATIC APPERCEPTION TEST (T.A.T.)

Binet, Burt, and others have used picture interpretation as a means of studying intellectual and emotional qualities, but the test in its present form was first described by Morgan and Murray.[1] They also collected the standard series of 30 photographs (10 for men, 10 for women, 10 for both). The subject is shown each picture and asked to make up a story describing the situation, the events leading up to it, and the outcome, together with the thoughts and feelings of the characters. Prompting is allowed. A verbatim record is kept for later analysis. The session does not usually exceed an hour, though the subject may not cover all the pictures in this time. A second interview may be held, or it may be used for discussing the previous stories and asking the subject himself to help in interpretation.

Several other sets of pictures have been used ; generally ten are regarded as sufficient. They should be sufficiently ambiguous in content to give free rein to fantasy, and should show a variety of incidents. But each of them should portray an individual of the same sex and about the same age as, or younger than, the subject, so that he can readily identify himself and project his own needs and sentiments, frustrations and conflicts, and resistances, on the ' hero '. The test is widely used, also, in group written form, pictures being projected by slides for a few minutes each. Thus it was included in War Office and Civil Service selection, and by the Office of Strategic Services. It is very desirable that a standard procedure and standard pictures be used, so that the results of different investigators can be compared. Moreover, if the common themes or ' norms ' of performance are established, interpretation can more readily be based on any unusual elements (just as with expressive movements, cf. p. 50). Rapaport, Gill and Schafer publish such a list of expected responses for the Murray set. An interesting continental version of T.A.T. is Van

---

[1] Morgan, C. D., and Murray, H. A., ' A Method for Investigating Fantasies : the Thematic Apperception Test '. *Arch. Neurol. & Psychiat.*, 1935, 34, 289–806. Test published by Harvard University Press, 1943.

Lennep's [1] 4-Picture test.   Jackson's [2] set of 6 pictures, *A Test of Family Attitudes*, appears suitable for use with children in this country (Fig. 6).

Unfortunately the approach to interpretation varies widely with the theoretical background of the psychologist.   Those

Fig. 6.—Reproduction, about two-thirds actual size of Picture II in Lydia Jackson's Test.

who follow Murray [3] have adopted his elaborate system of needs and presses (external forces that the individual regards as beneficial or harmful).   But Rotter, Harrison, Rapaport, and Wyatt present simpler schemes. [4]   These are based on the style

[1] Van Lennep, D. J., *Four Picture Test*.   The Hague : Nijhoff, 1948.

[2] Jackson, L., ' Emotional Attitudes Towards the Family of Normal, Neurotic, and Delinquent Children '.   *Brit. J. Psychol.*, 1950, 41, 35–51, 173–185.   Test published by Methuen, London, 1952.

[3] Murray, H. A., *et. al.*, *Explorations in Personality*.   New York : Oxford University Press, 1938.   Sanford, R. N., *et. al.*, ' Physique, Personality and Scholarship '.   *Monogr. Soc. Res. Child Develpm.*, 1943, 8, No. 34.   Tomkins, S. S., *The Thematic Apperception Test*.   New York : Grune and Stratton, 1947.

[4] Harrison, R., ' The Thematic Apperception and Rorschach Methods of Personality Investigation in Clinical Practice '.   *J. Psychol.*, 1943, 15, 49–74.   Rotter, J. B., ' Thematic Apperception Tests : Suggestions for Administration and Interpretation '.   *J. Person.*, 1946, 15, 70–92.   Wyatt, F., ' The Scoring and Analysis of the Thematic Apperception Test '.   *J. Psychol.*, 1947, 24, 319–330.   Rapaport, *et. al.*, Bibliography.

or structure—compliance with instructions, language characteristics, logical coherence, consistency of stories with one another,
realisticness, etc., and on the content of recurrent themes—
predominant emotional tone, social and sexual or other attitudes,
conscious strivings (particularly of the hero), and unconscious
motivations and defences.   It is essential for the scorer-
interpreter to be trained and experienced; the amateur clinical
psychologist who uses any old set of pictures and interprets the
responses largely by intuition should certainly be discouraged.

Burt and Sen [1] advocate a still more straightforward
approach, owing little or nothing to abnormal psychology.
They assess the strength of a number of qualities such as Level
of Organization or Coherence, Observation of Details, Verbal
Richness, Imagination, Extraversion-Introversion of the main
themes, Maturity vs. Childishness, Integration vs. Neuroticism.
Symonds,[2] on the other hand, claims that the stories mainly
represent repressed drives which may be the very reverse of the
overt personality traits.

Many writers have testified to the value of T.A.T. in mental
hospitals, clinics, etc., especially when used along with other
tests such as Rorschach.   But scientific evidence is more
conflicting.   Harrison and Rotter [3] have been able to show that
interpretations of the same material by different testers are
reasonably consistent, and have achieved a high degree of
success in matching interpretations with independent case
histories.   Bell gives an extensive list of the characteristics of
stories produced by various types of psychotics and neurotics.
Thus it should be genuinely useful for differential diagnosis.
But it is much less successful when used for predicting suitability of personality for some occupation (Army officer, clinical
psychologist, etc.).[4]   Harrison [5] was able to estimate the IQs

[1] Unpublished memorandum.
[2] Symonds, P. M., ' Interpreting the Picture Story (TAT) Method '.
Amer. Psychologist, 1947, 2, 288–289.
[3] Harrison, R., and Rotter, J. B., ' A Note on the Reliability of the
Thematic Apperception Test '.   *J. Abn. Soc. Psychol.*, 1945, 40, 97–99.
[4] Cf. Kelly and Fiske, Bibliography.   Guilford, J. P., and Lacey, J. I.,
Printed Classification Tests.   Army Air Forces Aviat. Prog. Res. Rep.
No. 5.   Washington, D.C. : U.S. Government Printing Office, 1947.
[5] Harrison, R., ' Studies in the Use and Validity of the Thematic
Apperception Test with Mentally Disordered Patients '.   *Char. & Person.*,
1940, 9, 122–138.

of 37 cases, with a validity of ·78. Sen [1] finds the reliability
of assessments by different scorers on Burt's qualities to
average only ·4 ; nevertheless such qualities as Observation,
Verbal Ability, Level of Organization and Maturity gave very
promising correlations with follow-up results among high-grade
civil servants. Some attempts have been made to objectify the
test by providing multiple-choice questions or stories to choose
from, but this seems to be a blind alley.

OTHER PICTURE TESTS

Shneidmann's *Make a Picture Story Test (MAPS)*.[2] This
consists of 22 background pictures, and 67 figures, some of
which are arranged on the background by the subject, while he
tells a story about what they are doing. So far this has been
used chiefly with schizophrenic patients, and a series of objectively scorable characteristics (in addition to qualitative
features) have been found to differentiate them from normals.

Rosenzweig's *Picture-Frustration (P-F) Study*.[3] Although
this picture test also involves somewhat subjective scoring and
interpretation, its limitation to a few fairly clear-cut personality
trends is an advantage. It is based on Rosenzweig's classification of people's reactions to frustrating situations : some tend
to blame others or the environment (extrapunitive) ; some find
fault with themselves (intropunitive) ; while some tend to
minimize or evade the frustration (impunitive). Adults' and
children's tests are available, and they can be given in group
form. They consist of two dozen cartoons or line drawings,
in which one person describes a situation or makes a remark
which deprives, disappoints, accuses, harms, or incriminates
another. The subject is instructed to write the first words that
come to mind as the response of the second (frustrated) person.
A number of categories of response are distinguished, and
specimen answers are provided to help in scoring. There is as

[1] *Op cit.*

[2] Shneidmann, E. S., ' Schizophrenia and the *MAPS* Test '. *Genet.
Psychol. Monogr.*, 1948, 38, 145–223.

[3] Rosenzweig, S., ' The Picture-Association Method and its Application
in a Study of Reactions to Frustration '. *Char. & Person.*, 1945, 14, 3–23.
Tests published by S. Rosenzweig, Western State Psychiatric Hospital,
Pittsburgh, 1944. Cf. also Bernard, J., ' The Rosenzweig Picture-
Frustration Study '. *J. Psychol.*, 1949. 28, 325–343.

yet little evidence to prove that the resulting scores do correspond to typical frustration reactions in everyday life. However, one of the categories—need-persistence (measured by responses that stress searching for a solution)—correlated positively with the persistence factor in MacArthur's research (cf. p. 14).

The Szondi Test.[1] This is the most bizarre in our catalogue. It consists of 6 sets of 8 photographs. In each set of 8 is a homosexual, a murderer, an epileptic, an hysteric, a catatonic, a paranoiac, a manic, and a depressive. The subject chooses 2 pictures in each set which he likes most and 2 which he dislikes. This should be repeated on several occasions. According to Szondi, it is not those who show these personality characteristics overtly who like the corresponding pictures, but those in whom the tendencies are latent (owing to recessive genes). Repressed, rejected, or sublimated tendencies are represented by dislikes. Although the chief English-speaking proponent of the test, Deri,[2] has put forward a less esoteric account of the theoretical basis and uses of the method, there seems to be no evidence of its value, apart from case-study material.

THE RORSCHACH INKBLOT TEST [3]

This is far and away the most popular projection technique, and it is probable that more work has been done in standardizing and developing it into a scientific as well as a clinical instrument, and in training psychologists to use it properly, than on all the others put together. On the other hand, there is an unfortunate tendency for Rorschach testing to become a cult, like psychoanalysis, with the same tendency to dogmatism, to an elaborate jargon and to dissenting sects, and the same implications that only the initiated can understand it, and that it is immune from ordinary scientific standards of reliability and validity because it is concerned with the ' total ' personality. More than 1000 books and articles have been published on it to date.

---

[1] Szondi, L., *Szondi Test.* New York : Grune and Stratton, 1937.

[2] Deri, S., *Introduction to the Szondi Test.* New York : Grune and Stratton, 1949.

[3] Rorschach, H., *Psychodiagnostics.* New York : Grune and Stratton, 1942 ; London : Methuen. *Blots* (4th edit.), same publisher, 1946. A useful introduction for British readers is Mons, W., *Principles and Practice of the Rorschach Personality Test.* London : Faber, 1948.

Since 1937 the *Rorschach Research Exchange* has been published, a journal exclusively concerned with the test, though this has now been expanded into the *Journal of Projective Techniques.*

Many psychologists from Binet onwards have used meaningless inkblots as material for investigating the imagination.[1] Rorschach, a Swiss psychiatrist, tried out a large number of rather elaborate blots with mental hospital patients before

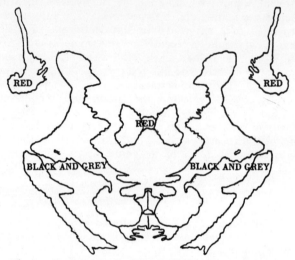

Fig. 7.—Outline reproduction of Rorschach's Blot No. III.
(Nine-sixteenths original size.)

publishing the standard set of 10, together with his monograph, *Psychodiagnostik*, in 1921. Administration is very simple. The blots (some black-grey-white, some coloured (cf. Fig. 7)) are presented in turn, and the subject is asked what he sees in each, what it makes him think of. He is encouraged to produce as many associations as possible, and to turn the cards round if he wishes. The examiner records unobtrusively, usually on a specially prepared form.[2] After completing the series, the

[1] Cf. Tulchin, S. H., ' The pre-Rorschach Use of Inkblot Tests '. *Rorschach Res. Exchange*, 1940, 4, 1–7. Cf. also Hertz, Bibliography.

[2] E.g. Klopfer, B., and Davidson, H. H., *Record Blank for the Rorschach Method of Personality Diagnosis.* New York : Rorschach Institute, 1939.

responses are discussed in order to elucidate what determined them, and to which parts of the blots they refer. In Klopfer's ' testing the limits ', there is a third stage where the tester probes deeper and prompts responses which were not produced spontaneously. For a normal production of about thirty responses, testing usually takes less than half an hour, but there are enormous variations ; some patients give less than ten responses, some several hundreds. Scoring and interpretation may take several hours.

Each response is scored under three headings :

I. Mode of apperception—whether the whole blot (W response), an ordinary detail (D) or unusual detail (Dd), or based on a white space in the blot (DS), etc.

II. The determinant—the form or shape (F+ or − according to aptness), colour (C), shading or chiaroscuro (K), or a response implying movement (M). The relative proportions of colour and movement responses yield the Erlebnistypus or experience balance—extratensive (excess of colour), introversive (excess movement), many of both types (dilated ambiequal), few or none (constricted).

III. Content—original (O+ or −), or common response (P) ; human (H), animal (A), anatomical, object, geographical, nature, architecture, plant, etc.

Beck and Klopfer,[1] the leaders of the main American ' sects ', suggest a number of more detailed scoring categories. Each of the main types of response is summed to give the psychogram or profile, and interpretation is based mainly on these scores and their inter-relations. The profile epitomizes, as it were, both the intellect and the affective life of the subject. Thus intelligence is shown by good form, original and movement responses ; but an excess of W shows a more abstract and synthetic, of D a more practical, and of Dd a pedantic, kind of intellect. Colour corresponds roughly to emotionality, and if the colour responses show little influence of form, this emotionality is poorly controlled. Movement responses represent

[1] Beck, S. J., ' Introduction to the Rorschach Method '. *Res. Monogr. Amer. Orthopsychiat. Ass.*, 1937, No. 1. Klopfer, B., and Kelley, D. M., *The Rorschach Technique.* Yonkers, N.Y. : World Book Company, 1942.

a rich inner life rather than overt emotion, somewhat like Jung's introversion, and the various kinds of shading responses show sensitivity and anxiety. Some of the content categories have special significance; thus the commonest responses, animals, show lack of imagination, anatomical responses, morbidity,[1] etc. Though particular responses are sometimes explored, e.g. along psychoanalytic lines, content plays a much smaller part in interpretation than it does in the clinical application of word association tests or in T.A.T. Indeed many psychologists regard Rorschach and T.A.T. as complementary, and prefer to apply both to their subjects. The sequence of Rorschach responses, and the context in which certain ones appear, may also help in the interpretation of neurotic trends and resistances. The significance of any score naturally depends on the extent to which it deviates above or below the normal score for other similar people. Numerous tables of norms have been published, but there are such wide variations with age and education of the subjects, probably also with the manner of giving the test, and with productivity or total number of responses, that these are far from satisfactory.

The above account is much over-simplified, and reference should be made to Klopfer's and/or Beck's manuals. It is most essential for the Rorschach tester to receive thorough training, and fortunately this is fairly readily available in U.S.A. and in England.

Reliability and validity are difficult to investigate, because Rorschachites insist that no category should be considered in isolation.[2] (The dependence of every category on the total number of responses, and the skewness of score distributions, constitute additional snags.)[3] Nevertheless, interpretations are frequently based on small differences in category scores; for example, 3 Colour-Form and 1 Form-Colour would be regarded

[1] Sandler and Ackner have recently classified types of content by factor analysis. On comparing their categories with psychotic diagnoses and symptoms, anatomical responses were found to be strongly associated with an insecure-aggressive, rather than an hypochondriacal, syndrome. Sandler, J., and Ackner, B., ' Rorschach Content Analysis : An Experimental Investigation '. *Brit. J. Med. Psychol.*, 1951, 24, 180–201.

[2] Cf. Ainsworth, M. D., ' Some Problems of Validation of Projective Techniques '. *Brit. J. Med. Psychol.*, 1951, 24, 151–161.

[3] Cf. Cronbach, L. J., ' Statistical Methods Applied to Rorschach Scores '. *Psychol. Bull.*, 1949, 46, 393–429.

as very different from 1 Colour-Form and 8 Form-Colour responses. Thus it is desirable that such scores should possess stability and consistency. The ordinary split-half and retest methods of studying reliability have been used, but are open to criticism. Perhaps the fairest method is to compare with the results of a parallel series of blots, two of which are available —one by Behn-Eschenburg, one by Harrower.[1] Meadows [2] obtained correlations averaging only ·50 for 25 score categories between Rorschach and Behn responses of 100 normal persons and 100 neurotics. They ranged up to ·84, but many coefficients were very low. The reliability of scoring might also be queried, but several experiments have shown that different experts do agree very closely. Tables have been published to assist in the scoring of doubtful responses (good vs. poor forms, normal vs. rare details, etc.). Other researches indicate that it is scarcely possible for a subject to fake a good or poor personality, unless of course, he has been primed. Temporary mood, however, and the rapport between the subject and the particular tester do seem to have some influence.[3]

Claims for the diagnostic significance of the categories are by no means as fanciful as might appear, since a vast amount of evidence is available on the trends in different neurotic and psychotic groups. A typical manic patient, for example, gives a very different psychogram from a typical depressed case. Moderate correlations are often obtained between certain scores and intelligence tests ; Hertz [4] quotes higher ones with neuroticism, though these have not been confirmed. Sen [5] has shown by factorizing the various category scores that they can be reduced to three main components which might be termed—associative fluency or productivity, intelligence, and neurotic tendency. Correlations of around ·5 were obtained between

[1] Behn-Eschenburg, H., *Psychische Schüleruntersuchungen mit dem Formdeutversuch.* Bern : Bircher, 1921. Harrower-Erickson, M. R., *Psychodiagnostic Inkblots : A Series Parallel to the Rorschach Blots.* New York : Grune and Stratton, 1945.

[2] Meadows, A. W., *An Investigation of the Rorschach and Behn Tests.* Ph.D. Thesis, University of London, 1951.

[3] Cf. Lord, E., ' Experimentally Induced Variations in Rorschach Performance '. *Psychol. Monogr.,* 1950, 64, No. 316.

[4] Hertz, M. R., ' The Rorschach Inkblot Test : Historical Summary '. *Psychol. Bull.,* 1935, 32, 33–66.

[5] Sen, A. ' A Statistical Study of the Rorschach Test '. *Brit. J. Psychol.,* *Statist. Sec.,* 1950, 3, 21–39.

the factor scores of students and associates' ratings on these traits. This type of piecemeal validation is, of course, entirely foreign to the manner in which the Rorschach is normally used, though the fact that it is successful suggests that it might be turned into a more objective personality test. Matching methods of validation have been tried, though they, too, have their disadvantages. Undoubtedly they show that diagnoses based on the psychogram as a whole (even when interpretation is done ' blindly ', without seeing the subjects themselves) can be identified with case-studies or clinical data with considerable success.[1] Thus the skilled Rorschach tester can certainly help in the differential diagnosis of mental patients. He seems, however, to be less able to make valid predictions about normal persons. Thus the test was of very little value in selecting clinical psychologists. Nor did any of the scores correlate with success among U.S. Army Air Force pilots, but predictions made from the complete psychograms did yield an appreciable validity coefficient.

Several modifications of technique have been tried. Harrower[2] has worked out a method of group examination, where the blots are shown by slides and subjects write their responses on prepared forms. This seems to yield similar material to the usual method, but rather less complete. Munroe[3] developed an ' inspection technique ' for rapid and relatively objective scoring. The presence or absence of twenty-eight signs of emotional instability in group records was counted, and these sign-scores gave rather promising validity in identifying students whose academic work fell below the level expected from intelligence tests and previous examinations. Similar is Bühler and Lefever's[4] method of scoring for adequacy vs. malfunctioning

[1] Cf. Vernon, P. E., ' The Significance of the Rorschach Test '. *Brit. J. Med. Psychol.*, 1935, 15, 199–217. Krugman, J. E., ' A Clinical Validation of the Rorschach with Problem Children '. *Rorschach Res. Exchange*, 1942, 6, 61–70. Benjamin, J. D., and Ebaugh, F. G., ' The Diagnostic Validity of the Rorschach Test '. *Amer. J. Psychiat.*, 1938, 94, 1163–1178.

[2] Harrower-Erickson, M. R., and Steiner, M. E., *Large Scale Rorschach Techniques*. Springfield, Ill. : Thomas, 1945.

[3] Munroe, R. L., ' Prediction of the Adjustment and Academic Performance of College Students by a Modification of the Rorschach Method '. *Appl. Psychol. Monogr.*, 1945, No. 7.

[4] Bühler, C., Bühler, K., and Lefever, W. D., *Development of the Basic Rorschach Score with Manual of Directions*. Los Angeles, Cal. : Rorschach Standardization Studies, No. 1, 1948.

of personality. Unfortunately Munroe's technique failed to yield appreciable correlations with college grades in another experiment by Cronbach,[1] with a rather different type of student population, though there was moderate agreement with dormitory staff ratings of social adjustment. Harrower also devised an entirely objective multiple-choice test. The blots are shown on slides and nine possible responses to each are presented, some commonly given by normal people, some by neurotics (these are listed by Eysenck). The subject ticks those which he thinks appropriate and his score is the number of neurotic choices. This seems to have very poor validity, but a more reliable method suggested by Eysenck, where the subjects rank each set of nine responses, has given small correlations with neuroticism.

ARTISTIC PRODUCTIONS

Lowenfeld's *Mosaic Test*.[2] The subject is given a box containing some 2 to 400 small squares, triangles, and diamond-shaped pieces, coloured white, black, red, green, blue, and yellow—together with a wooden tray lined with a sheet of white paper. He is told to make anything he likes with the pieces, and is encouraged to go on until he is satisfied with his construction. A permanent record can be made by drawing round the pieces before removing them and chalking in their colours. A few subjects make concrete or representational patterns, but more commonly they create abstract ones which are classified into various types : compact, scattered, incoherent, also according to success or the completeness of the Gestalt, the use of edge or frame designs, winged and arrow patterns, etc. Though a considerable amount of data is available on the types of designs occurring in different psychopathological groups,[3] and among children of different ages, the test can hardly be said to provide an objective method of diagnosis. Lowenfeld, and those whom she has trained, can give remarkably penetrating

[1] Cronbach, L. J., ' Studies of the Group Rorschach in Relation to Success in the College of the University of Chicago '. *J. Educ. Psychol.*, 1950, 41, 65–82.

[2] Lowenfeld, M., ' The Mosaic Test '. *Amer. J. Orthopsychiat.*, 1949, 19, 537–550. Test material published by Institute of Child Psychology, London, and Psychological Corporation, New York.

[3] Summarized by Bell.

accounts of personality structure, but they are less successful so far in laying down definite principles of interpretation which others can follow. Kerr, and Himmelweit and Eysenck [1] quote experiments in which experienced testers successfully matched Mosaics with personality sketches, or wrote sketches from the Mosaics which were identified by psychiatrists. The tester was, however, unable to predict the answers of neurotic patients to a personality questionnaire. Notable advantages of Mosaics over other projection tests are that it is quite brief, and that it can be given many times over. Thus it is particularly useful for following through personality changes during psychological treatment.

Drawings and Paintings. Psychological studies of art [2] have concentrated chiefly on :

(*a*) Developmental stages—A useful application of such work is Goodenough's ' Draw-a-Man ' performance test of intelligence ;

(*b*) Cultural influences ;

(*c*) Artistic productions of psychotic patients, e.g. schizophrenics [3] ;

(*d*) the therapeutic value of drawing and painting among maladjusted children, and the changes that occur during the course of treatment. Among adult neurotics also, particularly those who are treated by followers of Jung, drawings are sometimes analysed in the same manner as dreams ;

(*e*) Tests, and factorial analysis of types, of artistic taste.

It is very widely assumed in child guidance that the style and content of drawings provide valuable diagnostic hints. Bell gives a lengthy table of aspects or elements and the significance of each for personality which has been alleged by various authors. But there is an astonishing dearth of evidence other than case-study material which, without a control group,

[1] Kerr, M., ' The Validity of the Mosaic Test '. *Amer. J. Orthopsychiat.*, 1939, 9, 232–236. Himmelweit, H. T., and Eysenck, H. J., ' An Experimental Analysis of the Mosaic Projection Test '. *Brit. J. Med. Psychol.*, 1945, 20, 283–294.

[2] Cf. Goodenough and Harris, Bibliography.

[3] Cf. Anastasi, A., and Foley, J. P., ' A Survey of the Literature on Artistic Behavior in the Abnormal '. *Psychol. Monogr.*, 1940, 52, No. 237.

proves nothing. For example, one cannot claim that such-and-such a feature is characteristic of ' anxious ' children, unless one has also shown that this feature is relatively absent from drawings of normal children. Even the matching method, which gave strong support to the validity of T.A.T., Rorschach, and Mosaics, has been neglected.[1] It is far too easy to read adult associations into children's productions—for example, to say that fences represent repressions, dark colours or shading, anxieties, etc. Distorted human figures, houses with tiny windows and the like often arise merely from backwardness or from defective drawing skill. (Some authors recommend finger-painting as making fewer demands than paint-brush, crayon, or pencil.) [2] However, Goodenough and others have proved that there tend to be more incongruities in drawings of a man by maladjusted and delinquent children than in those of normals ; and such children often score below their Binet Mental Ages on her test. Buck [3] uses as a test for adults drawings of a house, a tree, and a person (H-T-P Test), and accompanies these by a series of questions. His method of interpretation, largely based on Freudian symbolism, is highly subjective and lacking in validation.

In conclusion, we do not deny that drawings and paintings are expressive of personality, nor that they are valuable as an exploratory tool in clinical treatment. There are also well-established abnormalities in the productions of various psycho-pathological groups. But the origins of any feature are so complex that interpretation is in much the same state as was graphology 50 years ago.

AESTHETIC APPRECIATION

Many writers on art, such as Herbert Read, have attempted to classify modes of appreciation, as well as types of artistic

[1] Waehner describes a system of analysis of adult drawings and shows that personality sketches derived from this can be matched very success-fully with sketches based on Rorschach. Waehner, T. S., ' Interpretation of Spontaneous Drawings and Paintings '. *Genet. Psychol. Monogr.*, 1946, 33, 3–70.

[2] Cf. Napoli, P. J., ' Finger Painting and Personality Diagnosis '. *Genet. Psychol. Monogr.*, 1946, 34, 129–231.

[3] Buck, J. N., ' The H–T–P Technique : A Qualitative and Quantitative Scoring Manual '. *J. Clin. Psychol.*, 1948, 4, 317–396.

production, and have suggested relationships with Jung's or other systems of personality types. On the basis of introspective experiments, Bullough, Valentine, and Myers derived four main types of response to colours, musical tones, and other aesthetic stimuli : the objective or technical, the subjective or emotional, the associative, and the characterizing types. They did not claim, however, that individuals adhere consistently to one type, nor did they attribute these differences to personality traits. This is a problem which is amenable to experimental investigation, using Burt's technique of factorizing correlations between persons. Individuals are asked to rank a set of pictures or other artistic objects in order of appreciation (or rate them on an appropriate scale). When their orders are inter-correlated, a fairly high degree of overlapping is usually found even between experts and untrained adults and children. The correlation between each individual's order and the average or standard order may be taken as a measure of his artistic taste. Eysenck [1] finds some consistency in taste even when measured by such different sets of materials as reproductions of portraits, landscapes, statues, furniture, abstract figures (polygons), pieces of poetry, and odours. But over and above this general factor, he finds that one or more bipolar factors can be extracted, showing that some people have a fairly consistent preference for one type of art, others for another. The most clear-cut of these dichotomies is that between highly coloured, fairly simple, and impressionistic artistic styles and more complex, subtle and formal, or classical styles. Eysenck provides some evidence that preference for the former type is associated with extraversion, also with radical vs. conservative attitudes and (inversely) with age.

Similar factors have been distinguished in the appreciation of poetry and music, though there is less evidence of their connection with personality traits. Burt [2] claims, however, that persons belonging to his four main temperamental types (cf.

[1] Eysenck, H. J., ' Some Factors in the Appreciation of Poetry, and their Relation to Temperamental Qualities '. *Char. & Person.*, 1940, 9, 160–167. ' The General Factor in Aesthetic Judgements '. *Brit. J. Psychol.*, 1940, 31, 94–102. ' " Type "-Factors in Aesthetic Judgements '. *Brit. J. Psychol.*, 1941, 31, 262–270.

[2] Burt, C. L., ' The Factorial Analysis of Emotional Traits '. *Char. & Person.*, 1939, 7, 238–254, 285–299.

p. 16) tend to show characteristic tastes in all the arts, as follows :

> Unstable extraverts like romantic, emotional, and dramatic productions, with strong human interest, e.g. Titian and Rubens, flamboyant Gothic architecture, Wagner and Strauss, Byron and Shakespeare.
>
> Stable extraverts like more objective and realistic art, for the associations it arouses rather than the emotions, e.g. Raphael and Chardin, Handel and Verdi, Johnson and Macaulay.
>
> Unstable introverts like mystical and impressionistic art, e.g. El Greco and Blake, early Gothic, Debussy and Delius, Shelley and Yeats.
>
> Stable introverts like intellectual and formal productions, e.g. Van Eyck, Vermeer, and Cézanne ; Bach ; Wordsworth and Henry James.

In one experiment with postcard reproductions, people judged as belonging to these types did express liking for 73% of the corresponding and only 42% of the non-corresponding types of pictures. The other attributions are plausible, but there is no published evidence for them so far.

PLAY METHODS

Older theories explained play as resulting from surplus energy, or as practising the instincts, or as recapitulating the evolution of the race. Nowadays it is generally regarded as a medium of self-expression in which wishes, anxieties and conflicts, and socially unacceptable impulses are worked out. Thus it is particularly valuable in the psychotherapy of young children, for whom language is such a difficult means of communicating emotions. Like artistic productions, however, it certainly does not provide a straight-forward diagnostic tool. One would expect that fantasy behaviour would often be compensatory, and that quite different attitudes would be expressed, e.g. in doll play, from those normally shown to the family, teacher, or other children. Inevitably, therefore, subjective interpretation enters in the use of play as a clue to personality, and there are grave dangers in jumping to conclusions about children on the basis of casual observations and a slight acquaintance with psychoanalytic theories.

A further difficulty in adapting play as a projection technique is that it does not normally leave a permanent record ; descriptions by an observer or play therapist introduce many possible sources of error. Researches under Sears [1] at Iowa show that valuable results from the standpoint of personality theory can be obtained by the application of exact observational techniques to various aspects of doll play. An alternative approach is to employ a standard set of toys with which the child constructs a scene, or plays out a drama, and to photograph the resulting constructions. This is the basis of Lowenfeld's [2] ' World ' test, so called because the child portrays, as it were, his view of the world with miniature people, animals, houses, trees, etc. Bühler and Kelley have collected and published a set of materials for this test, which they regard as a test of emotional disturbance. The method has been found useful also with adults.[3] Moreno's [4] psychodrama is a more elaborate method of involving adults in play for diagnostic and therapeutic purposes. It is far too dependent on the skill of the director-interpreter to be considered seriously as a diagnostic test. However, it connects up with the group observational methods of Chap. VI.

Although play provides such a rich field for personality investigations among children, and has a very extensive literature, it seems unlikely to yield any convenient or practicable tests. We should recall, however, that it does not only reflect unconscious motives. As described in Chap. VI, valuable measurements of social and character traits were obtained from time-sampling and tests based on play. Obviously, too, it provides an indication of interests. It would take too long to

[1] Cf. Pintler, M. H., Phillips, R., and Sears, R. R., ' Sex Differences in the Projective Doll Play of Pre-school Children '. *J. Psychol.*, 1946, 21, 78–80.

[2] Lowenfeld, M., ' The Nature and Use of the Lowenfeld World Technique in Work with Children and Adults '. *J. Psychol.*, 1950, 30, 325–331. Bühler, C., and Kelley, G., *The World Test. A Measurement of Emotional Disturbance*. New York : Psychological Corporation, 1941.

[3] Cf. Bolgar, H., and Fischer, L. K., ' Personality Projection in the World Test.'. *Amer. J. Orthopsychiat.*, 1947, 17, 117–128.

[4] Moreno, J. L., *Sociodrama : A Method for the Analysis of Social Conflicts*. New York : Beacon House, 1944.

observe and record all a child's play activities in order to survey his interests ; and the results might have poor predictive value ; (for example, early mechanical interests among boys are notoriously unstable). But the Pressey X-O and Strong Interest Blank try to cover the same ground at a more sophisticated level.

SENSE OF HUMOUR TESTS

The mechanism of projection certainly enters into our appreciation of the comic, and there have been some attempts to base personality tests on the types of jokes appreciated. Eysenck [1] found that when people rank jokes or other humorous material in order of funniness, or rate their appreciation, there is remarkably little agreement between them. Some persons, however, consistently tend to rate the simpler sexual and aggressive jokes more highly, whereas others consistently prefer more subtle and clever humour. In statistical terms, there is no clear general factor in the correlations between raters, but there is a prominent bipolar. Some correlations were found between the latter factor and extraversion-introversion, as measured by a personality questionnaire in normal subjects, and there was a slight tendency for hysterical patients to rate the sexual type more highly than did dysthymics. A much more elaborate test has been published by Cattell and Luborsky,[2] where some 200 jokes have been classified by factor (cluster) analysis into 11 pairs of types ; for example :

> Carefree, sexual vs. mordant and morose.
> Derision of stupidity, etc. vs. stable acceptance.
> Disregard of conventions vs. light badinage.

High positive or negative scores on each of these are claimed to derive from repressed personality tendencies, and certain correlations have been found with personality-questionnaire factors. For example, the first type connects with traits akin to surgency-desurgency. The scheme is probably too elaborate ;

[1] Eysenck, H. J., ' The Appreciation of Humour : An Experimental and Theoretical Study '. *Brit. J. Psychol.*, 1942, 32, 295–309.
[2] Cattell, R. B., and Luborsky, L. B., ' Personality Factors in Response to Humor '. *J. Abn. Soc. Psychol.*, 1947, 42, 402–421. *C-L Humor Test.* Champaign, Ill. : Institute for Personality and Ability Testing, 1950.

for many of the scores have low reliability, and they overlap considerably. Indeed when they are factorized they appear to resolve largely into the same bipolar dimension that Eysenck found. Moreover, the significance of the various kinds of jokes is dubious. When several judges were asked to classify them under Cattell's 11 types, they showed little agreement. Nevertheless, the test is both genuinely projective and objective, and clearly merits further development.

XI

Conclusions and Future Developments

IN trying to sum up the practical implications of our survey, it is advisable to distinguish three main situations in which personality tests or assessments are required—selection, experimentation, and diagnosis or guidance. The field of selection is the most straightforward because it is the least affected by the difficulties of personality theory and the many unsolved problems discussed in Chap. I. For example, there is no need to reach agreement as to the main traits or dimensions of personality. The value of any proposed test or other method can be determined directly by comparison with some external criterion such as educational or vocational success and failure. At the same time, progress along purely empirical lines is likely to be slow ; the choice of suitable methods depends largely on adequate personality theory, and on advances in the experimental and diagnostic study of personality. And, as Vernon and Parry point out, follow-up research and the discovery of good external criteria are far from easy. The application of tests for selection is handicapped, too, by the need for such tests to be short and simple, not dependent on highly trained testers nor on elaborate apparatus, and so forth.

We therefore naturally ask first how useful are paper-and-pencil tests, since they can generally be applied to groups of candidates, and scored, by slightly trained testers, at little cost. Tests of interests and attitudes such as the Strong Blank (p. 163), the *Kuder Preference Record* (p. 163), and the *Study of Values* (p. 162) have certainly proved their worth in America, though nothing similar is immediately available in Britain ; and it is doubtful how far they are suitable for average adults or for 11- to 14-year-old children, as contrasted with college students. The forced-choice questionnaire covering a limited number of main types of interest (like Kuder's) appears more promising than Strong's or any simple check list of interests and inclinations, because it eliminates response sets (cf. p. 167). It is also easier to standardize and to score. A grave defect of such tests is their susceptibility to faking, and they should at least be supplemented by objective information tests (p. 91). When a small number of interests is involved, as in selection for technical schooling, Peel and Lambert's technique (p. 91) may be an improvement. Other aptitude tests to some extent reflect personality and interests; for example, Moss's Social Intelligence Test (p. 92) might well be superior to ordinary intelligence tests in selecting for appointments involving social contacts.

It is difficult to see any use whatever in selection for miscellaneous personality inventories like the Bernreuter, Bell, Guilford, Boyd, etc., valuable though it would be to have measures of such traits as instability, extraversion, and ascendance. The reasons are fully set out in Chap. VIII. The only type worth considering would have to be at least as disguised as the Bennett-Slater (p. 125), and should preferably employ the forced-choice principle. That is, self-rating items should be tried out in actual selection situations; a small number of valid items should be chosen on the basis of correlations with an external criterion, and combined with invalid ones in such a way as to defeat the faker or the malingerer.

More factual biographical inventories, perhaps containing a few relatively innocuous self-description items, are worth developing but, as pointed out on p. 136, they necessitate large numbers and a rather stable selection set-up. In the case of children we advocated (p. 121) the construction of a similar third-person questionnaire and rating scale for teachers to apply, whose items would be empirically scored after validation against, say, secondary school success.

Few of the well-known projection tests are suitable. They are too lengthy, much too dependent on the subjective judgment of the tester-interpreter, and evidence for their validity is poor. Thus it seems unlikely that the group Thematic Apperception contributed anything worth while to the selection of British Army officers or civil servants. Sentence Completion (p. 177) is most free from these defects, but needs to be put across very carefully if candid responses are to be obtained. Picture Frustration (p. 184) might be tried, and group Rorschach scored by inspection technique would be worth validating against external criteria. A useful, quick, and objective controlled association test might be developed from Malamud's and Crown's Word Connection List (p. 177) and Pressey's Interest-

Attitude test (p. 176), given sufficiently large numbers for the preparation of up-to-date scoring keys.

Physical and physiological measurements and tests of behaviour must be approached very cautiously. The electro-encephalograph does indicate certain types of abnormality, and it is possible that the psychogalvanic reflex or other measures of autonomic functioning might prove relevant to certain jobs. Probably, however, they are too variable, and involve too elaborate recording. Static ataxia (p. 80) is one test of proven validity, and Sheldon's somatotypes (p. 37) may be significant. Even if the correlations of any such measure with the criterion are low, provided they are stable, it can contribute something to selection.

Most of the objective tests fall into two classes, described in Chaps. V and VI respectively. The former are too simple and specific, for example most of the f, p, and o tests. The latter, which approximate more or less closely to samples of everyday life behaviour, are too dependent on the subject's attitudes and on the way they are put across, and, therefore, too readily distorted by his desire to display an acceptable personality. Nevertheless, there are some exceptions : body sway (p. 80), manual dexterity and bodily co-ordination (p. 80) are certainly connected with emotional stability ; and the discrepancy between verbal and spatial-mechanical abilities (p. 74) has some significance. More hopeful are indirect measures including handwriting pressure characteristics (p. 60), oral fluency and the verb/adjective quotient in speech (p. 56), muscular reactions in the Luria apparatus (p. 54) and, particularly, measures of tension and breakdown under stress in complex reaction, co-ordination and learning tests (p. 85). The Q-score in Porteus Mazes (p. 63) and 'carefulness' at group tests (p. 66) fall under the same heading. Persistence can be measured in complex performance tests and in resistance-to-discomfort, but an adequate battery of persistence tests tends to involve too elaborate arrangements and too much time to be practicable.

It is a moot point whether a psychological tester's assessments of such traits as stability, impulsiveness, persistence, etc. based on observation of behaviour at apparatus tests (p. 66), would not be more reliable and valid than objective measures of such behaviour. Both might be employed. The various group observation methods developed by War Office Selection Boards (p. 96) are highly acceptable to employers and candidates but, being far more complex, they involve more subjective interpretation on the part of the observer and allow more scope for the candidate to modify his normal behaviour. Thus they depend greatly on the skill of the particular observer, and are generally less valid than might be expected. By contrast, time-sampling (p. 94) or other techniques of recording specified categories of behaviour are highly objective, but are too time-consuming and elaborate to be employed in selection. A compromise might be worked out, where the situations would be more structured than in most group exercises used at present, and the recording scheme more standardized.

Another interesting contrast may be drawn between group exercises and ordinary ratings by associates. The former make use of rather artificial situations, which are usually too brief to provide representative samplings of the candidates' normal behaviour (though superior in this respect to the conventional interview situation). The latter are based on normal behaviour, usually observed over a considerable period, but in a casual rather than systematic fashion. The prime defect of ratings is that they represent crystallized emotional attitudes of the raters towards the ratees, even when the rating scales attempt to emphasize observed behaviour. Observers of group exercises, or psychologists who judge qualitative behaviour at performance tests, are better able to maintain impartiality in comparing one candidate with another. Thus there is much to be said for arranging—where possible—trial periods of a week, a month, or more, on the job (or in the case of children, at the school) for which they are being selected. Their performance during this period should be assessed, not by generalized ratings, but by careful recording of specified types of behaviour ; and these should be made by a trained observer rather than by an employer, head teacher, or supervisor. The objection will doubtless be raised that ' specified types of behaviour ' are too narrow, and that an overall picture of the candidate's personal and social adjustment to the job is needed. But a great deal of evidence indicates that a few really reliable measurements of people provide better predictions of educational and occupational success than do subjective generalizations about their personalities as wholes.

Although we have seen that ratings seldom contribute anything more than do school marks in educational selection, they can nevertheless be of value in occupational selection. It is most desirable that each rater should be acquainted with thirty or more candidates, in order that relative—not absolute—judgments can be used. Possibly, however, a carefully constructed forced-choice scale would overcome the distortions due to variations of standards among raters of small numbers. If neither of these approaches is practicable, the best alternative is for the rater to fill in a highly concrete third-person questionnaire, accompanying this with a qualitative personality sketch or testimonial, and for the selecting psychologist to interpret this material so as to reach a final rating which will be comparable from one candidate to another. The Vineland Social Maturity scale (p. 110) fits in well with this conception, and there is a need for other scales along the same lines. Several other points regarding the technique of rating are made in Chap. VII, for example, the desirability of getting judgments from raters with varied outlooks, and of making rather more use of ratings or nominations by peers, less of ratings by superiors (teachers or previous employers, etc.).

Finally, the functions of the selection interview should be severely restricted, for the reasons given in Chap. II, though it can seldom be dispensed with because of its acceptability to candidates and employers, and its greater practicability than that of more objective techniques. It does have value in marshalling the evidence about a candidate's previous educational or occupational career, and it can provide useful indications of such traits as social aplomb, fluency, physical appearance, etc. As a diagnostic technique for assessing personality in general, or for synthesizing data from all sources into a final judgment of suitability, it is—on the average—extremely unreliable and invalid, although some interviewers (not necessarily psychologists or psychiatrists) are much better than others.

EXPERIMENTAL RESEARCH

There is scarcely a method either praised or condemned in this book which could not be clarified by further investigation. Results are so variable in the personality field that the repetition, extension, and interlocking of previous researches would be more useful than the continued construction of more or less novel tests. The concentrated effort which has gone into the improvement of social attitude scales, and made them into a genuinely useful instrument for sociological and opinion surveys, might well be applied to the measurement of autonomic variables, to time-sampling and systematic observation among older children and adults, to interest classification and measurement, to the selection and training of good interviewers, to the development of apparatus tests which will indirectly evoke really significant personal behaviour, to the improvement of ratings or measurements ' within persons ' and of techniques for the quantitative treatment of patterns of scores, and to a host of other fruitful problems.

Perhaps the greatest need is for more studies like those of Hartshorne and May, Eysenck, MacArthur and others, of particular traits by the trait-composite, syndrome, and factorial approaches, though unfortunately they have to be extremely elaborate. This is the only approach which provides satisfactory criteria of the validity of different tests, rating or other techniques, and so indicates those that can be most profitably employed in selection, diagnosis, and guidance. We must rely on it also for the discovery of the main personality dimensions or factors—those which cover the greatest amount of variance. For though it is true that the personalities of a set of individuals differ in innumerable ways, and that no two persons possess just the same traits differing only in amount, yet if we could but measure even three or four of the chief emotional-social and character dimensions and half a dozen or so of the chief interests and social attitudes, we would probably be able to make as accurate predictions about personality as we already can about abilities by means of a short battery of ability tests. And we could afford to neglect the diverse shadings in different persons and dispense with subjective interpretations of the ' total personality '. The greater the variety of tests or assessments included in such composites or factors the better. But it is particularly desirable to make more use than hitherto of measures based on time-sampling or records of specified categories of behaviour. This approach can, of course, readily be combined with the engineering of diagnostic situations, as in Burt's and Hartshorne and May's researches.

From the viewpoint of psychological science, there are two

main defects in the trait-composite approach—that it is ' cross-sectional ' rather than dynamic, and that it abstracts personality traits as though they were wholly properties of individuals. Direct recording of behaviour should help to reconcile trait-psychology with field theory and the study of social groups and processes on the one hand, and with ' longitudinal ' studies of personality development on the other hand. Although we have used the framework of trait psychology throughout this book, there is good reason to hope that some more fruitful system will eventually replace it. Obviously there are many other types of contemporary research—into experimental depth psychology, into the relations between perception and social and personality factors, etc.—which will help in constructing an adequate theory of personality, although at present they have little relevance to problems of personality assessment.

DIAGNOSIS AND GUIDANCE

The testing or assessment of personality for purposes of diagnosis, guidance, treatment, or control, is much the most intractable problem. For there is neither an external criterion of its value (as in selection), nor an internal criterion—the consistency of the results with one another (as in experimental research). The success of vocational guidance has indeed been followed up, but it is not possible to attribute this to any particular element in the procedure. Agreement with psychiatric diagnoses among mental patients also appears promising, but actually leads to such variable results that it is hardly possible to dissociate the test from the tester. One clinical psychologist does well with interviewing or with Rorschach, another with Thematic Apperception or drawings, another with deterioration tests or expressive movements, and so on. Hence in order to prove the worth of these or other methods, the diagnostician has to rely chiefly on evidence provided by the selector or the experimentalist. Unfortunately he is much too apt to trust to the face-validity of his case-studies and to his own experience ; these may be supremely good in individual instances and worthless in others. The lack of any generally accepted framework for the description of personality creates further difficulties ; the graphologist, Rorschachite, Freudian, or the average non-medical vocational psychologist, talk in quite different

15

languages. That is why we have stressed making the maximum use of a small number of operationally defined composite variables, in spite of their apparent narrowness.

The diagnostician is often less limited by time and cost than the selector, and may well spend a dozen hours on a single case if he applies Rorschach, T.A.T., Minnesota Multiphasic, and a biographical interview. Kelly and Fiske's results throw the gravest doubts on this intensive approach, and justify some resort to instruments which have received more objective validation, even though they seem less helpful in providing insights. Any of the techniques mentioned earlier in this chapter under selection could play a useful part in guidance, since any which have been successfully validated provide the clinician with checks on his intuitions. In addition, personality inventories are more worth while than in selection, because of the generally better motivation of candidates for guidance. Incidentally there is no need for questionnaires to be as long as MMPI or Strong's Blank, even if these are at present the best of their kind. Needless to say, their results must be interpreted with caution, but at the same time the psychologist should remember that his main object in using them is to correct biases in his own subjective summing-up of the personality he is studying. Another step which would be salutary in a vocational, psychiatric, or other clinic with a large staff, would be for different members to carry out the interviewing and the favoured projection or other tests involving subjective judgment, instead of expecting a single psychologist to improve his diagnoses by applying several techniques. Finally, there is no evidence that psychiatric interviewers or psychologists who make use of the concepts of abnormal psychology are any more consistent or capable of making more valid educational or vocational predictions than those trained in normal and applied psychology. However valuable the medical approach may be in therapy, the bulk of research shows that it has little to contribute to selection or guidance.

Thus we conclude as we started, that the testing or assessment of human personality is fraught with so many difficulties—it is more complex indeed than any other problem in individual psychology—that even the application of the highest psychological skill and technical accomplishment cannot be expected to bring about rapid success.

SHORT BIBLIOGRAPHY OF SUGGESTED READING

Allport, G. W., *Personality : A Psychological Interpretation.* New York : Holt, 1937.

Allport, G. W., and Vernon, P. E., *Studies in Expressive Movement.* New York : Macmillan, 1932.

Bell, J. E., *Projective Techniques.* New York : Longmans Green, 1948.

Buros, O. K., *The Nineteen-Forty Mental Measurements Yearbook.* Highland Park, N.J., 1941. *The Third Mental Measurements Yearbook.* New Brunswick, N.J. : Rutgers University Press, 1949.

Burt, C. L., ' Personality, a Symposium. I. The Assessment of Personality.' *Brit. J. Educ. Psychol.*, 1945, 15, 107–121.

Cattell, R. B., *An Introduction to Personality Study.* London : Hutchinson, 1950.

Eysenck, H. J., *Dimensions of Personality.* London : Kegan Paul, 1947.

Hartshorne, H., and May, M. A., *Studies in Deceit. Studies in Service and Self-Control. Studies in the Organization of Character.* New York : Macmillan, 1928–1930.

Fryer, D., *The Measurement of Interests.* New York : Holt, 1931.

Hollingworth, H. L., *Vocational Psychology and Character Analysis.* New York : Appleton, 1929.

Hunt, J. McV. (ed.), *Personality and the Behavior Disorders.* Chapters by Jones, Maller, White, Sheldon, Lewin, Hunt and Cofer. New York : Ronald Press, 1944.

Kelly, E. L., and Fiske, D. W., *The Prediction of Performance in Clinical Psychology.* Ann Arbor, Mich. : University of Michigan Press, 1951.

Paterson, D. G., *Physique and Intellect.* New York : Appleton-Century, 1930.

Rapaport, D., Gill, M., and Schafer, R., *Diagnostic Psychological Testing.* Chicago, Ill. : Year Book Publishers, 1945–1946.

Stagner, R., *Psychology of Personality.* New York : McGraw-Hill, 2nd. edit., 1948.

Strang, R., *Counseling Technics in College and Secondary School.* New York : Harper, 2nd. edit., 1949.

Symonds, P. M., *Diagnosing Personality and Conduct.* New York : Appleton-Century, 1931.

Thurstone, L. L., and Chave, E. J., *The Measurement of Attitude.* Chicago, Ill., University of Chicago Press, 1929.

Vernon, P. E., and Parry, J. B., *Personnel Selection in the British Forces.* London : University of London Press, 1949.

ARTICLES IN THE *PSYCHOLOGICAL BULLETIN*

Arrington, R. E., ' Time Sampling in Studies of Social Behavior '. 1943. 40, 81–124.

Berdie, R. F., ' Factors Related to Vocational Interests '. 1944, 41, 137–157.

Campbell, D. T., ' The Indirect Assessment of Social Attitudes '. 1950, 47, 15–38.

Ellis, A., ' The Validity of Personality Questionnaires '. 1946, 43, 385–440

Ellis, A., and Conrad, H. S., ' The Validity of Personality Inventories in Military Practice '. 1948, 45, 385–426.

Frank, J. D., ' Recent Studies of the Level of Aspiration '. 1941, 38, 218–226.

Goodenough, F. L., and Harris, D. B., ' Studies in the Psychology of Children's Drawings '. II. 1928–1949. 1950, 47, 369–433.

Hertz, M. R., ' Rorschach : Twenty Years After '. 1942, 39, 529–572.

Jenkins, W. O., ' A Review of Leadership Studies with Particular Reference to Military Problems '. 1947, 44, 54–79.

McNemar, Q., ' Opinion-Attitude Methodology '. 1946, 43, 289–374.

Orlansky, H., ' Infant Care and Personality '. 1949, 46, 1–48.

Ryans, D. G., ' The Measurement of Persistence : An Historical Review '. 1939, 36, 715–739.

Sanford, F. H., ' Speech and Personality '. 1942, 39, 811–845.

Sargent, H., ' Projective Methods : Their Origins, Theory, and Application in Personality Research '. 1945, 42, 257–293.

Vernon, P. E., ' The Matching Method Applied to Investigations of Personality '. 1936, 33, 149–177.

INDEX OF AUTHORS

INDEX OF SUBJECTS